The Quest for the Perfect Pub

13.9.89.   PORTUGAL

Sorry Ron - you will have to wait until you get back home to start looking!

Cheers. Barbara & Bob

The Quest for the Perfect Pub

A JOURNEY THROUGH ENGLAND AND WALES

Nick and Charlie Hurt

SIDGWICK & JACKSON
LONDON

First published in Great Britain in 1989 by Sidgwick & Jackson Limited

Copyright © 1989 by Nick and Charlie Hurt

All rights reserved. No part of this book may be reproduced or transmitted in any form or by any means, electronic or mechanical, including photocopying, recording or by any information storage and retrieval system, without permission in writing from the Publisher.

ISBN 0-283-99807-5

Typeset by Rowland Phototypesetting Limited
Bury St Edmunds, Suffolk
Printed by Billing and Sons Limited, Worcester
for Sidgwick & Jackson Limited
1 Tavistock Chambers, Bloomsbury Way
London WC1A 2SG

*Dedicated to the venerable landladies
and all the old boys*

Contents

Map	x
Key	xii
Introduction	1
Section One: Gloucestershire, Herefordshire, The Marches and Much of Wales	11
Gloucestershire	13
Herefordshire, The Marches and the Welsh Border	20
South, Mid and West Wales	32
Section Two: The West Country	57
Cornwall	59
Devon	70
Avon and Somerset	82
Section Three: The Peak District and the East Midlands	93
Section Four: Cheshire and North Wales	113
Section Five: Greater Manchester, Lancashire and Cumbria	123
Greater Manchester	125
Cumbria and the Lakes	128
Section Six: The North-East	139
County Durham	141
Northumberland	146
Tyne and Wear	153
Section Seven: The Yorkshires, Cleveland and Humberside	157

THE QUEST FOR THE PERFECT PUB

Section Eight: East Anglia	173
Lincolnshire and Cambridgeshire	175
Norfolk	184
Suffolk	196
Essex	201
Section Nine: Middle England	205
East Shropshire and the West Midlands	207
Warwickshire, Northamptonshire, Bedfordshire and Hertfordshire	214
Section Ten: Buckinghamshire, Oxfordshire, Berkshire and Wiltshire	219
Buckinghamshire	221
Oxfordshire	224
Berkshire	227
Wiltshire	229
Section Eleven: The Southern Counties	233
Dorset	235
Hampshire	238
Sussex	241
Kent	244
Section Twelve: Surrey and The Perfect Pub	249
Surrey	251
The Perfect Pub	252
Index	255

The Quest for the Perfect Pub

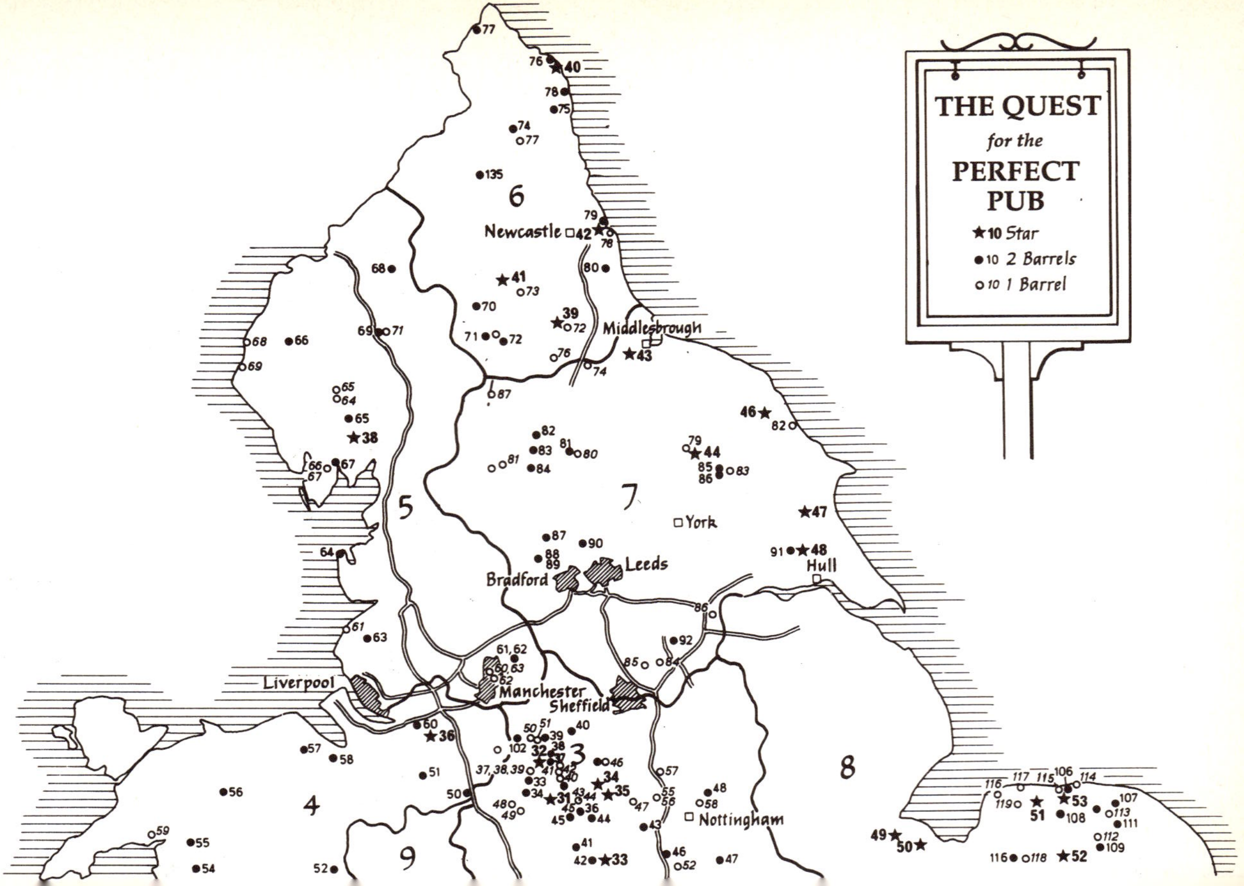
THE QUEST
for the
PERFECT
PUB
★10 Star
●10 2 Barrels
○10 1 Barrel
Newcastle
Middlesbrough
York
Leeds
Bradford
Hull
Liverpool
Manchester
Sheffield
Nottingham

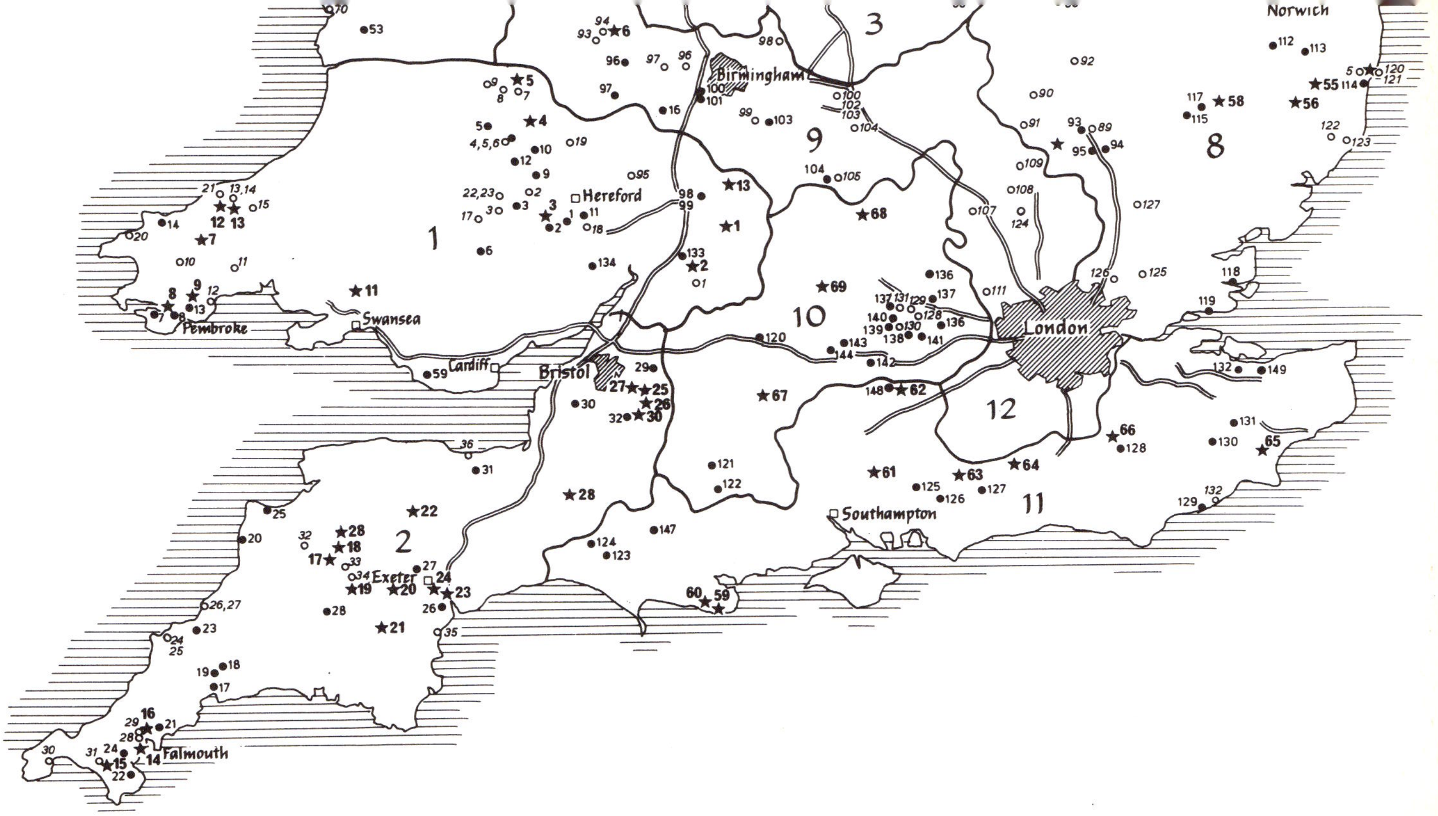

Norwich
Birmingham
London
Hereford
Swansea
Pembroke
Cardiff
Bristol
Exeter
Southampton
Falmouth

Star Pubs

1. **The Plough, Ford**
   Gloucestershire *L. and A. Carter*
2. **The Five Mile House, Duntisbourne Abbots**
   Gloucestershire *M. Ruck*
3. **The Cornewall Arms, Clodock**
   Herefordshire
4. **The Sun Inn, Leintwardine**
   Herefordshire *C. Lane*
5. **The Three Tuns, Bishops Castle**
   Shropshire *J. and D. Wood*
6. **The All Nations, Madeley**
   Shropshire *E. Lewis*
7. **The Presselli Arms Hotel, Rosebush**
   (Pembrokeshire) Dyfed *M. Lewis*
8. **The White Hart, Pembroke Dock**
   Dyfed *H. Lancaster*
9. **The Cresselly Arms, Cresswell Quay**
   (Pembrokeshire) Dyfed *M. and J. Cole*
10. **The Nag's Head, Abercych**
    (Pembrokeshire) Dyfed *David Jones*
11. **The Dyfryn Arms, Gwaun Valley**
    (Pembrokeshire) Dyfed
12. **The Mason's Arms, Cilgerran**
    (Pembrokeshire) Dyfed *R. Ray*
13. **The Fleece, Bretforton**
    Worcestershire *D. and N. Davies*
14. **The Seven Stars, Falmouth**
    Cornwall *J. Barrington Bennets*
15. **The Blue Anchor, Helston**
    Cornwall *S. and P. Cannon*
16. **The Pandora Inn, Restronguet Creek**
    Cornwall *R. and H. Hough*
17. **The Tally Ho, Hatherleigh**
    Devon *G. and S. Scoz*
18. **The Duke of York, Iddesleigh**
    Devon *J. Colville*
19. **The Oxenham Arms, South Zeal**
    Devon *J. Henry*
20. **The Drewe Arms, Drewsteignton**
    Devon *M. Mudge*
21. **The Rugglestone Inn, Widecombe**
    Devon *A. Lamb*
22. **The Mason's Arms, Knowstone**
    Devon *D. and E. Todd*
23. **The Bridge, Topsham**
    Devon *E. and P. Chefers*
24. **The Double Locks, Alphington**
    Devon *J. Stuart*
25. **The Star, Bath**
    Avon *Allen Perrett*
26. **The Packhorse, South Stoke**
    Avon *T. Brewer*
27. **The Crown, Kelston**
    Avon *M. Steele*
28. **The Rose and Crown, Huish Episcopi**
    Somerset *E. Pittard*
29. **The Seymour Arms, Witham Friary**
    Somerset *J. Douel*
30. **The Tucker's Grave, Faulkland**
    Somerset *I. and G. Swift*
31. **The Yew Tree, Cauldon**
    Staffordshire *A. East*
32. **The Royal Cottage, Royal Cottage**
    Staffordshire *Olive Prince*

KEY

33 **The Coopers Tavern, Burton-on-Trent**
Staffordshire *H. and T. Knight*

34 **The Olde Gate Inn, Brassington**
Derbyshire *P. and E. Burlington*

35 **The Barley Mow, Kirk Ireton**
Derbyshire *M. Short*

36 **The Holly Bush, Little Leigh**
Cheshire *A. Cowap*

37 **The Harrington Arms, Gawsworth**
Cheshire *M. Bayley*

38 **The Mason's Arms, Strawberry Bank**
Cumbria *H. and N. Stephenson*

39 **The Dun Cow, Billy Row**
Co. Durham *S. Parkin*

40 **The Olde Ship, Seahouses**
Northumberland *A. Glen*

41 **The Lord Crewe Arms, Blanchland**
Northumberland *P. Gingell*

42 **The Wolsington House, North Shields**
Tyne and Wear *Hugh Price*

43 **The Sun Inn, Stockton**
Cleveland *M. Walker*

44 **The Star, Harome**
North Yorkshire *P. Gascoigne-Mullett*

45 **The George, Hubberholme**
North Yorkshire *J. Frederick*

46 **The Moorcock, Langdale End**
North Yorkshire *M. Martindale*

47 **The Eagle, Skerne**
Humberside *R. and S. Edmond*

48 **The White Horse, Beverley**
Humberside *B. Thurnaby*

49 **The Saracen's Head, Saracen's Head**
Lincolnshire *J. Moss and A. Hill*

50 **The Bull Hotel, Long Sutton**
Lincolnshire *Mrs Mitchell*

51 **The Lord Nelson, Burnham Thorpe**
Norfolk *L. Winter*

52 **The Bell, Brisley**
Norfolk *A. Griggs*

53 **The Horseshoes, Warham**
Norfolk *I. Salmon*

54 **The Harbour, Southwold**
Suffolk *R. Westwood*

55 **The King's Head, Laxfield**
Suffolk *J. Parsons*

56 **The Victoria, Earl Soham**
Suffolk *C. and J. Bjornson*

57 **The Butt and Oyster, Pin Mill**
Suffolk *R. Mainwaring*

58 **The Black Fox, Thurston**
Suffolk *J. Ong*

59 **The Square and Compass, Worth Maltravers**
Dorset *R. Newman*

60 **The Fox, Corfe Castle**
Dorset *G. White*

61 **The Flowerpots, Cheriton**
Hampshire *P. Bartlett*

62 **The Mill, Dipley**
Hampshire

63 **The Duke of Cumberland, Henley**
Sussex *R. Seaman*

64 **The Blue Ship, The Haven, Billingshurst**
West Sussex *J. Davie*

65 **The Red Lion, Snargate**
Kent *D. George*

66 **The Queen's Arms, Cowden Cross**
Kent *E. Maynard*

67 **The Bruce Arms, Easton Royal**
Wiltshire *E. Raisey*

68 **The Peyton Arms, Stoke Lyne**
Oxfordshire *N. Oxlade*

69 **The Dun Cow, Northmoor**
Oxfordshire *J. Douglas*

Two Barrel Pubs
(represented on map by ●)

1 **Cupid's Hill, Pontrilas**
Herefordshire
2 **The Carpenter's Arms, Walterstone**
Herefordshire
3 **The Bull's Head, Craswall**
Hereford and Worcester
4 **The Farmer's Arms, Presteigne**
Powys
5 **The Greyhound, Llangunllo**
Powys
6 **The White Hart, Talybont-on-Usk**
Powys
7 **The Point House, Angle Bay**
(Pembrokeshire), Dyfed
8 **The Navy, Pembroke Street**
Pembroke Dock (Pembrokeshire), Dyfed
9 **The Three Horseshoes, Norton Canon**
Herefordshire
10 **The Stagge Inn, Titley**
Herefordshire
11 **The Cottage of Content, Carey**
Herefordshire
12 **The Tavern, Kington**
Herefordshire
13 **The Carew Inn, Carew**
(Pembrokeshire), Dyfed
14 **The Fishguard Arms, Fishguard**
(Pembrokeshire), Dyfed
15 **The Fox and Hounds, Cwmcych**
(Pembrokeshire), Dyfed
16 **The Plough, Shenstone**
Hereford and Worcester
17 **The New Inn, Tywardreath**
Cornwall
18 **The Crown, Lanlivery**
Cornwall
19 **The King's Arms, Luxulyan**
Cornwall
20 **The Bush Inn, Morwenstow**
Cornwall
21 **The Roseland Inn, Philleigh**
Cornwall
22 **The New Inn, Manaccan, St Keverne**
Cornwall
23 **The St Kew Inn, St Kew**
Cornwall
24 **Trengilly Wartha, Constantine, Nancenoy**
Cornwall
25 **The Clovelly Inn, Bratton Clovelly**
Devon
26 **The Turf, Exminster**
Devon
27 **The Beer Engine, Newton St Cyres**
Devon
28 **The Castle Inn, Lydford**
Devon
29 **The Catherine Wheel, Marshfield**
Avon
30 **The Crown, Churchill**
Avon
31 **The Notley Arms, Monksilver**
Avon
32 **The George, Norton St Philip**
Somerset
33 **The Sealion, Leek**
Staffordshire
34 **The Boat, Cheddleton**
Staffordshire

xiv

KEY

35 **The George, Alstonefield**
Staffordshire
36 **The Sycamore, Parwich**
Derbyshire
37 **The Butcher's Arms, Reapsmoor**
Staffordshire
38 **The Jug and Glass, Newhaven**
Derbyshire
39 **The Baker's Arms, West Street, Buxton**
Derbyshire
40 **The Red Lion, Litton**
Derbyshire
41 **The Swan, Draycott-in-the-Clay**
Staffordshire
42 **The Burton Bridge Brewery Tap, High Street, Burton-on-Trent**
Staffordshire
43 **The Malt Shovel, Potter Street, Spondon**
Derbyshire
44 **The French Horn, Rodsley**
Derbyshire
45 **The Queen Adelaide, Snelston**
Derbyshire
46 **Cap and Stocking, Kegworth**
Leicestershire
47 **The Crown, Old Dalby**
Leicestershire
48 **The Cross Keys, Epperstone**
Nottinghamshire
49 **The Red Lion, Birchover**
Derbyshire
50 **The White Lion, Barthonley**
Cheshire
51 **The Traveller's Rest, Alpraham**
Cheshire
52 **The Horseshoe, Llanyblodwel**
Clwyd
53 **The Slater's Arms, Corris**
Gwynedd
54 **Tyn-y-Groes, Ganllwyd**
Gwynedd
55 **The White Lion, Trawsfynydd**
Gwynedd
56 **The White Horse, Capel Garmon**
Gwynedd
57 **The Fox, Ysceifiog**
Clwyd
58 **The White Lion, Pen-y-Myndd**
Clwyd
59 **The King's Head, Broughton**
Clwyd
60 **The Chetwode Arms, Lower Whitley**
Cheshire
61 **The Station Buffet, Stalybridge**
Greater Manchester
62 **The Horse and Jockey, Stanedge, Delph**
Greater Manchester
63 **The Heaton's Bridge, Heaton's Bridge, Scarisbrick**
Lancashire
64 **Fleetwood Arms, Dock Street, Fleetwood**
Lancashire
65 **The Tower Bank Arms, Near Sawrey**
Cumbria
66 **The Black Cock, Eaglesfield**
Cumbria
67 **The Racehorse, Arran Foot, Near Ulverston**
Cumbria
68 **The Hare and Hounds, Talkin**
Cumbria
69 **The Agricultural Hotel, Cromwell Road, Penrith**
Cumbria
70 **The Cows Hill Hotel, Cows Hill, Weardale**
Co. Durham
71 **Langdon Beck Hotel, Teesdale**
Co. Durham
72 **The Bridge, Middleton-in-Teesdale**
Co. Durham
73 **The Ship, Low Newton-by-Sea**
Northumberland

xv

THE QUEST FOR THE PERFECT PUB

74 **The Star, Netherton**
Northumberland
75 **The Oddfellows Arms, Narrowgate, Alnwick**
Northumberland
76 **The Black Swan, Seahouses**
Northumberland
77 **The Mason's Arms, Norham-on-Tweed**
Northumberland
78 **The Jolly Fisherman, Craster**
Northumberland
79 **The Wooden Doll, Hudson Street, North Shields**
Tyne and Wear
80 **The Golden Lion, The Broadway, Houghton-le-Spring**
Tyne and Wear
81 **The White Bear, Masham**
North Yorkshire
82 **The Blue Lion, East Witton**
North Yorkshire
83 **The Thwaite Arms, Horsehouse**
North Yorkshire
84 **The Fox and Hounds, Starbottom**
North Yorkshire
85 **The Blue Ball, Malton**
North Yorkshire
86 **The Spotted Cow, Malton**
North Yorkshire
87 **The Swan, Main Street, Addingham**
West Yorkshire
88 **The Turkey, Goose Eye**
West Yorkshire
89 **The Grinning Rat, Keighley**
West Yorkshire
90 **The Bay Horse, Market Place, Otley**
West Yorkshire
91 **The Royal Standard (Dolly's), North Bar Within, Beverley**
Humberside
92 **The Woodlands Hotel, Great North Road, Woodlands**
South Yorkshire
93 **The Free Press, Prospect Row, Cambridge**
Cambridgeshire
94 **The Tickell Arms, Whittlesford**
Cambridgeshire
95 **The Queen's Head, Newton**
Cambridgeshire
96 **The Railwayman's Arms, Platform, Severn Valley Railway Station, Bridgenorth**
Shropshire
97 **The Fox and Hounds, Stottesdon**
Shropshire
98 **The Old Swan (Ma Pardoe's), Halesowen Road, Netherton**
West Midlands
99 **The Little Dry Dock, Windmill End, Netherton**
West Midlands
100 **O'Rourke's Pie Factory, Hurst Lane, Tipton**
West Midlands
101 **The Vine (Bull and Bladder), Delph Road, Brierley Hill**
West Midlands
102 **The Brewery Inn, Station Road, Langley**
West Midlands
103 **The Case Is Altered, Five Ways, Haseley Knob**
Warwickshire
104 **The Marston Inn, Marston St Lawrence**
Northamptonshire
105 **The 4.30 Liverpool Street to King's Lynn Special**
(British Rail)
106 **The Anchor, Morston**
Norfolk
107 **The Chequers, Gresham**
Norfolk
108 **The Bull, Walsingham**
Norfolk
109 **The Earle Arms, Heydon**
Norfolk
110 **The Hare and Hounds, Baconsthorpe**
Norfolk
111 **The Buckinghamshire Arms, Blickling**
Norfolk

xvi

KEY

112 **The Greyhound, Tibbenham**
Norfolk
113 **The Cherry Tree, Harleston**
Norfolk
114 **The Bell, Walberswick**
Suffolk
115 **The Pickerel, Ixworth**
Suffolk
116 **The Bennett Arms, Rougham**
Suffolk
117 **The Nutshell, The Traverse, Bury St Edmunds**
Suffolk
118 **The White Harte, Burnham-on-Crouch**
Essex
119 **The Crooked Billet, High Street, Leigh-on-Sea**
Essex
120 **The New Inn, Coate**
Wiltshire
121 **The Beckford Arms, Fonthill Gifford**
Wiltshire
122 **The Horseshoe Inn, Ebbesbourne**
Wiltshire
123 **The Tiger's Head, Rampisham**
Dorset
124 **The Fox, Corscombe**
Dorset
125 **The White Horse, Prior's Dean, Petersfield**
Hampshire
126 **The Three Horseshoes, Elsted**
West Sussex
127 **The Black Horse, Byworth**
West Sussex
128 **The Dorset Arms, Withyam**
East Sussex
129 **The Palace Bars, White Rock, Hastings**
East Sussex
130 **The Three Chimneys, Biddenden**
Kent

131 **The Bell, Smarden**
Kent
132 **The Mounted Rifleman, Luddenham**
Kent
133 **The Golden Heart, Birdlip**
Gloucestershire
134 **The Dog and Muffler, Joyford**
Gloucestershire
135 **The Holly Bush, Tarset**
Northumberland
136 **The Lions of Bledlow, Bledlow**
Buckinghamshire
137 **The Bull and Butcher, Turville**
Buckinghamshire
138 **Clayton Arms, Quoiting Square, Marlow**
Buckinghamshire
139 **The Old Ship, Cadmore End**
Buckinghamshire
140 **The Lamb, Rotherfield Grays**
Oxfordshire
141 **The Crooked Billet, Stoke Row**
Oxfordshire
142 **The Black Horse, Checkendon**
Oxfordshire
143 **The Old Hatch Gate, Cockpole Green**
Berkshire
144 **The Pot Kiln, Frilsham**
Berkshire
145 **The Crown and Horns, East Ilsley**
Berkshire
146 **The Ibex, Chaddleworth**
Berkshire
147 **The Fiddleford Inn, Fiddleford**
Dorset
148 **The New Inn, Stratfield Saye**
Hampshire
149 **The Shipwright's Arms, Ham Street, Oare**
Kent

One Barrel Pubs
(represented on map by ○)

1. **The Daneway Inn, Sapperton**
   Gloucestershire
2. **The Red Lion Hotel, Bredwardine**
   Herefordshire
3. **The Abbey Hotel, Llanthony Priory, Llanthony**
   Gwent
4. **The Barley Mow, Presteigne**
   Powys
5. **The Bull, Presteigne**
   Powys
6. **The Radnorshire Arms, Presteigne**
   Powys
7. **The Powis Arms, Lydbury North**
   Shropshire
8. **The Crown, Newcastle-on-Clun**
   Shropshire
9. **The Anchor, Anchor**
   Shropshire
10. **The Crown, Walton**
    Powys
11. **The Fishers Hotel, Whitland**
    Gwent
12. **The Royal Oak, Saundersfoot**
    (Pembrokeshire), Dyfed
13. **The Black Lion, Cardigan**
    Dyfed
14. **The White Hart, Cenarth**
    (Pembrokeshire), Dyfed
15. **The Emlyn Arms, Newcastle Emlyn**
    Dyfed
16. **The Brunant Arms, Caio**
    Dyfed
17. **The Radnor Arms, Talgarth**
    (Breconshire), Powys
18. **The British Lion, King's Caple**
    Herefordshire
19. **The Stockton Cross, Kimbolton**
    Herefordshire
20. **The Sloop Inn, Porth Gain**
    (Pembrokeshire), Dyfed
21. **The Castle, Bridge End, Cardigan**
    Dyfed
22. **The Blue Boar, Hay-on-Wye**
    Herefordshire/Powys
23. **The Three Tuns, Hay-on-Wye**
    Herefordshire/Powys
24. **The London Inn, Padstow**
    Cornwall
25. **The Old Ship Hotel, Padstow**
    Cornwall
26. **The Hotel on the Strand, Trebarwith Strand**
    Cornwall
27. **The Mill House Inn, Trebarwith Strand**
    Cornwall
28. **The Lemon Arms, Mylor Bridge**
    Cornwall
29. **The Seven Stars, Penryn**
    Cornwall
30. **The Union Hotel, Chapel Street, Penzance**
    Cornwall
31. **The Angel Hotel, Helston**
    Cornwall
32. **The Devil's Stone Inn, Shebbear**
    Devon

KEY

33 The New Inn, Sampford Courtenay
Devon
34 The Devonshire Arms, Sticklepath
Devon
35 The Teign Brewery, Teignmouth
Devon
36 The Bell, Watchet
Somerset
37 The Flying Horse, Leek
Staffordshire
38 The Britannia, Leek
Staffordshire
39 The Merrie Monk, Compton Street, Leek
Staffordshire
40 The Cavalier, Grindon
Staffordshire
41 The Royal Oak, Welton
Staffordshire
42 The Manifold Valley, Hulme End
Staffordshire
43 The Horns, Ashbourne
Derbyshire
44 Smith's Tavern, Ashbourne
Derbyshire
45 The George and Dragon, Ashbourne
Derbyshire
46 The Three Stags' Heads, Wardlow Mires
Derbyshire
47 The Hurt Arms, Ambergate
Derbyshire
48 The Black Lion, Consall Forge
Staffordshire
49 The Plough Inn, Kingsley
Staffordshire
50 The Bull I' Th' Thorn, Hurdlow Town, Buxton
Derbyshire
51 The Duke of York, Buxton
Derbyshire
52 The Swan in the Rushes, The Rushes, Loughborough
Leicestershire

53 The Bluebell, Belmesthorpe
Leicestershire
54 The Star, West Leake
Nottinghamshire
55 The New White Bull, Eastwood
Nottinghamshire
56 The New Inn, Newthorpe Common
Nottinghamshire
57 The Miner's Arms, Huthwater
Nottinghamshire
58 The Woodlark, Church Street, Langley
Nottinghamshire
59 The Ship, Lombard Street, Porth Madog
Gwynedd
60 The Tandle Hill Tavern, Thornham Lane, Slattocks, Middleton
Greater Manchester
61 The Ship Inn, Cable Street, Southport
Merseyside
62 The Ram's Head, Ripponden Road, Denshaw
Greater Manchester
63 The Wasdale Head Inn, Wasdale Head
Cumbria
64 The Old Dungeon Ghyll Hotel, Langdale
Cumbria
65 The Britannia Inn, Eltwater
Cumbria
66 The Devonshire, Victoria Road, Ulverston
Cumbria
67 The King's Head, Queen Street, Ulverston
Cumbria
68 The George IV Inn, Stanley Street, Workington
Cumbria
69 The Central, Whitehaven
Cumbria
70 The Wheatsheaf, Barrow-in-Furness
Cumbria

THE QUEST FOR THE PERFECT PUB

71 **The Museum Inn, Castlegate**
   Cumbria
72 **The Newton Cap, Bishop Auckland**
   Co. Durham
73 **The Firtree, Cornsay Colliery**
   Co. Durham
74 **The Black Swan, Parkgate, Darlington**
   Co. Durham
75 **The High Force Hotel, Teesdale**
   Co. Durham
76 **The Cross Keys, Gainford**
   Co. Durham
77 **The Turk's Head, Rothbury**
   Northumberland
78 **The Holborn Rose and Crown, East Holborn, South Shields**
   Tyne and Wear
79 **The Malt Shovel, Oswaldkirk**
   North Yorkshire
80 **The Bay Horse, Masham**
   North Yorkshire
81 **The White Lion, Cray**
   North Yorkshire
82 **The Leeds Arms, St Mary Street, Scarborough**
   North Yorkshire
83 **The Royal Oak, Old Malton**
   North Yorkshire
84 **The Cadeby Inn, Cadeby**
   South Yorkshire
85 **The Terrace, Kilnhurst**
   South Yorkshire
86 **The Winning Pot, Moorends**
   South Yorkshire
87 **The Tan Hill Inn, Keld**
   North Yorkshire
88 **The Swan Inn, Parson Drove**
   Cambridgeshire
89 **The Cambridge Blue, Gwydir Street, Cambridge**
   Cambridgeshire
90 **The Victoria, Ouse Walk, Huntingdon**
   Cambridgeshire
91 **The Wheatsheaf, Church Street, St Neots**
   Cambridgeshire
92 **The Ship, Chatteris**
   Cambridgeshire
93 **The New Inn, Ironbridge**
   Shropshire
94 **The Bird In Hand, Ironbridge**
   Shropshire
95 **The Waggon and Horses, Reddal Hill Road, Cradley Heath**
   West Midlands
96 **The Struggling Man, Salop Street, Dudley**
   West Midlands
97 **The Crooked House (Glynne Arms), Himley**
   West Midlands
98 **The Maid of the Mills, Atherstone**
   Warwickshire
99 **The Durham Ox, Shrewley**
   Warwickshire
100 **The Shoulder of Mutton, Stretton-on-Dunsmore**
    Warwickshire
101 **The Engine, Bridget Street, Rugby**
    Warwickshire
102 **The Raglan Arms, Dunchurch Road, Rugby**
    Warwickshire
103 **The Squirrel, Church Street, Rugby**
    Warwickshire
104 **The Dun Cow, Daventry**
    Northamptonshire
105 **The George and Dragon, Chacombe**
    Northamptonshire
106 **The Swan, Newton Bromswold**
    Northamptonshire
107 **The Sow and Pigs, Toddington**
    Bedfordshire
108 **The Musgrave Arms, Shillington**
    Bedfordshire
109 **The Cock, Broom**
    Bedfordshire
110 **The Plough, Ley Green**
    Hertfordshire

KEY

111 The Swan, Park Road, Bushey
Hertfordshire
112 The Old Brewery House,
Reepham
Norfolk
113 The Walpole Arms,
Itteringham
Norfolk
114 The King's Arms, Blakeney
Norfolk
115 The Bluebell, Langham
Norfolk
116 The Lifeboat, Thornham
Norfolk
117 The Jolly Sailors, Brancaster
Staithe
Norfolk
118 The Ostrich, Castleacre
Norfolk
119 The Chequers, Binham
Norfolk
120 The Crown, High Street,
Southwold
Suffolk
121 The Lord Nelson, East
Street, Southwold
Suffolk

122 The Oyster, Butley
Suffolk
123 The Jolly Sailor, Orford
Suffolk
124 The Green Man, Little
Braxted
Essex
125 The Viper, Mill Green
Essex
126 The Mole Trap, Stapleford
Tawney
Essex
127 The Rising Sun, Duton Hill
Essex
128 The Stag and Huntsman,
Hambledon
Buckinghamshire
129 The Old Crown, Skirmett
Buckinghamshire
130 The Crown, Nuffield
Oxfordshire
131 The Fox and Hounds,
Christmas Common
Oxfordshire
132 The Duck, Pett Bottom
Kent

Introduction

There are 83,000 public houses in Britain. Our task seemed simple. It was the Mesmerizing Brunette Editor (MBE) at the publishers' office who had given us our brief.

'Find the best 200 pubs in the country,' she snapped, dousing her cheroot in our glass of low-alcohol Masson Lite, 'and don't show your faces in Bloomsbury until you've written about them. You have three months.' She checked her Cartier watch. 'Starting from now. Get out.'

We left her luxurious office. Over the next few days, as we made our fevered preparations, the queue of friends turning up at our front doors and jockeying for a place in the back seat of the car grew ever longer.

'Lucky beggars,' they whined, 'what a job! Count me in; you must need a navigator.'

Yes indeed. What a job! We smiled smugly to ourselves as we headed down the M40 towards the Welsh Borders. A piece of cake.

There are 83,000 pubs in Great Britain. Now, after travelling 20,000 miles down motorway, backroad and dirt-track, we wish there weren't. For in spite of visiting over 2,000 of the 'best' of these, relying either on our own research, inside information in the areas concerned, or other publications, it proved an almost impossible task to find 300 that we can wholeheartedly recommend.

We had fondly imagined that lurking in the lanes of each county were scores of gems, from tiny one-room drinkers to great all-round inns, full of contented people and run by solicitous and dedicated licensees.

The truth came as a bitter blow. In the last two decades and with gathering momentum, the breweries (for it is mainly they who are to blame) have systematically ripped out not only the interiors, but also the very heart of the English pub. This is a continuing act of legitimized vandalism that the public are only now beginning to comprehend, just as it took fifteen years for the full horrors of the architectural blackguardism that took place in the High Streets of the 1960s to permeate the national consciousness.

The sad fact is that as we approach the last decade of the century, the British public house as we know it, that venerable and cherished institution, is threatened with extinction. It is as bad as that. Despite sterling work from CAMRA and other pressure groups, the brewery bulldozer rolls on, flattening all before it. It is almost too late to stop the destruction and salvage the survivors. Almost. The decision by the Monopolies Commission to limit the number of pubs owned by a brewery is obviously very welcome, but it has come several years too late and most of the damage has already been done.

As these pages will reveal to you, we have winkled out approximately 300 'proper' pubs of all types – the best 300 in the country; some of these are threatened with extinction and need your support, some have survived against all the odds, and some – usually free houses – are in the vanguard of an encouraging backlash against mindless brewery uniformity.

There are also a fair number of near-misses – those pubs that just failed to make the top 300 but are still worthy of your attention. We have listed these as well.

Let us take you back, and retrace with you some of the origins and traditions that made the British pub what it was until so recently.

A public house is 'an establishment providing alcoholic liquors to be consumed on the premises.' So says the *Macropaedia Britannica*, and as a basic definition that is perfectly accurate. But oh Lord, how very much more there is to it than that.

Since the ale-houses of Saxon times, pubs have been an integral part of the English way of life. (Scotland has by no means the same tradition; there is a strict delineation between bar and hotel, or drinking house and place in which to stay. The concept of the all-rounder is unknown there and hence we have not ventured north of the border.)

Quite early on, Common Law declared that the inns – where, in addition to drink, accommodation is available – and the taverns – where food is also provided – must receive all travellers who are in reasonable condition and who are able to pay the price.

It is popularly supposed that the public house reached its zenith in the sixteenth and seventeenth centuries, and this is probably correct.

If you were able to choose one night's entertainment at one pub anywhere and at any time, you could do worse than to drop into the Mermaid Tavern, Cheapside, on the first Friday evening of any month in the early 1600s. Here would meet the Friday Street Club, famous for its sparkling wit and consumption of Canary wine. On a good night you might bang into Walter Raleigh, the doomed founder-member, John Donne, the great metaphysical poet later to take the cloth, even Willie Shakespeare himself. At a table in the corner you might observe the misogynist drinking companions Francis Beaumont and John Fletcher, hard at work composing such immortal lines as 'Nose, nose, jolly red nose/ And who gave thee this jolly red nose?' or, during a particularly perceptive session, 'There is no drinking after death.' Indeed, Beaumont was so bored during an enforced absence from his favourite boozer that he wrote to fellow member Ben Johnson: 'I lie and dream of your full Mermaid wine.' He continued:

> *What things have we seen*
> *Done at the Mermaid! heard words that have been*
> *So nimble, and so full of subtil flame,*
> *As if that every one from whence they came,*
> *Had meant to put his whole wit in a jest,*
> *And had resolv'd to live a fool, the rest*
> *Of his dull life.*

However, things were not all sweetness and light in the taverns of those times. One of the greatest poets of them all, Christopher Marlowe, was struck down at the untimely age of 29 by one Ingram Frisar in a Deptford dive after an argument over the bill. And as far as the Mermaid was concerned, it must have been quite a blow to the regulars when it was burned down in the Great Fire of 1666. At least they were not forced to repair to a Chef and Brewer.

The great days of the coaching inn are well chronicled, and many fine examples of these buildings survive, though the interiors of most have been desecrated (see The Old Coaching Inn House, Chudleigh, Devon, p. 77). Contemporary drawings and cartoons have combined to create a legacy of jolly, red-faced travelling companions drinking tankard after tankard of mulled wine by a roaring fire and a table groaning with victuals, while outside in the frosty stable-yard the trusty horses stand snorting and stamping. The reality was rather less cosy and considerably more uncomfortable. Many are the tales of swindling landlords and murderous ostlers, of horses being cut in half in the accelerating race between coaches to get there first, of the 'outsiders' being found frozen to death on their arrival, and of the constant threat from marauding bands of highwaymen (the first of whom were former Royalist officers left penniless and disaffected at the end of the Civil War). The coaching days reached their high point around 1825, just when the steam engine that was to bring about their decline was taking its first tentative lurch along the iron road of the Stockton and Darlington Railway.

By the mid 1800s public houses in general were regarded as superior to the ginshops and beerhouses which had proliferated in the cities, and the continuing rise of the middle classes led landlords to divide their houses into several different bars to distinguish between the various ranks of drinkers. In the North there are still rare examples of large pubs with many small rooms. It is only now that the practice of keeping separate public and saloon bars is being sacrificed in favour of the soulless open-plan concept so beloved of the big breweries.

This brings us up to date and to the point of this book. There is no doubt that since the war the public house has sunk to the nadir in which it is now floundering, a degradation which revealed itself to us more and more as we travelled the country. When, from the end of the 1950s, a good proportion of the smaller independent breweries, who had been serving their area well with a network of perhaps twenty or thirty tied houses and presenting a truly local identity to the world, were sucked, Jonah-like, into the maws of the conglomerate whales – Watneys, Courage, Allied, Bass and others – then the fate of the pub seemed to have been sealed.

Once the big breweries had made the beer all taste the same, it needed only a logical extension of this magic formula and – hey presto! – everything would become the same. The glitter-

INTRODUCTION

eyed zealots from the marketing departments who didn't know a pub from a Ford Escort set about recreating the food and decor of their premises in such a way that you actually couldn't tell one from the other.

By the time of the bleak and inflationary three-day weeks of the early Seventies a similar scene was being enacted in similar pubs on any night of the week:

'Yes?'

'Two Babychams, three scampi platters and a pint of urine, please.'

'Garnish?'

'I beg your pardon?'

'A tired piece of lettuce and an onion ring?'

'I really don't care.'

'Twenty-seven pounds fifty.'

How the marketing director and his fellow conspirators must have guffawed between sips of the chairman's claret as they reaped the rewards of this gigantic con-trick. They had proved that you can fool some of the people all of the time.

Luckily, a few inspired souls realized what was going on and started to rebel. It is easy to ridicule the Campaign for Real Ale as a bunch of earnest, bearded, pipe-smoking, Lefty beer-bores with leather elbow-patches and knitted ties, but their achievement is undeniable. They took on Moby Dick and beached him. Watneys were forced to remove Red Barrel from the market and learn how to brew beer again, and other breweries followed suit, up to a point.

It has to be said that drinkable beer is now available in 70 per cent of public houses and that independent breweries such as Adnams, Brakspears, Samuel Smiths and many others are thriving again. But the conglomerates can take none of the credit for this and in most areas their alleged marketing skills still hold both pub and punter in thrall.

But this book is not about beer, and the sad truth is that what is now needed is a Campaign for Real Pubs. The good old-fashioned English boozer is an endangered species at the mercy of many horrific modern enemies: decors of unparalleled artificiality, astonishing nylon carpets that send shockwaves searing through the body, appalling piped music, microwaved pizza and other Eurostodge, bleeping video-games, bland juke-boxes, American designer 'beer', unsuitably-flavoured potato 'snax'. One by one the old pubs are being swallowed up by the catering chains, whose thrusting, Next-clad young executives are at this very moment roaming the country. Their acquisitions are speedily turned into half-hearted 'theme' pubs, probably called Funsters, Hank's or the Raj, where a plastic mill-stream, bar staff in Stetsons, or a yellowing pith-helmet on the wall are considered to be bold and radical statements in 'Leisure-time programming'. If you feel like blowing up such places, or merely hitting the landlord, then this is the book for you.

It is not intended as a guidebook. There are several of these on the market. If you wish to know they will tell you about the 'well-kept Squiffington's on handpump which may be sampled in the charming oak-beamed lounge where nautical prints are a feature'. What they won't tell you is that this is a hoity-toity, pretentious, chintzy little hell-hole where you have to wade your way through Alan and Judith's home-cooked horror-story of a menu before you can safely get your face round a drink.

Instead, this book sets out to be a celebration of the fact that there are, thank God, a few proper pubs still left in England, true to the old traditions and upholding the values of privacy and simple pleasure which are so scorned in modern life. However, in the writing, these pages have also become a lament that the few oases left are increasingly few and far between, far scarcer than we had ever imagined, and it can be no coincidence that the disappearance of proper pubs mirrors the general decline in the quality of rural life and the encroachment of the New Town, the Shopping Mall and the fast-food outlet.

The 200 main entries in this book are a careful selection of places that we consider to be the best 200 pubs in the country, that is to say in the countryside, villages and smaller towns of England and Wales. We have left the cities and large conurbations for a future book.

You may take issue with our choice; everyone has his or her favourite pub, and there are many excellent places that we have enjoyed but left out for one reason or another.

Bear in mind also that this book is not written by committee or local contributors. We have covered all the ground ourselves, and where a region proved to have no pub worthy of our selection, we have made no attempt to include one merely for the sake of geographical balance.

INTRODUCTION

So, what is the definition of a perfect pub? There are many different types, and a dogmatic attitude is counterproductive. The basic criteria are: attractive interiors, quality of service, good conversation, a variety of non-electronic pub games, good real ale, good real fires, commitment to the local community. They come in many shapes and sizes from one-room drinkers to thriving and well-known inns: some have superb food, some merely baps; some have excellent accommodation, some but a bar, a barrel and a bench or two. What they all share in common is that they are proper pubs, exciting to discover, fun to frequent and hard to leave.

Each in its own way is as near as you can get to the perfect pub and we have categorized them as follows:

ORD: The One-Room Drinker. Not always one room, but old-fashioned, unspoilt, basic, often without a bar, usually no food to speak of, possibly under the same licensee for many years.

GLL: The Good Little Local. As it sounds, be it in a village, on a street corner, in the countryside, with a good local feel.

LLL: The Lively Little Local. A more boisterous version of GLL, often with other attractions, music, games, etc.

GMTH: The Good Market Town Hotel. Rare these days and not necessarily in a market town, but a civilized and traditional place offering food and beds.

GAR: The Good All-Rounder. An establishment, be it primitive or de luxe, which offers a particularly good combination of any of the following ingredients: bar life, conviviality, welcome, food, beds, games, entertainment, conversation, fun.

GGAR: The Great All-Rounder. An accolade awarded only to the best of the GARs.

GITS: The Good In A Tight Spot. The near-misses.

We do not list the beers or comment on the food unless the quality is exceptional. Qualifying symbols have been limited to the following, any of which may appear with the categories above.

THE QUEST FOR THE PERFECT PUB

★ (star)
with **BOLD TYPE**:
Awarded to the very best pubs in the country, regardless of category.

🛢🛢 (two barrels)
with **BOLD TYPE**:
Denotes other near-perfect pubs that just fall short of ★ rating.

🛢 (one barrel)
with ORDINARY TYPE:
Denotes pubs of high merit in the Second Division.

FC
(Flat Caps):
Pubs frequented by the old boys to whom the book is dedicated, who know what a good pub is, and are always the best conversationalists in the bar.

I
(Isolated):
Pubs in an isolated position, often fun/difficult to find and all the better for it.

W
(Welcome):
Pubs giving a particularly warm welcome, where you will easily fall into conversation.

F (Food):
Pubs providing particularly good food within their range, from baps to beef bourguignon.

B (Beds):
Pubs with accommodation, where it is a pleasure to stay, or with a billet if the session downstairs gets too much for you. Telephone numbers are given only for these establishments.

M (Music):
Pubs with live music, from singsong to a blues band, but always worth catching.

OP
(Oiled Precision):
Pubs run with a sure hand, lack of fuss, and maximum efficiency and charm.

E
(Eccentric):
Pubs of particular eccentricity, be it of the landlord, locals or building.

VE
(Very Eccentric):
Speaks for itself.

We have listed the licensee's name for all pubs awarded a star. Remember that a pub is only as good as its landlord, so check above the front door as you enter. The turnover can be very swift these days.

To those who feel that we are too critical of the current state of affairs, may we point out that in our opinion a good pub is one of the most enjoyable things in the world and essential to the wellbeing of humanity. In this view we are not alone. The great Dr Johnson pointed out: 'There is nothing which has yet been contrived by Man, by which so much happiness is produced as by a good tavern or inn.' This well-known and much-quoted dictum was echoed by his contemporary, the poet William Shenstone:

> *Whoe'er has travel'd life's dull round,*
> *Where'er his stages may have been,*
> *May sigh to think he still has found*
> *The warmest welcome, at an inn.*

And because we do feel so strongly on the subject we rather naturally detect the slipping of standards where other less prejudiced observers might not. After all, ever since a forward-thinking, Saxon ale-wife first erected a wattle roof to keep out the rain, people have been banging on about the Decline of the Pub and the End of the World As We Know It.

In conclusion, let us offer you a post-war quotation from a writer not known for his love of either ale or company, but one whose judgment on social issues was unerringly accurate and often prophetic:

> My favourite public house, 'The Moon under Water' . . . consists mostly of regulars who occupy the same chair every evening and go there for conversation as much as for beer. If you are asked why you favour a particular public house, it would seem natural to put the beer first, but the thing that most appeals to me about 'The Moon under Water' is what people call its 'atmosphere' . . . it has no glass-topped tables or other modern miseries and, on the other hand, no sham roof-beams, inglenooks or plastic panels masquerading as oak. . . . 'The Moon under Water' is my ideal of what a pub should be . . . but now is the time to reveal something which the discerning and disillusioned

THE QUEST FOR THE PERFECT PUB

reader will probably have guessed already. There is no such pub as 'The Moon under Water'.

George Orwell, *9th February 1946*

Our quest was to try to prove wrong the former Burma policeman and *plongeur*; was the perfect pub the modern equivalent of the Holy Grail, mythical, wonderful, unattainable? The next three months would take us from giddy heights to soul-numbing depths as we pursued our odyssey across the island, from Beer to Eternity.

Section One

Gloucestershire, Herefordshire, The Marches and Much of Wales

Gloucestershire

September 1st, Wednesday
Full of optimism, the advance jingling in our pockets, ski boots, butterfly nets and fishing rods stacked neatly in the dicky, we set off jauntily down the A40(M) on the first stage of our journey. Leaving Oxfordshire for later, we aimed for a safe house, one we had known for many years, which would put us in the right frame of mind to sally forth on our quest.

Let us, for a moment, consider the horror of present-day Gloucestershire and the Cotswolds. Because this area is pretty, within easy reach of London and recently en-royaled, it has in the last decade become infested with the worst type of Englishman and his chattels.

Every Friday, swathed in a waxed cotton cape, gripping the wheel of his Range Rover and talking urgently into a Voda-Fone, Damian leaves Parsons Green at 4 pm. Beside him is Annabel. She almost made the British Equestrian Team in 1971 and is now increasingly reliant on Harrods' beauty counter. In the rear are Tamsin, Rollo and Aubrey, all spoilt and about ten, and Ingrid, the au pair. Behind them a pair of under-exercised chocolate Labradors sprawl gloomily.

At 6 pm, after two hours of brutally arrogant driving, they are pulling up outside a sweet little wisteria-covered cottage the size of Blenheim Palace; the weekend has begun.

The next two days are a frenetic round of activity. There is Tamsin's first meet to be video'd, the OAP gardener to be bullied, and extravagant forays to butcher and wine merchant to be organized. There are gamebirds to be slaughtered, lunch for fifteen to be cooked, the proximity of the house to 'The Waleses' to be emphasized whenever possible, and endless gossip about friends in London to be exchanged. Then, at last, when the *Trivial Pursuit* board has been boxed for the evening, comes the moment when the chaps can sneak noisily out to the 'local'.

THE QUEST FOR THE PERFECT PUB

And this is where our story really starts. For the local has long gone, and with it the locals.

So if you, cosily ensconced in your own favourite pub, are thinking to yourself 'Yes, yes, I know the type they're on about, but isn't he too easy a target?'; or if, safe in the fastness of your remote stronghold, your thoughts perhaps lie more in the mould of 'Bugger Gloucestershire', then let us issue this stern warning: *Weekend Man is coming.*

It matters not where you may live, be it in the far Marches of the Welsh Border, aloft in the high peaks of Derbyshire, or under the wide, sweeping skies of East Anglia, you can be certain of one thing: he is coming. And he comes not alone, but with goods, hangers-on, chequebook and credit card.

What happened to Hampshire in the Sixties, to Gloucestershire in the Seventies, and what is happening so tragically now to Suffolk and Norfolk will, in time, be it ten, twenty or fifty years, also happen to the piece of country that you love. Weekend Man is multiplying, soon to be ubiquitous, omnipotent. Be honest with yourself. Examine yourself closely. Are you one of them? Is your best friend? Are we?

Except in very isolated areas almost all the pubs in Gloucestershire have fallen prey to this vicious animal, and are catering for him, aiding and abetting him. But there is a glimmer of hope that brightens as you travel West. In small villages and hamlets, away from the main roads, it is still possible to find the occasional, simple, decent pub, and here we highlight three of our favourites.

The backroad (B4077) from Stow-on-the-Wold to Tewkesbury offers one of the most pleasant drives in middle England. For some unaccountable and merciful reason the planners and developers have forgotten to spoil it. It winds, rises and falls, aggravates, charms. Between Stow and Toddington, in that part of the country where all signposts seem to point to Guitings, Swells and Slaughters, and on a tricky left-hand bend, is a huddle of buildings, caravans, barns and old buses. The chances are that on your arrival you will sweep past it and have to retrace your skid marks.

SECTION ONE

★ **THE PLOUGH, Ford, Gloucestershire. GGAR (FC, W, B, M, OP, E). Tel: 038 673-215. Les and Anne Carter.**
There is an unusual feeling about The Plough. You are at first perplexed, then you define it. It is the atmosphere of people enjoying themselves.

The pub is divided into three rooms, neither rough nor smart, and all as welcoming as each other. Good home cooking (excellent real chips and special seafood nights on certain Thursdays – worth enquiring), is provided for the hungry, and for the tired or lazy there are two rooms upstairs that may be rented at a fair price. On tap there is Donningtons and first-class cider. Most importantly there is a relaxed and unhurried efficiency of service that is the hallmark of a fine operation. Nothing is seen to be done, but everything happens on time – or thereabouts.

The classic way to experience The Plough is to book both rooms one weekend in the depths of winter. Carefully choose a small group of your best friends to accompany you and accommodate the surplus in the nearby, sympathetic bed and breakfast, High Trees.

A typical Saturday may well unfold in the following manner.

At 8.30 am the fires are lit in the bars and a dog or two takes up position in front of them, but you will not be turfed out of bed. It will have been suggested that you do not breakfast before 10.30, particularly if the previous night you were at the bar taking residents' privilege until the early hours. Indeed it is a common occurrence, on arriving here at lunchtime, to see a couple of hangovers just beginning to toy with the cornflakes, coffee and toast. These are followed by an enormous plateful of eggs and bacon, and as you sit before them and the fire, the landlord's son Richard will be setting up the bar. An enthusiast himself, he has been well trained by his father, Les, in the proper arts of inn-keeping.

For it must be said that this is the magic of The Plough. It retains its status as a first-class local pub, but thanks to the landlord's personality can accommodate all sorts of people and mix them up superbly. A typical Saturday lunchtime crowd might combine regulars, travellers, children, dogs, dipsomaniacs, jockeys en route for Cheltenham, Irish priests keeping tabs on the jockeys, a couple of itinerant musicians playing for pints, Members of Parliament, second-hand car dealers, stockbrokers, farmers, a lone TV soap star, straightforward thieves, millionaires, labourers, lovers and losers. There may even be a stray triplet of American tourists who just can't believe their luck. All topics may be discussed. Most behaviour, as long as it doesn't inconvenience others, is tolerated. The line is drawn only, firmly and obscurely at the wearing of hats, as a close friend of the authors can testify.

It is now time to introduce yourself to the resident pianist, Reg, the finest and most approximate musician in the Cotswolds. Do so with respect, for you are in the presence of a genuine living legend. Reg is a delightful man who, fuelled by gallons of shandy (doctor's orders), will embark upon marathon piano-playing stints made up of all manner of songs, from nostalgic pre-war hits to such controversial and post-modernist stompers as 'Let's Twist Again' and 'If I Had a Hammer'. He also has a wide repertoire of popular classical pieces.

So spirited is Reg's playing that it is possible to overlook one or two minor inaccuracies in his performance, though repeated reminders by his many supporters that 'he's never had a lesson in his life' are not strictly necessary.

There are moments when his playing surpasses the hopes of even his most fervent admirers. Such times have passed into local legend. Everything has to be right and it helps if the moon is in an auspicious phase.

The first indication that there is magic in the air comes when Reg slips cannily into his moving and highly personal (some would say wayward) version of the 'Warsaw Concerto'. As the last notes of this fine work die away, the whole pub holds its collective breath. The suspense is almost unbearable. Will he? Won't he? The waitress suspends the delivery of tripe and onions. Revellers freeze, their glasses halfway to their lips. Then, at last, come the first sweet notes.

The origins of 'The Chicken Song' are, some might say thankfully, lost in the mists of time, although Reg is vaguely certain that it comes from America. Suffice to say it is a heady and eclectic brew, somewhere between a barrelhouse twelve-bar and the unsuccessful finale of an amateur operatic production.

Pandemonium breaks out. Children begin to cry. Strong men break down and repeatedly thump the table. Hardened cynics stare in dumbfounded amazement as though witnessing the rendition for the first time. At the piano, unperturbed, Reg accompanies his bizarre and eccentric playing with a high-pitched and blood-curdling howl.

And this is only lunchtime.

To be seated here at The Plough by the fire on a winter's day or night, drink at hand, Reg on the piano, surrounded by friendly faces – this, for the true connoisseur of the public house, is to be somewhere very close to paradise.

Oh the innocence of those early days of the quest. Oblivious to the pressures of time, we lingered three nights at The Plough, having encountered a mandolin-playing friend who had just won a bundle on the Getting-Out Stakes at Cheltenham and was intent on spending it. We helped him.

September 4th, Saturday

★ **THE FIVE MILE HOUSE, Duntisbourne Abbots, Gloucestershire. ORD (W, E). Miss M. Ruck.**
Miss Ruck is still operating what is probably the last old one-room drinker in Gloucestershire. As one might expect, the pub has been in the family since 1930, and Miss Ruck took over a few years ago from her mother.

The Five Mile House is on the main Cirencester–Gloucester road (A417(T)), about four miles out of Cirencester on the right hand side. You will need to drive slowly and keep your eyes open, since the building is set down in a slight dip and the pub sign is discreet to the point of invisibility, which is a very good thing, for there is not much room inside.

As you enter, you will notice on the left an open area, with a tiny snug made from two, old, high-backed settles placed at right-angles to each other and in front of the fireplace. This is the place for private chinwags, for as you enter the main bar you will observe that the conversation here is general, and you will be expected to join in.

Miss Ruck sits behind her tiny bar/servery at one end, nursing what appears to be orange juice, and occasionally getting up to tap excellent Courage bitter from her cask into someone's glass. She is the first of the regiment of venerable landladies you will meet in these pages and to whom the book is dedicated. She immediately points out: 'This is a proper pub. People come here to talk.'

And indeed they do. The big table in the bay window is the perfect place to sit, listen and make a contribution to the banter. Standing at the fire, the youthful local vicar is telling mildly risqué jokes about the Pope, while his wife confides to her friend about how her family disapproved of her marrying a priest. A local architect swaps gardening lore with a capped old boy in the inglenook.

Seated to our left is Tom, a true eccentric who lives in a hut in the woods with his cat. He is a master carpenter and also something of a Classical Greek scholar.

'What a magical morning it's been,' he begins. 'D'you know, the Ancient Greeks had a word for it – Thurgia – natural magic; that's the kind of morning when you could walk alone through a beechwood and come across a string quartet playing Bach in a clearing – and not think twice about it. Ah, the imagination's the only private place left in the world today.'

He continues in this fascinating and lyrical way for some time, and lubricates the imagination with constant applications of barrelled cider. He likes living in the woods, and occasionally hitches into Cirencester for groceries.

'But I only come in here once a week.'

This seems doubtful. When?

'Only on Sundays, boy.'

But it's Saturday today.

'Ah well, this week I've come out in sympathy with the Jews,' he says, and a twinkle dances in his eyes.

The Five Mile House is a true delight, from Ziggy the Labrador crisp addict, through the landlady and her patrons, to the outside lavatories, complete with wooden seats and hard, shiny Bromo paper. Go at a weekend lunchtime or any evening; it will be a rewarding experience.

Miss Ruck does no food. She will sell you one of her tasty home-pickled eggs, served with a packet of potato crisps, but that is the extent of it.

While on the subject of pub food, it is necessary to issue some general warnings. Too many pubs these days serve too much very bad food to too many people, making free with frozen ingredients and microwaves. The better pubs either regard food as an irrelevant diversion from the main business or put some thought and style into it and do the job properly, as many of the establishments in this book demonstrate.

As an intelligent reader you must use your own discretion. It is worth making a long detour around anything called a Carverye (Succulente Roaste Beefe of Olde Englande) and whatever you do give a wide berth to the 'salad bar' which purveys tired vegetable matter swimming in a sea of fermenting salad cream and is usually presided over by a bottle-nosed old cove in a chef's toque, with slurred speech and nicotined fingers.

The point that has to be made is that pubs should primarily be places in which to drink, talk and have fun, not to eat, and an acceptable compromise is that offered by several of the houses in this book: baps. To see a mound of these on the bar, filled with nothing more than good Cheddar and a slice of onion, or a thick cut of ham from the bone, is to know that here is a pub that has not been deflected from its proper purpose.

The best establishments of all, like The Five Mile House, simply refuse to serve food of any sort, rightly taking the view that if you must eat, then for goodness sake do so quietly, quickly and without fuss in the privacy of your own home.

Before leaving Gloucestershire, we paid one more call, to a lesser, but highly enjoyable establishment.

THE DANEWAY INN, Sapperton, Gloucestershire. GLL.
Sitting by the canal, just off the Cirencester–Stroud (A419) road, The Daneway, at most times of the year, remains fairly unspoilt, though beware of summer weekends, when you might as well be in Surrey. The simple, whitewashed building holds three different rooms – public bar, lounge and smoke room (children admitted), and the landlord is a friendly Yorkshire-man. The beer is good, and may include Wadworth's, Archers or their own brew, Daneway. The public bar gossip is lively and spicy.

Also recommended in Gloucestershire are:

THE GOLDEN HEART, Coberley (off A436), Birdlip, Gloucestershire. LLL.
A wide range of beers from the cask (Adnams, Hook Norton,

THE QUEST FOR THE PERFECT PUB

Marston's and others) are available at this characterful and relaxing old village inn.

🍺🍺**THE DOG AND MUFFLER, Joyford, Nr. Coleford (off A4432), Gloucestershire. GLL (W).**
This is an unspoilt rural delight with Sam Smith's on pump, a warm welcome and plenty of diversions.

Herefordshire, The Marches and the Welsh Border

From Sapperton we intended to head north-west through the lanes towards Herefordshire, but some strange magnetic force appeared to draw the car back the other way, and unaccountably we found ourselves in the wooded hills around Stanway and Toddington. We were back where we started, handily placed for a further night's revels at **THE PLOUGH** at **Ford** (see p. 15). Resisting the temptation, we corrected the steering and pulled ourselves together. Luckily it was only a few minutes drive to the Severn Valley and the M5 interchange.

We passed thankfully over this, only to get caught in a stream of slow-moving traffic winding through a vista of industrial estate and Army Ordnance depot on the edge of Tewkesbury. A two mile stretch of rocket-launchers and personnel carriers was punctuated by the futuristic British HQ of Dr Robert Moog, whose pioneering synthesizers were tinkled by many a caped and posturing 1970s keyboardsman, and eventually led to the delightful High Street, a pleasing jumble of architectural styles.

SECTION ONE

Closing our eyes to the Sixties' shopping precinct we scuttled over the Severn, through the firm and pointed Malvern Hills, and into Herefordshire. Our destination was the Black Mountains.

We took the backroads from Hereford to the Golden Valley. At Bredwardine the Wye flows slow and fat between the Rectory where Reverend Francis Kilvert (also of Clyro) wrote and ministered his flock, and the RED LION HOTEL, GITS, where a simple but decent room with a stunning view and a sound dinner can still be had. Here the road climbs dramatically up Dorstone Hill, from the top of which the Golden Valley is unfurled below you like a scroll, fertile and many-hued, framed by the brooding backdrop of Hay Bluff and the Black Hill.

Turn right at Vowchurch for Pontrilas, and with the thirst raging within you, look carefully for the hamlet of Cupids Hill.

CUPIDS HILL, near Pontrilas (B4347), Herefordshire. ORD (FC, W).

A hundred yards into Wales there is a small white house on a hill, with no distinguishing marks, keeping its own counsel in the quiet, hidden evening; but over the door is inscribed: 'J. Godding, licensed to sell spirits, ale and wine . . .', and you may find, as we did, Joe Godding himself tending his beans and his hanging baskets.

Almost completely untouched by the last twenty years, Cupids Hill is a wonderful place to stop for a drink; a smallish, square parlour-style room with a bagatelle table in the middle, good solid chairs and a tiny bar from which Joe and his wife dispense refreshment. There is no draught beer, since local trade does not demand it, but bottled ales and local ciders go down very well.

Joe Godding inherited the licence from his father who, on taking the pub at the tender age of 19, was enjoined by the local beak merely 'to behave himself'. He died fifteen years ago, aged 87, after a lifetime's intense social drinking, which goes to prove, as Mrs Godding says, that 'It's not the drink that kills you.' A splendid establishment, where much passion can be aroused in a discussion about the merits of different types of bailer twine; long may it remain so.

A few miles north-west, in the lee of the Merddin Mountain and on the other side of the hill, lies Llanthony Priory, where the Victorian poet Walter Savage Landor attempted to build a house for years, only to have it dismantled by the locals every time he turned his back; whether this was an anti-English protest, or merely a pithy comment on the quality of his poetry, is not known, but Llanthony is now a pony-trekking and walking centre, popular in summer, and best visited in the bleak months of winter when The Abbey Hotel reverts to being a proper local.

As a general rule, most of the more picturesque pubs described in these pages are visited in summer at your own risk for obvious reasons, especially if you want to meet the locals, whose hibernation pattern is the direct opposite to that of the hedgehog, and is activated, as the days lengthen, by the first tide of motorized visitors. It lasts generally from Whitsun until after the August Bank Holiday.

🛏 **THE ABBEY HOTEL**, Llanthony Priory, Llanthony, Gwent. GAR (I, B, VE). Tel: 08732-487.
Llanthony is magnificently situated on the lonely and often impassable mountain road that leads south from Hay-on-Wye to Abergavenny. The Abbey Hotel is part of the undercroft of the ruined Norman priory that was established here in 1108, and is an eccentric establishment with a proprietor whose sense of humour may not be to everyone's taste. We had known it for several years, and thoroughly enjoyed our return. The Brain's beer, among other guesting ales, is drawn with fluency from the cask. There is a beautifully furnished, old-fashioned dining room for those brave enough to stay the night; tales of strange after-hours happenings in the pub and the graveyard that surrounds it are legion but cannot be substantiated.

From here, head back into England, and aim your sights on The Cornewall Arms at Clodock, next to Longtown.

★ **THE CORNEWALL ARMS, Clodock, Hereford and Worcester. LLL (FC, W, E).**
We were, as usual, late for our rendezvous, and we careened round the treacherous mountain lanes, treating blind corners with the contempt which they deserved, fearing that we might be too late. Thank God, when we screeched, tyres smoking, to a halt outside the low white building, a familiar car and attendant bicycle were parked outside. What was quite extraordinary,

SECTION ONE

when we opened the doors, was the thickness of the fug, the hubbub of voices and the sheer energy of activity that seethed behind those whitewashed walls.

The Cornewall Arms is as fine an example of a true local as you will find anywhere in the Marches. This Saturday night the place was bursting at the seams with people out for a good time: men whose working lives were spent on the bleak, sheepy hillsides, brothers, physical and spiritual, to Lewis and Benjamin Jones from Bruce Chatwin's *On The Black Hill*, were drinking and playing skittles with an almost manic fervour, wearing old tweed jackets and luminous green kipper ties (a Christmas present in 1975), and nearly all of them sporting that most distinguished of local trade marks, a fine pair of Cider Ears. (These are acquired usually in early middle age, when the combination of the weather, the products of Messrs Bulmer and Weston, and a propensity for falling asleep in uncomfortable positions on the way home conspire to produce a pair of appendages that stick out at right-angles from the head and have a raw, inflamed look about them; they are fire-engine red and very much a feature of the countryside around here.)

The noise in The Cornewall Arms was staggering; the clink of rapidly-emptied sleevers, the crash of skittles, the rattle of dominoes, the thud of darts, the slap of cribbage cards, the thrum and burr of local talk – all combined in a benign and friendly cacophony that was irresistible. Fighting our way through the throng and the haze, we observed, waiting for us by the window, deep into his second pint, head full of concertos for violin and chainsaw, the modern composer Anthony Powers, and his wife, restaurateuse and opera administrator Helen Priday, in a very fetching pair of black bicycling britches.

'This is a wonderful place, Anthony,' we exclaimed.

'Yes, yes,' he replied, 'wonderful. But look, just one more here, boys, we want to take you to The Gluepot.'

The Gluepot?

'Well, it's The Carpenters Arms at Walterstone, actually, but the locals call it The Gluepot . . . and then there's The Bull's Head at Craswall. Do you know that?'

No, we didn't.

'Ah, the Bull's Head . . .' and his spectacles misted over with emotion. The composer had his drinking boots on.

The authors remember little of the rest of that evening. With the composer at the wheel, humming strange atonal excerpts from his works, we drove up into the hills.

🍺 THE CARPENTER'S ARMS (THE GLUEPOT), Walterstone (off A465), Hereford and Worcester. LLL (FC, W).

Of The Carpenter's Arms we can recall fragments of conversation, the landlord's wry gin 'n' lemon leer, a lurid blue jukebox room, the amazing rococo flourish with which Anthony unearthed a barrel of Wadworth's 6X from behind the bar, and above all the unquestioning friendliness with which we were treated, down to the veiled suggestion that we might care to accept the local hospitality and linger into the night. The authors would have happily accepted, but the composer's eyes now shone with evangelical light; he bundled us back into the car, and soon we found ourselves at The Bull's Head at Craswall.

🍺 THE BULL'S HEAD, Craswall (off B4350), Hereford and Worcester. LLL (FC, I, M, E).

This is well worth a visit, being on a lonely mountain road and almost entirely unchanged inside. There is a massive fireplace and a landlady of deceptively stern aspect, and if you go there sober you might notice all sorts of interesting architectural features. What our notes tell us is that The Bull's Head has a fine selection of dogs, the Worst Cheese Sandwich in the World, a tiny bar in the corner, and a solid mixture of local flatcaps and German and Irish hillwalkers toasting their feet by the fire and getting a sing-song going.

We could have stayed here and sung all night, as the extraordinarily dire quality of the singing was opening new lines of research for Anthony Powers, but unfortunately a fracas developed when one of our company, a road-gang boss or 'civil engineer' from Battersea, became involved in a heated exchange over the correct text for 'The Green Green Grass of Home' and we were all most unfairly ejected without further ado. Anthony was constrained from punching an enormous Prussian backpacker, and drove us back to our lodgings, where to our relief he deposited us, leaving us to sleep it off and, the next day, venture deeper into The Marches.

SECTION ONE

September 5th, Sunday
50 years ago, Presteign(e), or Llandandras, or, in the Saxon, *preosta haemed*, or household of priests, was the capital of Radnorshire, a fine old county which has now been subsumed into the administrative district of Powys. It boasted a handsome Courthouse (assizes still operative, as one of the authors knows to his cost), a thriving livestock market, the handsome church of St Andrew where, in the 17th century, it took thirteen priests to exorcize the evil spirit of Black Vaughan of Hergest Court and imprison it forever in a snuff box, and *twenty-six* pubs.

Though this number has diminished along with the town's commercial importance, Presteigne is still one of the best drinking centres in the West, and enjoyed something of a second golden era at the turn of the Eighties.

Those were the days when Ken and Mal Carswell kept **THE FARMER'S ARMS, LLL (FC)**, when Saturday afternoons were Saturday afternoons and you could place a bet with the evasive Taffy over a half of dark; when Ghillie and Griffer, the senile delinquents, would drink ten pints of GL (a local beverage tasting of fermented apples and kerosene) and climb into Griffer's 1963 bench-seat Consul to go chasing a woman over by Llangunllo and return with a rabbit and two black eyes; when Weedo got so pissed that he fell asleep over 'Match of the Day', and Squealer and Luggsy super-glued a golf tee to the end of his nose and stuck his hands together too; when Hedley Simcock the coalman, 'the Dark Man' as he was known (see **THE CRESSELLY ARMS, Cresswell Quay**, p. 41), rammed a London immigrant's head through the stud wall by the dartboard for calling Griffer a silly old git.

They were also the days when a colourful couple kept The Duke's Arms (we will call them Brian and Elaine). Their incumbency ended the day Brian barricaded himself into the upstairs with a case of whisky and a shotgun, convinced that the SAS from nearby Hereford had surrounded the pub and were about to launch a mortar attack. It was only the heroic efforts of PC Alf Roberts which persuaded Brian to give himself up, and he came meekly out to spend the next six months banged up in the local 'Sanatorium' at Talgarth (see THE RADNOR ARMS, Talgarth, p. 48 and THE BLUE BOAR, Hay-on-Wye, p. 55).

Things are a little quieter in Presteigne these days; The Farmer's is under new, but sympathetic, management, and

The Duke's lies sadly empty and neglected, but you will certainly find a warm welcome in THE BARLEY MOW, GLL (FC, M), THE BULL, GITS, or even THE RADNORSHIRE ARMS, GITS, though stick to the bar there (the hotel is under the dreaded ownership of THF, and the food reveals this all too clearly). Do pay a visit to Presteigne if you're close, and don't be tempted to sweep by on the ill-made bypass known with local irony as 'the motorway'.

As a footnote, there still exists the legend of a black hound which roams the hills and valleys around Presteigne and down towards Brilley; this hound had connections with a prominent local family, whose arms the pub in Clyro still bears, with whom a famous author once stayed, and, it is claimed, was inspired to write one of his best-known stories: the name of the pub in Clyro is The Baskerville Arms.

The local tradition of drinking goes back a long way, as the following, reprinted from a 19th century issue of Punch, goes to prove:

HELL IN HEREFORDSHIRE
'THERE IS MUCH SECRET CIDER-DRINKING IN HEREFORD'

Excerpts from the evidence of the Bishop of Hereford before the Licensing Commission.

> *The wild white rose is cankered*
> *Along the Vale of Lugg,*
> *There's poison in the tankard*
> *There's murder in the mug;*
> *Through all the pleasant valleys*
> *where stand the pale-faced kine*
> *Men raise the Devil's chalice*
> *and drink his bitter wine. . . .*

We left Presteigne amid rumours that the Carswells, late of The Farmer's Arms, had been seen the previous night carousing in their old haunts, but we were unable to substantiate this. Feeling dreadful, we motored north out of town on the old farm roads. Leaving the ruins of Stapleton Castle to the left, we climbed to the bleak heights of Stonewall Hill, where one of the

SECTION ONE

least known but most spectacular views in all the Marches took our breaths and our hangovers away at a stroke.

We were standing on a high, treeless ridge; to one side stretched the wild hills and copses of the Radnor Forest and Mid-Wales, The Warren, Cwm Whitton Hill, Harley's Mountain, tumps, settlements, the still-visible hump of Offa's Dyke; to the right, the ground fell away into the rolling well-tended farmland of Shropshire and the lush valley of the Teme, with the battlements of Ludlow Castle sometimes appearing, mirage-like, in the far distance. Nowhere is the contrast between Wales and England, the very real sense of two separate and hostile territories, made so clear and so dramatic as on Stonewall Hill.

Skirting the very north of Herefordshire, we passed through Brampton Bryan, where Lady Brilliana Harley, of the great Cromwellian family, refused to surrender to the Royalists in the absence of her husband; this brave act cost her her life and castle, whose remains are now incorporated in the 14th-century gatehouse to the present mansion.

A few minutes later, we came to our first port of call, Bravonium, or to give its more recent appellation, Leintwardine. Over the old stone bridge, where the River Clun joins the Teme, turn right down the street parallel to the river, and there it is – a small terrace of stone cottages, outside one of which is a faded, peeling, painted sign: THE SUN INN C. Lane, licensed to sell Ale and Wine.

★ **THE SUN INN, Leintwardine (off A4110), Herefordshire. ORD (FC). C. Lane.**
Here nothing has changed since the 1940s. You sit in Mrs Lane's tiny parlour, where there are two wooden tables and a couple of faded chintz armchairs, and she disappears into her back kitchen to pour you your beer; it arrives in a jug and tastes very good.

She has run the pub for many, many years, and still, mercifully, is not touched by the rampant tourist trade which is sweeping the Borders. She is happy to cater for her regulars, who have grown old with her, and her little cottage is a centre for gossip, family matters and the odd game of cards. But she will welcome you warmly, as she did us, so long as you are prepared to enjoy The Sun's simplicity and atmosphere, and do not start fretting about boeuf bourguignon or seafood lasagne. A very special place indeed; go there before Mrs Lane retires.

As we had a lot of ground to cover, we confined ourselves to one drink at The Sun. Leaving Leintwardine by the Ludlow Road, we swung off to the left after a mile, and plunged deep into South Shropshire and Housman country, the silent, deep Clun Forest, where the black-faced native sheep stare wisely at you, and very little is going on.

> *Clunton and Clunbury, Clungunford and Clun
> are the quietest places under the sun.*
>   A. E. Housman, 'A Shropshire Lad'

We had a brief stop at Lydbury North for a swift half of reasonable Woods in THE POWIS ARMS, GITS, a decent, stone-built village local which was only marred by a regular's obsessive monologue about his root canal work, and reached Bishop's Castle at lunchtime.

King Offa of Mercia, as well as knowing all about dykes, seems to have been something of a rough diamond at the best of times, for legend has it that Ethelbert, King of East Anglia, was extremely keen on Offa's daughter, and came to Bishop's Castle, then known as Lydbury Castle, to ask for her hand in marriage. Offa, far from inviting him in for a man-to-man chat over a carafe of house mead, or even merely requiring him to declare his means and/or intentions, simply had him put to death in a foul and treacherous manner.

This came to the notice of the Bishop of Hereford, who hauled Offa over the coals and, as a penance, made him hand over possession of the town, thereby putting the monarch down a peg or two and gaining a nifty *pied-à-terre* in the neighbourhood.

Bishop's Castle flourished thereafter, at one time returning two MPs to Westminster, and remains a bustling little market town with, on its steep High Street, one of the best, and oldest (1642), of the Border pubs.

★ **THE THREE TUNS BREWERY, Bishop's Castle, Shropshire. GAR (FC, W, F, M). J. & D. Wood.**
The beer that they brew twice a week at The Three Tuns is delicious, a light golden, heady, hoppy nectar which creeps

very subtly upon you and at some time or other socks you over the back of the skull with a velvet sandbag. Don't be in a hurry here.

There has for many years been a tradition of live music at The Three Tuns, performed in the long room over the old tower brewery itself, which adjoins the pub and makes a fine courtyard. In the days when Peter Milner had the pub, bands from the nearby villages, Shrewsbury and as far afield as Wolverhampton used to play here, with such famous guests as the late great Alexis Korner, father of the British Blues scene, and the locally-based Jeremy Taylor, writer of the show 'Wait a Minim' and immortal songs such as 'Jobsworth' and 'Red Velvet Steering-Wheel Driver'.

One of the authors also used to play in a local combo, and it was on an R & B night that there he first met a large, bullish and extrovert man who lives mere yards from The Three Tuns, and practises the unlikely art of making medieval instruments; half-finished viols, sackbutts and lyres litter his bachelor townhouse. It was a long time since we had seen him, but we remembered vividly the demonic effect which the Tuns beer had upon him, releasing a latent arrogance bordering on the psychotic.

'Has he been in recently?' we enquired of the new landlord. His cheery demeanour clouded over, and he regarded us with suspicion.

'Who wants to know?'

'Oh . . . er . . . I used to know him years ago.'

'Well, you won't find him in here – ever again. He's banned.' He made it sound like excommunication, which, in a way, it was.

'Dare we enquire why?'

'For being grossly insulting to the landlord.'

This seemed unpardonable, but very much in character.

'Does he still live in the town?'

'Only just, boy,' said a voice from behind. He was one of a pair of red-faced, local wide boys, who had a ferret in a cage and were deep into celebration of a fine morning's bag.

'We got the bloody hounds onto him.'

'Good grief, why?'

'Once he weren't allowed in here, he used to have a few drinks at home like, and then play that ruddy Mozart so loud that people couldn't hear themselves think; and he used to saw at that fiddle of his over the top of it, see? Bloody racket it were. In the end we had to pay the beaters to set hounds at him. Soon stopped him, that did.'

By this time, the Tuns Bitter had done its trick and we were alternating between tears and laughter; suddenly feeling sorry for the poor mad bastard we stumbled over the square to hammer on his front door. But of the musical whittler there was no sign. Through the window a film of dust lay over everything; on a window-seat was tossed a viol (or possibly a sackbutt), broken in half, strings dangling.

What a bitter penalty one pays for being rude to the landlord of a good pub.

It was time to get out of town.

Two pm. We were running short of time. There is a perfectly good main road from Bishop's Castle to Newcastle-on-Clun, but semi-delirious with the Tuns Bitter and rejoicing in the countryside, we dived off into the lanes that cut through the Clun Forest. It is an astoundingly diverse enclave of moorland, upland pastures sprinkled with stone circles, menhirs and old camps (much venerated by local hippies at solstice time), and deep, folded valleys through which the River Clun ambles contentedly.

Within ten minutes we were totally lost, and closing time was looming. Round in circles we went, through Mainstone and Cefn Einion, until with minutes to spare we emerged from the shadow of Offa's Dyke and pulled into the car park of THE CROWN, GITS (M), at Newcastle-on-Clun.

The new landlord, Jeff Aldridge, a former brewer from Weymouth, is settling in nicely, and still running the jazz nights instituted by the former licensee 'Lord' Ted Bunting, well-known local saxophonist. We spent a pleasant two hours in his company, over lunch, with several pints of 'Weasel', as the beer is affectionately known, and lively conversation. The Crown is a good little oasis in a barren area where the only competition is THE ANCHOR, GITS (M), a lonely, windswept barn of a place, run by enthusiastic Watford immigrants, which features bouncers and music three nights a week.

Eventually Jeff threw us politely out of The Crown, and we staggered blindly up the nearest hill to try and sober up.

Breaking through the treeline, we reeled around the moor under a milky autumn sky; there was a soft western light and a stiffish breeze that rustled the heather, stirred the gorse and reeds and riffled the corn like a cardsharp showing off. Grouse got up out of the heather. A hare shot into the cornfield. Buzzards wheeled. We felt better.

🍺 THE GREYHOUND, Llangunllo, Powys.
ORD (FC, W, E).

Back on schedule and back in time. The Greyhound is run by Bill Theson, who's been there longer than he wants to remember, but he remembers everything and everybody. He also operates an elderly petrol pump at the back of the pub, so all thirsts are catered for.

Llangunllo still benefits from a train station, part of the surviving Mid-Wales Railway, and, while retaining a sleepy, untouched atmosphere, has acquired over the years a certain 'outlaw' reputation, centred round the pub. Seated here in the old bar, decorated with 1950s cigarette posters, you can often see rabbits, pheasant and other game changing hands over or under the bar, deals going down over a pint or two, whispered corner confabs, dark deeds being plotted.

The Greyhound is the nerve centre of the village, and a fine and colourful place, rough only in the sense that it is real; those who cherish local life and the wisdom of the elderly will love it and fall into good talk with any of the old boys in the bar. Others would do best to avoid it. That evening we had time only to say hello to Bill, collect a female companion and hightail it south.

South, Mid and West Wales

We sped through Pilleth where, in 1402, Owen Glyn Dwr killed 1,100 of Edmund Mortimer's army, and where the ploughshare still uncovers human bones. Turn right onto the B4594 after **THE CROWN** at Walton, GITS, where the annual coal-carrying race is always won by 'the Dark Man' (see **THE FARMER'S ARMS, Presteigne**, p. 25) and where Wordsworth stayed with relatives. Cut across the tops through Gladestry and Painscastle, left along the Wye leaving The Radnor Arms at Talgarth for another time, and soon you will be rolling into Talybont-on-Usk, ready for your drink at the first-rate and (as yet) completely unspoilt White Hart.

THE WHITE HART, Talybont-on-Usk (A40), Powys. GLL (FC, W).
This splendid establishment has had the same proprietors for over thirty years: Frank, his wife and her twin sister. They run a large, square, high-ceilinged room with comforting time-yellowed walls, bisons' horns, a big ceiling fan and an odd collection of paintings in ornate frames. The overall effect is bizarre, but wonderful. They have a strictly local following, except in high season, but are uncommonly welcoming and helpful to 'outsiders'. For some time they gave occasional sanctuary to the authors' sister who, while living a quiet life nearby, got deeply entangled in a volatile triangle. The back room at The White Hart became less a bolt-hole and more a home from home to the poor child. She was waiting for us now at the bar.

Frank, all 5'4" of him, twitched his whiskers confidingly from behind the pumps, and engaged her in local gossip.

'Good to see you, m'dear. Remember poor old Reg; he can't come in no more. The police made him prove he wasn't alcohol-dependent. Well, I mean, how do you prove you're *not* something?'

'What happened to old Ben?' asked our *femme fatale* of a sister.

'Did you hear about him at the Royal Show? He floated through it, drunk as a lord. He went to the Mercedes stand and ordered one of them big ones, see! £27,000 it were, and special colour scheme too; very particular about the colours, he was. Well, he signed for it and went home. The next day they come to deliver the damn thing!'

'What happened?'

'Ben got right angry about it. He said, "You take that thing from here now or I'll call the police (a popular local expression – see THE RADNOR ARMS, Talgarth, p. 48), I don't want it." Well, they showed him the paper he'd signed, and do you know – he didn't remember a damn thing about it!'

As we left to seek our lodging, Frank told us the sad news that due to his wife's illness he'd been forced to sell the pub; he just couldn't cope any more. Our hearts sank, until he told us that the buyer was a local, already a regular there, and that he had solemnly promised to keep The White Hart exactly the way it is, and not change a thing. If he is a man of his word, we will look forward to our next visit. Frank has assured us that he himself will merely be moving from one side of the bar to the other. Go there yourselves and see. The White Hart is a simple, unvarnished *treat* of a place.

September 6th, Monday

To those who have never visited it, Pembrokeshire comes as a revelation. It is one of the most beautiful and unspoilt counties – a land of mountains, rivers and wooded valleys, bordered by over 140 miles of fine coastline. It is also a rich and happy hunting ground for proper pubs.

The importation of Flemish settlers by the first two English King Henrys in the 12th century, and the subsequent building of castles at Haverfordwest and Tenby in order to protect the immigrants from marauding attacks by the Welsh princes, gave to the area the appellation 'The Little England beyond Wales', and though it is not uncommon to hear Welsh spoken in these parts, there is still an Englishness to the place, noticeable even in the softness of the local accent.

After an unpleasant and uncomfortable night at The Riding Stables, Crickhowell, where we were abused, possibly poisoned, and eventually fleeced by an unstable hotelier who bore a worrying resemblance to a former (Welsh) jockey, we drove swiftly away from the Usk Valley and deep into Gwent along the Heads of the Valleys road.

From the old county of Brecknock, we passed through the northern tip of Monmouthshire and into Glamorgan, keeping south of the Brecon Beacons and Black Mountains.

There is a sudden and intense change in both landscape and atmosphere. The pleasant, rolling countryside gives way to a desolate prospect of straggling rows of grey concrete dwellings, scattered like litter amidst the slag-heaps and mine workings. Complete housing estates lie abandoned near worked-out collieries, and rusting railway tracks lead in all directions to nowhere.

On windy street corners lurk the youth and flower of Wales, betrayed by both government and union, wishing away the best time of their lives. Their backdrop is a row of empty shops and broken windows, their outlook a vision of nothingness. They smoke half a cigarette. They clutch a small bag of groceries. They fuck the girl from number nine and borrow a pram. They dream.

On the border of Carmarthen and Pembroke we stopped at Whitland and refreshed ourselves at THE FISHERS HOTEL, GLL, a sound old pub with a good local trade. An enterprizing young Scots couple had recently taken over the tenancy. They told us of brave old boys with sticks and caps who even after two seizures still vie with each other to see who can polish off the neck of a gallon whisky bottle the fastest. But the brewery had plans. Things were uncertain. We continued on to our destination.

Haverfordwest was an agreeable town until the planners spotted it clinging to the hillside and trapped and ensnared it with all the roundabouts, pedestrian precincts and road-widening schemes that money and corruption could buy. After seven circuits of the one-way system we identified our given rendezvous. We had our instructions. 'There are two pubs with the same name in Haverfordwest,' we had been told. 'Whatever may befall you, never, ever, drink in the one at the top of the town, or, under *any* circumstances, in the front bar of the one at the bottom. I will meet you in the back bar.'

We made our way to the small room. There we met our connection. When we had sat down he leaned towards us furtively. There was mystery and intrigue afoot, he whispered. Skulduggery.

At the bar sat the three most powerful men of the town: a Freemason, a Druid and a Bent Solicitor. They were the worse for wear and locked in a conspiracy. Was it feasible, they were asking themselves, to turn the castle into a car park, or should they press ahead with the scheme for a shopping mall? Good God, it was half-past twelve on a market day and almost anything was possible. Another large pink gin.

We left Haverfordwest, where Augustus John grew up and where the fly-posters were advertising a gig by local heroes Kelvin and the Absolute Zeroes. We were on our way with pounding hearts to one of the greatest public houses in Wales, the fabled and fabulous Presselli Arms Hotel at Rosebush.

★ **THE PRESSELLI ARMS HOTEL,** Rosebush (off B4313), Pembrokeshire (Dyfed). **ORD (FC, I, W, M, VE). Margaret Lewis.**
We had heard several reports of this establishment, including a glowing account from a friend, Careena Farquhar, who was born in Pembrokeshire and did not speak English until she was ten. She had told us that to bypass the Presselli would be an act of supreme folly, and so we followed her advice unquestioningly.

Accompanying us as we drove the few miles north was one of Haverfordwest's favourite sons, an eccentric musician and songwriter. After a terrifying and colourful career as a drummer in the Sixties he then sat in a tree for several months outside his Oxfordshire mansion, eating only bananas, Twiglets and a wide range of chemical compounds. He recovered with dignity and aplomb to write a Number One with Ronnie 'Plonk' Lane called 'How Come?' A good question.

In the car there was speculation. We were heading towards the Presselli Mountains. A few miles away, in the bay of St Brides, was the island of St Elvis. Was this just coincidence, or could it be that the forebears of the great man once roamed these hills, quiffs aquiver, lips curled into sneers, frightening and exciting the ladies? The Welsh are able to sing, after all.

The history of The Presselli Arms Hotel can be simply told. In the last century a local man, Mr Owen, began working the surrounding land for slate, and indeed constructed the Maenclochog Railway by which to transport it from his quarries. It was not long before he obtained the prestigious contract to supply the roofing materials for the new Houses of Parliament, then under construction. It therefore came as a major setback to all concerned when it was found that the nature of the slate was such that after only a short time in situ at the Palace of Westminster it began to rot and crumble away.

The resourceful Mr Owen was by no means defeated by this body blow. He had noticed how no sooner were the quarries out of action, they began to fill with water from the hills. To him it was only a short step to imagining Rosebush as a thriving and fashionable place to take the waters – a little like Cheltenham perhaps, or even Bath itself. He began building dainty little Chinese bridges across his hideous pits. The local newspapers carried advertisements for the wonderful new spa resort. The quarry railway would bring to Rosebush the clamouring multitudes, the waters would comfort and delight them. All that was needed, surely, was an hotel in which to provide them with rest and refreshment.

Why Mr Owen chose to build the hotel in beige corrugated iron is one of those little mysteries that remains unsolved. For that is what The Presselli Arms Hotel is – a medium-sized corrugated iron shack on the tip of a tiny village at the end of a disused railway line.

Inside, the walls bear testimony to the hopes and disappointments of the good old days. There is a framed poster entitled 'And Thence to Rosebush', with wildly optimistic sketches of carriage-loads of happy revellers steaming into the bustling spa town.

Behind the bar stands the still-lively and charming Mrs Peg Lewis, who had been dispensing hospitality at the Presselli for as long as anyone can remember, and who still lives on the premises. Ask her for a glass of her excellent Worthington bitter from the cask. Admire her splendid 1953 television, still broadcasting murky pictures of Sir Anthony Eden failing to solve the Suez Crisis. Make enquiries as to when she next expects her son to be in. The nights when he coaxes tune after tune from the ancient organ that stands against a far wall are part of local folklore.

As we left the Presselli, silly smiles on our faces, our companion let it be known with some forcefulness that in his opinion, which, he pointed out, had not gained the wide respect in which it is held without being honed by years and years of the most arduous and taxing research, The Presselli Arms Hotel, Rosebush, was undoubtedly the finest public house in the world. Neither of us felt inclined to argue. For we knew something he didn't, that among its many fine attributes the Presselli, courtesy of Mr Owen, possesses something indisputably unique – the first flushing lavatories in West Wales.

Five pm. It was several stops later when we returned to the same pub at Haverfordwest. The Freemason, the Druid and the Solicitor were still at the bar, but by now so close had become the conspiracy, so secret the deal, so many were the pink gins that had been taken, and so complicated had become the special handshakes, that the three of them were inextricably entwined in an impossible tangle.

Sitting down at a table and enjoying the privileges of market day were Joffrey Swales and his son Peter. Joffrey is the band master of the Town and County Band, and under his benevolent eye all those years ago our musician friend had first knocked hell out of a snaredrum. Also the proprietor of the local music shop, he caused a considerable stir among the burghers in the 1930s by daring to display a saxophone in his shop window. Peter was Mick Jagger's personal manager in old Rubberlips' heyday and, having no doubt drawn considerably on that experience, is now a top psychiatrist in New York. They told us of the golden era of this particular pub when, on market days, the landlord would by mid-afternoon be quietly lying on the floor behind his bar while the drinking population of the lower half of the town got on with the business of helping themselves.

Just as we were leaving we witnessed a strange incident. The Solicitor, eyes firmly shut, suddenly sat bolt upright, knocking over an ice-bucket and a bottle of angostura bitters. There was a moment's eerie silence as he unravelled his arms from the melee and leaned in again toward his senseless caballers.

'There's plenty more,' he slurred thickly, 'where this came from.'

In one graceful and well-practised movement he with one hand made the shape of a rabbit's ears above his head and with the other slipped a roll of fifty-pound notes in the Freemason's top pocket. Then, very slowly, he toppled from his stool to the swirly orange carpet bringing down with him, physically if not metaphorically, both of his sleeping partners.

We left the Messrs Swales walking with some determination up the High Street towards their next destination, and were ourselves by 6.30 comfortably ensconced in The Point House at Angle Bay in the excellent company of 'Dusty Springfield', landlady of **THE THREE HORSESHOES,** Norton Canon (see p. 50).

THE POINT HOUSE, Angle Bay, Pembrokeshire (Dyfed). GLL (I).

There is something very comforting about drinking with an off-duty publican, rather akin to embarking on a battle campaign with the SAS in back-up. Dusty had just arrived with her daughter for a week's holiday in her caravan. A pleasant jumble of boats was moored in the bay, and the surprisingly elegant, if leaky, oil refinery at Milford Haven was reflecting the evening sun on the opposite shore. A handful of people were making the best of the beach.

The Point House lies at the end of a long, bumpy track which passes as close as possible to the water's edge. Most pub guides will tell you that the fire here has been alight for up to 300 years. When we arrived it was out. The Point House was probably at its best during the tenure of the present landlord's Irish father-in-law who used to ignore the dry Sunday rule then enforced in Wales, knowing that his establishment was too remote for the police to bother with. Sunday lunchtime at the Point House under his stewardship was an experience to savour. This evening we drank Guinness and enjoyed the following exchange:

Customer:	'Do you have anything to eat? We've been walking all day and we're hungry.'
Barman:	'Not until 7.30. The menu starts at 7.30.'
Customer:	'Oh.'
Barman:	'We have rolls.'

SECTION ONE

Customer: 'Oh good. What kind?'
Barman: 'Cheese, cheese and pickle, cheese and onion, cheese and lettuce, lettuce and pickle, pickle and onion, onion and lettuce . . . or prawn and tomato.'
Customer: 'What would you like, Elspeth?'
Elspeth: 'Prawn and tomato please.'
Customer: 'Six prawn and tomato please.'
Barman: 'Rolls don't start until 7.30.'

The evening wore on. We found ourselves in Pembroke Dock, a once thriving town where at the turn of the century two battleships had been built for the Japanese Navy. Now Pembroke Dock and neighbouring Pembroke constitute one of the worst unemployment blackspots in the country. It is a marvel that the local people bear their affliction with such fortitude and cheerfulness, and you won't find a nicer town in all Wales.

🍺🍺 THE NAVY, Pembroke St., Pembroke Dock, Pembrokeshire (Dyfed). GLL (FC).

At 9.30 pm we entered The Navy (not to be confused with the *other* Navy, in Melville St., a more up-market establishment), to the accompaniment of Tom Jones on the juke-box. ('It's Not Unusual' and 'Stranger On The Shore' make up the theme music of Pembrokeshire.) The Navy is a first-rate place, a one-room drinker with a fine example of striplighting, sensational flock wallpaper, a pack of grizzled terriers, a solid wooden bar at the right height, and some of the shiniest, reddest faces you could ever hope to see in a month of Sundays. If you are ever tempted, as we were, to board the ferry from Pembroke Dock to Rosslare, then The Navy, or The White Hart (see below) are exactly the places in which to strap on your seaboots beforehand.

★ THE WHITE HART, Pembroke St., Pembroke Dock, Pembrokeshire (Dyfed). LLL (FC, W). Harold Lancaster

At 10.10 pm we went next door to The White Hart, a similar sort of set-up. We were flagging, hungry. On the bar there were plates of expertly-made sandwiches and bridge rolls. There had been a celebration, a birthday party. We ordered whiskies and the man next to us began talking.

'Pembroke Dock,' he began, 'is the friendliest place on earth. I've had to move far away to find work, but I always come back at the slightest opportunity. And this,' he made an expansive gesture, 'is the best pub in Pembroke Dock. Help yourselves to the food. That's what it's there for.'

We needed no further bidding. As we unashamedly wreaked havoc on the bar we were watched with kindly old eyes by Mr and Mrs Lancaster, the landlord and his wife.

When we had tucked away the last of the sandwiches, Mr Lancaster nodded understandingly.

'A couple of my home-made curry puffs will see you right.' He disappeared and returned shortly with two delicious concoctions, waved away any mention of money, and while we basked in the warm glow of whisky, sandwiches, curry puffs and the thrilling hum of a proper pub in full swing, Mr Lancaster regaled us with hair-raising tales of transvestitism in Malaysia and racketeering in Korea, two subjects on which he was an unlikely expert.

As we left, we congratulated Harold Lancaster on his wonderful establishment. He looked embarrassed.

'We try to keep it tidy,' he replied.

Pembroke Dock is not high on the itinerary of most visitors, who perversely prefer to explore the dubious delights of the nearby castle, birthplace of the mealy mouthed and treacherous Henry Tudor. It presents the gritty side of the equation, and The White Hart merits its star for the great warmth of its welcome, the fierce loyalty which it inspires among its band of devotees and the old-fashioned courtesy and charm which eludes more polished and expensive establishments.

September 7th, Tuesday
It was a delightful autumn morning when we left Pembroke, with a light breeze, a blue sky and a strong sun. The stars were out. It was snowing.

We headed first for Saundersfoot. For those masochists who savour the inimitable atmosphere of the British seaside resort, Saundersfoot, east of Pembroke, is a necessity. When you have tasted the cockles, stared at the sea, and debated with yourself for the thousandth time which wrong turn at which particular crossroads it was that brought you to your present predicament, then turn away from the shoreline, step nimbly across the pay-and-display car park and walk the short distance up to the Royal Oak.

THE ROYAL OAK, Saundersfoot (B4316 – off A478), Pembrokeshire (Dyfed). GLL (E).

This is a pleasant place with a strong cast of local characters and that morning we were privileged to witness a pleasing performance by the first of the regulars. He came in, ordered a pint of Courage Best and sank it in one draught without fuss or ceremony. Then he turned to us and, with the air of a man who has against all the odds performed an act of great self-denial, announced: 'The first today.' It was 10.30.

He was followed in by an unconvincing looking 'major', complete with moustache. This gentleman produced a wineglass from each pocket and placed them on the bar. Then he ordered a large whisky.

'The reason I start drinking at 8.30,' he told us for no apparent reason, 'is because you get a much better class of person in the bar at that time of the morning.' It was 10.35.

By the time we left, twenty minutes later, the Oak was filling up with various co-stars and the windows that overlooked the town and beach were mercifully beginning to steam up.

At 11.30 we arrived in Heaven.

★ THE CRESSELLY ARMS, Cresswell Quay, Pembrokeshire (Dyfed). LLL (FC, I, W, OP).
Maurice and Janet Cole.

Cleverly hidden down a twisting cat's cradle of lanes that bear no signs, The Cresselly Arms overlooks the tidal creek of the Cresswell River, which is mud at low tide and around which are grouped a few houses. The pub is an attractive creeper-covered building, and outside it stands the coalman's lorry.

Never ignore the tell-tale sign of the coalman's lorry (see **THE FARMER'S ARMS, Presteigne**, p. 25). It invariably means that you have arrived at the best pub in the district. *Le charbonnier boit ici*. In this case, some people might go further and say that The Cresselly Arms is the best pub in Wales, Britain, Europe, the World, the Solar System . . . Amen.

Inside, at one end of the bar, the coalman stands in quiet conversation with the landlady, cap pulled sideways across his head, coalsack harness still on his back, Guinness in hand. The appealing room has a red and black tiled floor and is furnished with good, plain tables, benches and chairs. It features a long bar at which it is a pleasure to stand or sit. There is another room beyond with a working Aga and more tables.

The pub used, until recently, to be run by Alice Davies, but she is now 100 years old and it all suddenly became too much for her. She lives there still, occasionally becoming absent-minded and burning down her bedroom, looked after with great care by the present incumbents, Maurice and Janet Cole, publicans extraordinary.

Mrs Cole performs her neat slippered scuttle along the bar. She has a winning smile. You order a pint of her impeccable Hancocks which she taps with confidence into a jug and then into your sleever. She passes the time of day and returns to more pressing matters. The coalman's glass is empty. It must be filled.

Maurice Cole enters the pub very, very slowly, the reason being that on his arm is an old gentleman of one hundred and one in a flat cap and a 1930s suit. He has recently gone blind, so Maurice has fetched him down to the Cresselly for his lunch-time drink. He guides him to the table, fetches two halves and sits down with him. The Coles are the sort of publicans that put most of their rivals to shame.

The old man gropes for his drink.

'Did we win the football?' he croaks. His accent is ancient, from another century.

'We lost 4-0,' says Maurice, guiding the old man's hand to his glass.

'I dare say we won in the pub after,' rejoins the ancient. His features break into a wizened grin. He is remembering such a night at The Cresselly before the First World War when he was a stalwart of the village team and they lost the match but won the evening.

The pub is filling slowly. The Cresselly Arms is more than a pub. It is a meeting place, a way of life, the heart of the community. On summer evenings when the tide is high the boats sail in for an evening of frolicking and capers. It is an impossible place to leave. Do not stint yourself on time.

You order another pint of Hancocks. The coalman raises his glass and grins a sweet, slow Irish grin of contentment.

Mrs Cole tends to his Guinness and bends her ear again to his

SECTION ONE

wisdom. He must be attended to, looked after and comforted. Today is his 50th birthday.

Three pm. Leaving Cresswell Quay we drove north, and as the afternoon grew older, we penetrated deeper into Cardiganshire. It gave us an uneasy feeling. We had been made to feel so much at home in Pembrokeshire, how would we fare in the heartland? People spoke Welsh here, they set fire to houses. They went to Max Boyce concerts and got excited about rugby; they were strange and dark and weren't used to Sunday drinking. The least we feared was being dragged from our French car with English plates, tarred and feathered, and left for the carrion crows in Cardigan Bay.

Minding our Ps and Qs, we booked two rooms at THE BLACK LION, GMTH, an hotel in the High Street of Cardigan (Aberteifi). The River Teifi, boiling with salmon, has its estuary here, but the bay is shallow, with a sandbar, so Cardigan has never been a major shipping town, and now concentrates on its market and tourism. However, until fairly recently, men used to fish for salmon in coracles, a primitive Celtic form of boat, and the river is believed to have been the last British haunt of the beaver, now long extinct, but for the slaying of which very heavy penalties were exacted by the Royal Laws of Wales.

Six pm. We had some good inside information to follow up, so we set out south on the A478 to Pen-y-bryn, where there is a small left turn to Cilgerran. Choosing not to visit the castle there, we crawled through the village, looking for the little end-of-terrace building that is The Mason's Arms (The Ramp). We were not disappointed.

★ **THE MASON'S ARMS (THE RAMP)**, Cilgerran, Cardiganshire (Dyfed). ORD (FC, W, VE). Richie Ray.
Regulars in The Black Lion had warned us against The Mason's. 'There'll be nothing for you there,' they cautioned. 'He's a rude old bugger, the landlord, and he'd as soon bawl you out as give you a drink.' The opposite was, in fact, the case, and set a precedent; in general, The Mason's Arms is a lucky name for a pub, and we have had enjoyable times in many a house bearing it. This is worth remembering when faced with a choice of unknown pubs, one of which sports this hallowed sign.

Cilgerran has a glorious past as a drinking village. In the last century, in its heyday, there were thirteen working quarries here and fourteen pubs. Now there are two. The Ramp Inn was so called because it was built at the top of the ramp up which all the stone was hauled from the quarries for transportation elsewhere, and, since it was the first port of call for men knocking off work, built up a thriving trade. On paydays, the company took over the bar/snug to the right of the front door and handed out the weekly emoluments to the hard-working stonemasons. It soon became officially known as The Mason's Arms, but the locals still call it The Ramp.

It is a tiny two-room drinker, though most of the drinking goes on in the front bar, behind which sits the comfortable figure and beacon-like face of the proprietor, Richie Ray. Richie is not one of those landlords content to watch his clients supping up, while he himself nurses a mug of cocoa. Not at all. He is constantly checking the quality and freshness of his wares, hence his complexion, the convivial atmosphere and the sound state of the Bass from a cask. We felt immediately at home.

By the old range, in which a fire was blazing, two elderly regulars sat, with a whisky and a pint in front of them. Our trepidations about Wales fell away as they engaged us in polite but genuine conversation. Were we on holiday? Preserving our incognito we said yes, we were. How did we know about The Ramp? We were on a pubbing holiday, we liked the old places. The face of one of them lit up. He'd always enjoyed them, he said, and in forty years of holidaying in the British Isles, he'd kept a log of every pub he'd visited. But on the whole he liked The Ramp best. How we would have loved to have seen his list, had time permitted.

The Ramp is scruffy in the best sort of way: everything is crammed into a very small space, including the landlord, who goes for the collarless shirt and braces kind of chic; the lavatories are spectacularly primitive; dust lies like a waistcoat over most of the fittings, in the way turned into an art form by Quentin Crisp. If you are a cleanliness fetishist, it might appall you; but the beer is very good, the company as well, and in its very unchangingness, and unbroken links with the past, The Ramp is undoubtedly a little lump of Welsh gold in a gilt-and-tarnish world.

SECTION ONE

Eight-thirty pm. Ensconced in a corner of THE WHITE HART, Cenarth, GAR, (A484 out of Cardigan), a couple of miles on from The Ramp and just in Pembrokeshire, we were tucking into a pair of lamb chops each. The atmosphere was good, so were the chops. The waitresses were pretty and there was a fair sprinkling of locals.

Suddenly we heard a roll of drums from outside, and a crisp count. 'One – two – three – four!' With oiled precision (OP) and a good sense of swing, a brass band launched into 'In the Mood' with a fluent clarinet sailing over the top. We abandoned our dinner.

In the square, under rustling trees, dressed in smart red-and-white uniforms, the bells of their polished instruments glinting in the last rays of the sun, The Town and County Band from Haverfordwest were getting on down.

Fronting them, bow-tied and beaming, pint at his feet, and conducting with a practised flourish, was Joffrey Swales. An appreciative crowd had gathered, and the band, under Joffrey's benevolent dictatorship, played a lively half-hour set.

During a fine unaccompanied clarinet rendition of the local national anthem, 'Stranger on the Shore', we were joined by the landlord of The White Hart, a bluff Englishman with a reputation for a somewhat extreme form of patriotism.

'Good band aren't they?'

'They're all right.' He scowled. 'But I bet you couldn't get them to play "Land of Hope and Glory".'

Oh, the Welsh and the English. Even in the late twentieth century the age-old hostilities are always on the simmer.

At 9.30 pm as the strains of the Town and County Band vanished into the deepening dusk, we quickly covered the three or four miles to Abercych. We had very high hopes of The Nag's Head.

★ **THE NAG'S HEAD**, Abercych, Pembrokeshire (Dyfed). LLL (FC, W). David Jones.
On a corner by a bridge on the little River Cych, which debouches into the Teifi, stands a small row of cottages. This is Abercych, and The Nag's Head is one of these cottages. Across the road is a tip-top collection of old tractors.

It was Tuesday night. Probably a bit quiet in there. Still, it did look promising. We opened the door. A great blast of laughter, chatter and warm air hit us full on and nearly knocked us over. We pushed our way in.

The small bar was packed to bursting; you could barely have slid a cigarette paper between the drinkers. The Nag's Head was heaving with people having a really good time. The conversations were not casual, diffident affairs; they were intense, vital, animated, made more so by the press of people, so that faces were never more than a few inches apart; the talkers were looking each other in the eyes. There were some of the funniest jokes in the world being told, occasionally in Welsh, and some of the most genuine laughter ever heard was ringing round the room.

It was here that all our reservations about Wales were proven ill-founded. We moved through this rollicking throng to the bar, where a shy, gentle giant of a barman served us with a drink and a sweet smile. Everybody in the pub looked like someone we knew, or seemed familiar in some way. When we were befriended by three of the revellers, it came as no surprise that they were Robert Mitchum, John Wayne and Lee Marvin. Within moments we became bosom pals; it was clear that anybody in The Nag's Head would have given us a floor to sleep on for the night. They wanted us to have as good a time as they were. We did.

There were red faces galore, a well-bred handsome grey-haired woman with a diamond ring locked in harmonious debate with an old flat cap with string round his trousers, a winking wide-boy with a Brylcreem racecourse grin, one or two walkers with fringey beards and boots; there was a bucolic Breughelian distortion, there was a transport of delight.

And then there was the Rat. From a glass case above the bar glowers the Biggest Stuffed Rat in the western world.

One morning in 1952 Mayor Spudding of Abercych discovered the beast rooting amidst his vegetable patch. With great presence of mind he went indoors, fetched his shotgun and despatched the monster, fearing an invasion of super rats. It was subsequently identified as a coypu, and for thirty-six years it has kept a glassy but watchful eyes on the goings-on at The Nag's Head. But the locals still refer to it as 'That bloody rat'. If you only go to three of the Welsh pubs in this book, make sure this is one them.

SECTION ONE

September 8th, Wednesday
At 9.30 am, with The Nag's Head still ringing in our ears, we leave Cardigan with two very specific destinations in mind. The first is a pub in Llandovery, Carmarthenshire, recommended to us by our friend from Haverfordwest. It is run by two brothers, one of whom stands behind the bar and repeats any particularly choice snippets of conversation to the other – who remains in the private side room and is never seen in public. It is obviously a must. Unfortunately, the drummer cannot remember its name or where it is.

At Newcastle Emlyn, we stop at the EMLYN ARMS, GMTH, a market town hotel not quite so badly spoilt as most and conveniently next door to the bookmakers if you want to lie down after the last.

We pass through Lampeter and a stench of cabbage and gravy, as all the pubs in town compete to produce the worst lunch at the lowest price.

At Caio, a village in a pretty valley of the River Waldron, we refresh ourselves in the respectable BRUNANT ARMS, GITS, with a glass of Murphy's stout.

Midday. We arrive in Llandovery and make enquiries in one of the hotels. The proprietor eyes us warily. Yes, he knows the pub we're looking for, run by the two brothers. It is The Red Lion, but do we *really* want to go there? We do.

★ **THE RED LION, Llandovery, Carmarthenshire (Dyfed). ORD (W, VE). John Rees.**
We enter. It is minute and perfect. An old flat cap sits with stick and half-pint in the middle of the one room. The eccentric landlord, John Rees, emerges from his side room, whence comes the occasional mutter and growl (presumably from his invisible brother). He serves us with first-rate Buckleys from the barrel.

We felt perfectly at home in the 'neglected minimalist' decor and within seconds were deep into some interesting conversation. The old boy prefaced and ended each of his observations with a 'choo!', a sound halfway between a 'coo' and a spit that served equally well as an expression of disgust or wonderment at the strange ways of the world and the follies of the human race.

THE QUEST FOR THE PERFECT PUB

The landlord, he told us, was an idle good-for-nothing.

The landlord treated us to his own wild variation on a laugh.

Though the Prince of Wales was all right, the old boy continued, it was high time he and his wife got a house down here in Wales. High time. Choo.

And quite right.

As for his brothers, they should be castrated. Choo.

No comment.

The landlord was a worried man. Firstly, he was still a bachelor and had left it a little late to get married (about fifty-five). Secondly, if there was one thing he couldn't stand it was redheads. Thirdly, Buckley's Brewery was owned by Barlow Clowes, an organization that had just crashed in suspicious circumstances and he didn't in God's name know where he was going to get his beer from.

Choo. If there was one thing worse than redheads and Prince Andrew, interposed the old timer, it was filthy foreign milk in packets. Choo. It came from plastic cows in Hamburg, though they didn't dare write about it in the papers.

The landlord was warming to his theme. If there was one thing worse than Prince Andrew, redheads, Barlow Clowes, foreign milk, plastic cows, Sarah Ferguson, worse even than the awful, singing, dancing Prince Edward, it was the spectacle of Robert Maxwell, pictured recently in one of his own papers, wearing a Savile Row suit and trainers.

Trainers? Trainers! Choo!

We left The Red Lion at Llandovery with all expectations exceeded, a little light-headed, an hour or so older, and a great deal the wiser.

We had one more call to make on this first trip to Wales.

THE RADNOR ARMS, Talgarth (A438), Breconshire (Powys). GLL.

Apart from the mental hospital (see The Duke's Arms, Presteigne, p. 25 and THE BLUE BOAR, Hay-on-Wye, p. 55) there is little of note at Talgarth, save The Radnor Arms. At the time of our first visit, this was one of the best preserved 19th-century pubs in the world, and one of the simplest. There were two rooms, one a parlour, with lino and piano, and the other rougher, snugger, with magnificent flagstones and a fine fireplace. Between the two was a little central Victorian servery

SECTION ONE

with a hatch and shelves, but no bar. Your drink was brought to you at the table. Nothing had changed this century, save for the electric light and, a long time ago, a coat of paint. It was the closest thing to a time-slip we had felt.

Alas, the first tide of change had already overtaken The Radnor Arms. When we arrived, after lunch, it was to find the elderly landlord alone, having lost his wife (whose mother had run the pub before) only two weeks previously. He was clearly in mourning, and had not found the heart to open much since the funeral. However, he received us with immense courtesy, with just one caution: 'I'll have no bad language here, or you're out.' We were the only customers. He poured us bottled Whitbread and, perhaps feeling lonely, sat down to talk. The afternoon sun silhouetted his lined profile as it slanted through the dancing motes in the air. He wouldn't go on alone. He had just sold the pub to 'a man from Abergavenny who won't change it much.' Fingers crossed, we thought.

'Well, I wouldn't have sold it to just anybody. It's unique now, this place. I won't have it changed. I had four fellows came in from Merthyr once, and I caught them putting one of them jukeboxes in the other room, without no by-your-leave nor nothing. That's what they do, y'know. Then they've got you. I said 'You get from here now and take that thing with you before I call the police' (see **THE WHITE HART, Talybont-on-Usk**, p. 32). 'In a Jag they were, and all dressed up like bloody bunny-rabbits.'

We thought there might be hope yet for The Radnor Arms if the new owner kept his promise. For the outgoing widower, there will be his nest-egg, his warm new bungalow and his memories.

The vision we took away was of a frosty winter night, fire blazing, soft hubbub of voices, unthawing fingers and toes, tinkle of piano from the other room, and the landlord behind the hatch, filling his big jug to do one more round of the tables.

Postscript: So taken were we with The Radnor Arms, probably the most beautiful and perfectly preserved of all the pubs that we visited on our journey, that, fools and romantics that we are, we revisited the pub soon afterwards to see the new regime in action. We wished we hadn't. The promise had been broken. Gone was the servery, a jukebox was blaring, the lager was flowing; the settles were still there, the fireplace was smoulder-

THE QUEST FOR THE PERFECT PUB

ing, but the past was accelerating into the stratosphere, and the memories were riding its slipstream.

A cold chill of fear clutched at our hearts. Would we even complete our task before the last few places were crushed beneath the heel of progress? It seemed all the more important to chronicle and champion such establishments while the embers were still burning even though it might be a last futile attempt to fan the flames of a dying fire. We crossed the English border with the coals of new resolve glowing in our bellies.

Herefordshire, Worcestershire, South and West Wales is an area so rich in good drinking-houses that a research journey yields almost too much bounty. Here is a highly partial list of other recommended places well known to us. It would be inadvisable, however, at some of them, to mention the authors' names, unless you are not thirsty.

🍺 THE THREE HORSESHOES, Norton Canon, Herefordshire. LLL (FC, W).

A simple, but superb local on the Hereford–Kington (A480) road and kept by Linda and Frank Goodwin in a most relaxed manner. New licensing laws have made little difference to their Windmill 'we never close' policy; lively conversation, lino, quoits, darts, a serious drinking clientele, children welcome, guitars also, excellent home-made pickled eggs and a delectable landlady who is dead ringer for Dusty Springfield (see **THE POINT HOUSE, Angle Bay**, p. 38). Not to be missed.

🍺 THE STAGGE INN, Titley, Herefordshire. GLL (FC).

On a bend in Titley, between Kington and Presteigne on the B4355. Until recently The Stagge was kept by 83-year-old Frank Bingham, a retired bank manager who was one of the best-loved landlords in the county. Much patronized by Irish ukelele players and other musicians, it became a home from home and scene of many a fine evening, watched over by Frank's stern but fatherly eye. Only he was permitted to say when a patron had 'had enough', and he was entirely sensitive to the moods of his volatile clientele – when he said 'enough' enough it was. This patrician and always courteous gentleman can still be seen in the plain but cosy public bar at The Stagge,

SECTION ONE

nursing a Brewmaster or a Scotch, the old twinkle still in his eye. His successors are continuing the splendid Stagge tradition, and also said to be cooking well. Go there; you will enjoy it.

THE BRITISH LION, Kings Caple, Herefordshire. GLL.
Off the A49, not far from Hoarwithy, in the south of the county. A good, solid, higgledy-piggledy village pub with a big pot-bellied stove, a pillar of unlikely Doric aspect in the middle, and a quiet, friendly Northerner of a landlord with a slightly unnerving but endearing way of addressing all comers, regardless of sex, as 'luv'. Good conversation can be had here; a very sound village local.

THE COTTAGE OF CONTENT, Carey, Herefordshire. GAR (F).
Take the Hoarwithy turning off A49 and follow signposts from Hoarwithy.
   This opened-out old pub is well-known and fairly widely chronicled; at weekends and some evenings it is patronized by Jumping Jeremies from the smart bits of Herefordshire. We include it here for the following reasons. The modernization has been handled very well indeed. These people understand what a pub should be, and have kept all the original features, simply opening the space out a little. There are scrubbed tables, very good food, and one of the best pints of Marston's Pedigree in this part of the world. But the main triumph at The Cottage of Content is that the locals still drink here; no whipper-snappers have driven them away, and they clearly still enjoy it. The management are relaxed and charming and it is an excellent example of how to bring a pub into the modern world without ruining it.

THE STOCKTON CROSS, Kimbolton, Herefordshire. LLL (FC).
This is a village cider-pub of considerable character, two miles north of Leominster on the Ludlow Road (turn right for Leysters). It is attractively set on a grassy bank in the centre of the village, a pleasant place at which to sit, drink and watch life go by. Much frequented by fine old boys with gnarled hands

51

and local ears (see **THE CORNEWALL ARMS, Clodock**, p. 22) who enjoy greatly the local produce, be it from flagon or barrel. Two small bars make up the interior, and while there is little of architectural merit, the atmosphere is undeniably snug. On rare occasions, you may catch a glimpse of a tall, blond, leonine figure, inadequately disguised in a fishing hat, sneaking in through the side door clutching a clanking plastic bag, and several minutes later slinking furtively out again, carrying the same bag, which will now be heavier, but still clanking. This is the novelist, sailor and banjoist Sam Llewellyn, a local resident, purchasing fuel with which to pen another of his blockbusters; so powerful is this rocket fluid that Llewellyn once conceived, wrote and delivered to his publishers in *three weeks* a 550-page, perfectly-researched epic novel. The cider is very good at The Stockton Cross.

🍺 **THE TAVERN, Kington, Herefordshire.** ORD (FC, E).

Set in a backstreet and so low-profile that of Kingtonians probably only those over the age of 40 know of it, this very much deserves a detour. Run for many years by two maiden sisters, the second of whom, Miss May, has only recently been forced to give up, The Tavern is a superb one-room drinker, in muted brown and nicotine, with a solid bar, beautifully-engraved mirrors, amazing old pictures of village teams, and a licence to brew, which it has not done for a long time, though the yard out back still has the workings.

Miss May was a formidable character at first, until you had passed her rigorous standards which included above all, good manners. You could get as drunk as you liked as long as you did it with decorum. If you passed the test, she was a delightful companion, full of local history and with a wicked sense of humour. If you failed, she would serve you pints consisting of the slops from the drip-trays as a subtle way of dispensing with your custom. It never failed to work. Now run by a family friend, who hasn't changed a thing, The Tavern is an almost perfect example of an old Herefordshire pub.

★ **THE DYFRYN ARMS, Gwaun Valley, Pembrokeshire (Dyfed). ORD (FC, E).**

Down by the river, in the thickly-wooded and beautiful Gwaun

SECTION ONE

Valley, where eccentrically they celebrate New Year later in the calendar than most of us, is this gem of a pub, an unspoilt and individualistic drinker of immense character. Welsh is spoken here. Only locals frequent the place, but the more intrepid reader will on no account miss it. It would be his loss, not theirs.

🍺 THE CAREW INN, Carew (A4075), Pembrokeshire (Dyfed). LLL (W).

On the way to **THE CRESSELLY ARMS** (see p. 41), stop off at this welcoming, homely and traditional country inn, set above the estuary and close to Carew Castle. There are two small bars, good Worthingtons and a tidal water mill, presumably only working at high and low tide. Simple snacks and honest company can be assured. As you would expect, the same family have owned it for fifty years.

🍺 THE FISHGUARD ARMS, Fishguard, Pembrokeshire (Dyfed). LLL (M, E).

In its own little bay between the Heads of Strumble and Dinas, Fishguard is well worth a visit (even if you are not in a mind to take the ferry to Rosslare) for the character of the town and for the quality of the public houses, the best of which is The Fishguard Arms. It is a small, dark and single-minded establishment, where the ever more inflationary prices of beer over the years are chronicled on the ceiling. There is also a particularly enticing back bar with piano.

When we arrived, there was a heated discussion in progress between an old boy and two youngsters about the relative merits of Bass and Hancocks, a local beer. We drank good Marston's from the cask.

A stranger entered, ordered a vodka-and-tonic and unwisely asked for ice. The landlady fixed him with a stern eye.

'I do no ice at all,' she informed him, as if there were several varieties of ice she could have stocked had she wished but was unimpressed by all of them.

Next door in The Royal Oak, the Irish-American adventurer General Tate signed a peace treaty after the miserable failure of his 'Fishguard Invasion' of 1797 in which his army of some 1,400 Frenchmen capitulated to the local militia almost without striking a blow. For some time after there were severe problems

53

THE QUEST FOR THE PERFECT PUB

of overcrowding in the prisons of Haverfordwest and Pembroke.

🍺 **THE SLOOP INN**, Port Gain, Pembrokeshire (Dyfed). LLL.
The only pub in this tiny and almost-abandoned old grain port, where the harbour is enclosed by dramatic cliffs, and the surrounding coastland is good walking country. The Sloop appears to be open most hours, and Bertie and Margaret Phillips are always keen to oblige.

🍺🍺 **THE HOPE**, East End Square, Pembroke, Pembrokeshire (Dyfed). LLL (W).
The nicest pub in Pembroke is The Hope, a small and intimate house where the loyal and discerning regulars include the well-known character Ernie, who can neither read nor write and whose remarkable stories slip down inordinately well with the beer.

The Hope is run by the hospitable husband-and-wife team of David and Paddy Pratt. What David does not know about jazz drumming, flora and fauna, and Pembrokeshire pubs and history – 'It was at 9 am on the 3rd of March 1644 that the first cannon shot was fired from the castle walls . . . no, hold on, it must have been nearer 9.30' – is not worth knowing.

While Paddy indulges in drinks only of the soft variety, David claims that his short move from one side of the bar to the other was the best move he ever made.

🍺🍺 **THE FOX AND HOUNDS**, Cwmcych (off B4332), Pembrokeshire (Dyfed). GLL (I, E).
Two miles outside Abercych, down a lonely, wooded road that follows the valley (cwm) of the River Cych, stands one of the most isolated pubs in Pembrokeshire. For its dappled, sylvan location alone The Fox and Hounds is worth a visit. The landlord is a charming man of uncertain European extraction, and he keeps a spacious, one-room bar where the beer is good, the locals gather to play skittles, the dogs are large and friendly, and where, perhaps, a lone, well-spoken biker from Redditch, in earrings, khaki and leather, is listening intently to Frank Zappa and Public Image Ltd. Strangely, the locals do not seem to mind. Though often quiet, the general impression is that

SECTION ONE

anything could happen. 'They'll never spoil this place, not as long as I'm here,' asserts the landlord. Let's hope he's right.

🍺 THE CASTLE, Bridge End, Cardigan, Pembrokeshire (Dyfed). GLL (FC).
A small, one-room, striplight-and-lino drinker just before the bridge over the Teifi as you enter Cardigan. Unaffected by trends, this is a little bit of old Cardigan preserved. The elderly landlady has a girlish smile and a hyperactive spaniel; her son drinks at **THE RAMP, Cilgerran** (see p. 43). Over the bridge, Cardigan is still dry on Sundays, but Bridge End is just in Pembrokeshire (the river is the boundary), so go there then, when most of the town's drinkers troop over after church and chapel for a good liquid Sunday afternoon. An honest, unpretentious place, with good Hancock's beer.

🍺 THE BLUE BOAR, Hay-on-Wye, Radnorshire (Powys). GMTH.
The Blue Board has been through a few changes recently and has now been redesigned inside. The local planning officer caused the present landlord many problems about the siting of the drains, disrupted the building programme and was then removed to the local asylum at Talgarth, where there is, incidentally, a special ward set aside for cider casualties. Usually a good place to drink, The Blue Boar has, in the past, harboured many a 'red neckerchief' (see THE OLD BREWERY HOUSE, Reepham, p. 191) who abound in great numbers in the surrounding hills. Hay has become the secondhand book centre of the British Isles, thanks to 'King' Richard Booth who, while building up his empire, declared the town an independent State, crowned himself monarch, and, Caligula-like, made his horse Prime Minister. It is full of eccentrics, and The Blue Boar is still the favoured watering-hole of the celebrated trans-sexual April Ashley, when she is in residence at her townhouse here.

🍺 THE THREE TUNS, Hay-on-Wye, Radnorshire (Powys). GLL (E).
Run by Lucy Powell, an expert on the Royal Family (don't mention them unless you have all day), this pub features in the film of Bruce Chatwin's brilliant book about the area, *On The*

55

Black Hill. Drink the cider, not the beer. Observe the oldest dog in the world.

★ THE FLEECE, Bretforton, Hereford and Worcester. GAR (FC, OP). Dan and Nora Davies.
The venerable Lola Taplin, whose family owned The Fleece for five hundred years until her death in 1977, left this glorious building and the entire contents to the National Trust on the condition that they continue to run it as an old-fashioned pub. The NT have kept their word, and the current licensee is a dedicated and charming man.

There are three rooms, all with splendid fireplaces. One has a huge inglenook in front of which sit the village's old boys, on Sundays in their old tweed suits and polished shoes, talking shop and providing a link with the past. The furniture is magnificent, mainly 18th- and 19th-century (the licence began in 1848), and there is a renowned pewter collection.

Clientele range from locals to (at weekends) families out from Birmingham and Worcester, but they mix well. The Fleece is deservedly famous, and must be visited as it stands head and shoulders above the surrounding competition.

🍺 THE PLOUGH, Shenstone (off A450), Hereford and Worcester. LLL (FC, W).
The Roses have run The Plough for more than thirty years and never fail to provide a warm welcome to regular and visitor alike. It is one of a handful of pubs owned by Daniel Batham's brewery, and their excellent product fuels the good humour that pervades this relaxing local, which seems a world away from its real location – perilously close to the urban nightmare of Birmingham.

Section Two

The West Country

Cornwall

September 13th, Monday
'There aren't any decent pubs left in Cornwall,' observed Nice Brian gloomily, staring into his Bass. 'Too many bloody emmets around now, they've all been turned into food-factories. Five year ago it were different.'

There were sympathetic nods from the early-evening crowd assembled around the bar at The New Inn, Tywardreath, Cornwall. In addition to the authors and Nice Brian, also present were Mad Brian, Brian from London, Brian with wobbly legs and the imposing figure of George Truscott, the licensee.

Tywardreath is a largely unspoilt village just inland from the old Cornish china-clay port of Par, which is still thriving. It was here that Daphne du Maurier partly set her novel *The House on The Strand*, in which the drug-crazed hero, half in the 14th century and half in the 20th, scrabbles around in the moonlit graveyard at Tywardreath, unable to land successfully in either era.

🍺 **THE NEW INN, Tywardreath (off A390), Cornwall. LLL (FC, W, B). Tel: 0726-813901.**
The New Inn is a substantial stone building from which the church is visible. Remembering it from years before, we had made it our first port of call after a non-stop drive from Bristol, where we had been for the weekend and a much-needed medical checkup. We had planned a quick stop, intending to push on to Truro for the night, but the first pint of Bass from the cask had been so seductive that we were now on our third, and it was obvious that not much more driving should be attempted. So instead, we were picking the locals' brains for the best pubs in this part of South Cornwall.

Having made our decision to stay, we found the regulars more than willing to help us in our quest, and soon a short list of

THE QUEST FOR THE PERFECT PUB

suitable places was being drawn up. George attempted to sell us a dog-eared and much-thumbed copy of the (excellent) CAMRA *Guide to Real Beer in Cornwall* but desisted when called a 'hook-nosed bleeder' by one of the Brians, and instead offered to accompany us on our rounds. We accepted eagerly, but at that moment his wife entered the bar and caught mine host in the act of donning his hat and coat. 'Oh no, you don't,' she informed him sternly. 'Back behind that bar this instant.' We booked ourselves a couple of beds upstairs, left him whispering assurances that he closed at 'eleven-ish' and set off into the gathering dusk.

🍺 **THE CROWN**, Lanlivery, Cornwall. LLL.

🍺 **THE KING'S ARMS (THE BRIDGES)**, Luxulyan, Cornwall. LLL (FC).
Monday night is a very good drinking night in South Cornwall and the two establishments we visited on our whistle-stop rounds that evening (both off the A390) were in the same mould: good, thriving village locals. The beer in both pubs (Bass, Hancocks, Tinners) was first rate, as is the case generally in Cornwall, and the mix of people very lively and eclectic: locals, ruddy-complexioned women, the odd intellectual, and an interesting new breed of teenage hybrid, male and female, who are the exotic offspring of the union between local people and the commune dropouts of the 1960s, with Cornish accents and wild, romantic eyes. All proliferate in these hills and rocky creeks. In fact, the dramatic nature of the coastline in South Cornwall spares the area from the very worst excesses of summer tourism as witnessed on the wide beaches and criminally built-up north coast round Perranporth and Newquay. Here, in the pubs a few miles inland, can perhaps be seen the spirit of the Cornish people; it is a pity, however, that the local authorities have seen fit to light these pretty villages with the kind of hideous orange streetlamps you find on the sliproads to the M25.

We returned to The New Inn at 10.30 to find a fine session in progress. Arming ourselves with pints, we were soon engrossed in conversation and noted with grateful anticipation the practised way with which, at 11 pm, George Truscott closed the curtains, dimmed the lights, shut the till and locked the door. We were about to witness a demonstration of the gentle art of the Lock-In.

It must be explained here that the Lock-In is sacred. Nothing must disturb its flow, nothing must detract from the clients' enjoyment, nothing must interfere. That is the Law, unwritten but untransgressable, whatever the circumstances.

About thirty minutes into extra time, we became aware of a faint but pungent aroma emanating from the nether regions of the pub. Nobody our side of the bar appeared to notice, and George was attending to his business on the other so we thought nothing of it, until, a few minutes later, the smell became more pronounced and a few wisps of smoke began to curl around the door. The landlord remained unmoved, and the Bass continued to flow. We looked at each other. Was this the work of an arsonist, maddened at having been excluded from the drink-up? Was it the constabulary's way of warning George they knew what he was up to? Or was it the Free Cornwall Mafia ticking the landlord off for being a bit behind with his payments? There was no way of telling, so we watched with bated breath as Celine Truscott came running into the bar, accompanied by billows of black smoke, and spoke quietly into her husband's ear. Visibly annoyed at having to leave his friends, the landlord left the room, to appear a moment or so later with a grey, set expression on his face. Still saying nothing, he began to soak towels and rags in water and returned whence he had come. Braving the smoke, we ventured into the back room.

'Everything all right?'

'Yes fine, just a little chip fire,' came a reassuring voice that ended in a choked splutter. We peeped into the kitchen.

It was joyously aflame.

We went back to our seats, not wanting to raise the alarm. The bar was now clogged with thick, black, smoke that made it difficult to breathe. Yet everybody in The New Inn was behaving as if nothing unusual was happening at all. Drinks were being drunk, and conversations continued in an unsettlingly insouciant way for some minutes until George appeared at the bar door, face beetroot-red, holding a handkerchief to his mouth.

'Right, that's it, everybody out, just a tiny little mishap, nothing to worry about, just leave, bloody quick!'

THE QUEST FOR THE PERFECT PUB

Muttering and grumbling, as if they had been unfairly dismissed, the Brians and other regulars of the New Inn shuffled unwillingly out into the night, while behind them their favourite place was lit with dancing flames of the kind that burned down Manderley in du Maurier's most famous novel.

After heroic efforts by George and his wife, the fire was brought under control without recourse to the fire brigade, we all shared a nightcap and we retired to our smoke-filled bedroom above the kitchen. Throwing the window open to release the fumes we beheld a poignant sight; standing in the porch of The New Inn below us, swaying like an aspen in a stiff breeze, desperate not to go home and hanging on in the drunken misconception that the door of the pub might suddenly open again and a hand pull him back in for just one more, was Mad Brian. We watched him for several minutes, until his shoulders slumped in a final gesture of despair and he tacked diagonally home down the deserted street.

September 14th, Tuesday
There are no chemists' shops in Cornwall. Well, to be accurate, there appear to be none at all between Tywardreath and Falmouth, and that is quite a long stretch of road to travel if you are suffering from hangovers of the gigantic proportions that can be acquired at the New Inn. We drove on, through rainy, chemistless villages with surreal and outlandish names, until, somewhere between Sticker and Grampound, or it may have been Probus and Come-to-Good, we stared at each other with wild and rheumy eyes; we would have to venture into a town and locate an old-fashioned pharmacist who knew how to deal with our condition. They all had a patent remedy, an elixir compounded of raw eggs, toads' scrotums, Worcester sauce and milk of magnesia; we could take it, we weren't squeamish. We were only two miles from our destination, the Seven Stars in Falmouth, and we had to be in fair health.

Penryn is a small town tacked on to the end of Falmouth, a place of long and narrow streets that is the home of Our Lady of The Pharmacy, healer and benefactress to travellers.

We entered her spotless sanctum; her homely face shone with sympathy and caring. We began to blurt out an incoherent list of our symptoms, but she silenced us with a gesture and motioning us to wait, disappeared up into the altar of her preparations room. We hung about, self-consciously shifting from foot to foot. The shopgirl regarded us somewhat nervously. Could she help? No thanks, we were just waiting.

It was worth the wait. To our relief and the shopgirl's astonishment The Sister of Mercy of Penryn emerged, bearing brimming beakers of a strange yellow, foaming liquid which looked as if it had been dreamed up by the special effects department at The House of Hammer.

'Here you are, gentlemen.' She placed a glass into each of our shaking hands. 'It never fails to work on me.' Even this admission of worldliness did not tarnish her image as we downed the fluid in long, shuddering draughts. The shopgirl's eyes grew wider and wider, until she suddenly burst into peals of delighted laughter at our plight. So quick to work was the cure that before we had finished the glass we were both hopelessly in love with her. It was time to get back on the road before we caused any trouble.

★ **THE SEVEN STARS, The Moor, Falmouth, Cornwall. LLL (FC, W, E). John Barrington Bennetts.**
The sky was hurling torrents of stinging rain at the earth as we circled Falmouth town centre looking for a parking-space. Feeling better, but still frail, we needed something wonderful to happen, and it did.

Once you have parked your car, locate the Moor Shopping Centre. Unpromisingly located between it and the Post Office is an elderly building which is The Seven Stars. Only the thick steam on the windows gives any hint of the riches within.

The Seven Stars is effectively a one-room drinker that has been refreshing the town since 1660, and the fact that the current licensee is the fifth generation of his family to run it accounts for the totally unspoilt interior and atmosphere. Inside, at a long bar, sits a row of faces: weather-beaten, nautical, bright-eyed faces, clad in oilskins, fisherman's jerseys, stout boots. Occasionally one face replaces another as a stool becomes vacant, but the front line is never broken.

On the other side of the bar there is a row of lovingly-tended barrels of Bass, Courage Directors and St Austell, two of each kind, the second stillaged up for a smooth transition when the brisk pace of consumption empties the first.

Between the two, soft-voiced and welcoming, is one of the

THE QUEST FOR THE PERFECT PUB

best and most attentive barmen it was our pleasure to witness anywhere in the country. An ex-seafarer himself, he is dedicated to his clientele. Quietly, he patrols the line of drinkers, noticing instinctively when a glass is empty, knowing exactly with what to refill it, lighting a cigarette here, dispensing advice there, completely in tune with the needs of the crowd. If you are hungry he will sell you a Cornish Pasty but that is all. He will advise you on ferry times, tides, local landmarks, and if he does not know will find one of his customers who does. He will look after you. We sheltered from a two-hour rainstorm at The Seven Stars, and watched with pure joy the honest running of a serious, no-frills harbour-town pub, where the tattoos and rough-edged atmosphere need not alarm you; you may be an 'emmet', but the locals want to make sure you get the best out of your visit and are disposed to help you. Falmouth, especially out-of-season, is a straightforward, entertaining town. The Seven Stars turns it into a memorable one.

It was still raining when we left The Seven Stars, but our hearts were lighter and our optimism restored as we set course for Helston and The Blue Anchor. Here, indeed, was quality.

★ **THE BLUE ANCHOR, Coinage Hall St., Helston, Cornwall. LLL (W, M, E). Sid and Pat Cannon.**
The Blue Anchor is justifiably famous the world over, and well-documented in other publications. Here are our impressions.

The best way to visit The Blue Anchor is to arrive towards the end of the morning, say 11.30. Book yourself a room at THE ANGEL HOTEL, GMTH (B), tel: 0326-572701, just up the street. You will need it later. Park your car in The Angel car park, thereby avoiding the infamously zealous traffic-warden who, in the week of our visit, had already booked a police car and a hearse in the act of loading up a coffin. Walk the few hundred yards to The Blue Anchor and settle in.

The building started life as a monks' retreat in the early 15th century, and probably had a brewhouse even then. It has been a pub and brewery since 1550, uninterrupted by historical events, and its beers are still in the first league. There are two bars in the warren-like interior and a separate room across the covered alley where those who insist on eating are skilfully dealt

SECTION TWO

with by means of local pasties, toasted sandwiches and other simple and acceptable items.

Five beers are brewed here, including Blue Anchor Medium, Best, Spingo Special and Extra Special, of which Medium (the weakest) pitches in at a hefty OG 1050 (hence your room at The Angel). The first person we met in the front bar of The Blue Anchor was a Lizard-dweller in a bobble hat, who told us about the legendary Christmas Special (OG 1108) brewed for the festive season.

'We hired a minibus on the Lizard to bring us into Helston for our Christmas shopping. Well, we came in here for a quick one before lunch and none of us got any shopping done at all. I drank three pints of the Christmas Special, and I was still too drunk to go to work the next morning.'

Have a look round the brewhouse while you can still stand; like the interior of the pub itself, it is basic, efficient and full of atmosphere, and the landlord's enthusiasm is manifest.

'We still don't open all day,' he admits. 'The beer's too strong and they can't take it, so we do close in the afternoons.' You can usually find them open until 4 pm, however, on Saturdays.

It is wonderfully relaxed here; outsiders are tolerated with sardonic good-humour, and there is a colourful cast of characters.

We left for our siesta, noting the poster advertising an R & B gig, to be held in the skittle alley, featuring the raw blues of Slim Willy and the Guzzle Rustlers, and secure in the knowledge that The Blue Anchor has been a very special place for 500 years and is not about to change a great deal in the near future.

One siesta later, we were battling north-east through another rainstorm across the central Cornish plain, scarred with worked-out mines, crumbling chimneys and roofless, lichen-encrusted sheds. Unemployment is the highest in the county here, round Camborne and Redruth, and the aspect bleak and uncompromising. But there is a certain stark beauty in this ancient land, plundered for its wealth since the Romans, and the shrouds of water through which we saw it gave it a dream-like, soft-focus quality that was almost romantic.

At any rate, it was infinitely preferable to Perranporth, which we reached at about 5 pm. This part of the Cornish coast, because of its accessible, sandy beaches, has suffered appallingly at the hands of developers and the tourist industry. Nowhere in the world, from Benidorm to Torremolinos to the shanty slums of Rio or Soweto, can you find such architectural vandalism and opportunism; hotels, caravan sites, tea emporia, self-catering cellblocks are scattered like dirty white confetti over headland and valley, car parks mar the cliffs and beaches. The older, Edwardian villas and guesthouses are little better, huddled together in their overcoats of grubby grey stone, paint cracked and peeling, their age their only redemption.

In an off-season Perranporth, we trudged silently across the beach, where dogs were defecating into rock-pools, where litter clogged the sewer that ran over the muddy sands into a brackish sea, where even the seagulls looked depressed. Everything was closed; the Majestic tearooms lay under a blanket of guano, the sun had long since set on The Sunset Bar and Disco, and no string of golden surfer boys and girls were queuing outside The Last Wave Inn.

We left before our moods got the better of us. There were quite obviously no pubs anywhere near here. We took the coast road away from this scene of devastation, towards Padstow and the Devon border.

We passed the night in Padstow, whose old centre and harbour remain unspoilt and still discernible as a working fishing port. The outskirts are, of course, full of ring roads and golf-links, and you may well despair. It is, however, the best watering-hole on this part of the coast, benefitting from the superb cooking of Chris Stein at The Seafood Restaurant, where the food and ambience are of such quality that you feel you actually could be in the South of France. Spend your money there, drink a decent pint of St Austell Tinners at THE LONDON INN, GLL, and have an inexpensive night at THE OLD SHIP HOTEL, GITS, tel: 0841-532357, where the rooms are reasonably-priced and the Lock-In mildly amusing. Then, in the morning, on your way into Devon, you have two treats in store for you.

September 15th, Wednesday
Leaving Padstow on the Wadebridge road, and turning left to St Teath, you arrive at the small hamlet of Trebarwith. Leave your car here, and follow the footpath through a gate, down onto the downs. You tread a deep, rutted track through rumi-

SECTION TWO

nating kine until, breasting a small rise, you discover yourselves standing on a giddy headland, with the wind blowing hard enough to knock you over. To your left is a wooded gorge that descends to the water's edge. To your right is another, that ends half a mile from the sea and from where a straggle of houses leads down to a craggy inlet.

The Atlantic is roaring in on the autumn equinox, and the surf is crashing onto the cliffs with primaeval fury. Take the sheep-path down the cliff, and you will be standing on the rocks at the edge of Trebarwith Strand, which must have been a fine little smugglers' landing-place in times gone by. Here you can refresh yourself at THE HOTEL ON THE STRAND, GAR, with its 'Beastro', or at the MILL HOUSE INN, GAR (B), tel: 0840-770200, half a mile inland, prettily situated at the foot of a wood with a melodious stream gushing past it. There is a pleasant garden, an active piano in the middle of the room, single cigarettes for sale behind the bar, and, in mid September at least, an air of tranquillity.

Otherwise you can do as we did, walk back up the cliff, rejoin your car and head north again.

Tintagel is the legendary site of Camelot, but of Arthur and his Court there is no sign. Time, tourism and the memory of a raddled Richard Harris in ill-fitting tights singing 'How to Handle a Woman' have erased all traces. Instead there is Camelford, where, a few months before our visit, the South-West Water Authority had poisoned thousands of people with a surplus of 'clean water additives'. We did not prolong our stay.

Eighteen miles up the A39, we turned left just past Bude towards Morwenstow. The twisting lanes led up through the broadleaf woodland of Hartland Forest, past the astounding fortified manor farm called Stowe Barton, onto a high headland where suddenly we leapt five centuries when the great white, curved outlines of the satellite dishes of the CSOS installation reared up into our vision, surrounded by high fencing and 'Danger' signs. Leaving this behind we were soon back on lonely lanes again, and within a mile and a half we spied on the left an isolated promontory with spectacular views, and one of the finest old pubs in Cornwall.

THE BUSH INN, Morwenstow, Cornwall. GLL (I).
Everything about The Bush bespeaks longevity. Parts of the

walls date back to 950 AD, when the building was a Cistercian Chapel inhabited by monks who cared for the local lepers. There is an arrow-slit sized squinthole in the wall of the main bar through which the monks, untainted in their sanctum, kept an eye on their charges. It has been a pub for several hundred years and the present landlord has been there for twenty-nine of them. There are fine old carved chairs, worn slate floors, good beer from St Austells and a friendly barlady who cooks a good, simple beef stew and serves it with hot baps – the perfect pub lunch. Big fires roar in winter, when the locals reclaim their favourite chairs and play the old games.

The countryside around has a real feeling of prehistory about it, the quiet and isolation are palpable, and there is probably no more restful place to stop and drink than this. We were able to put aside the faintly sour feeling which Perranporth and Newquay had instilled into us, and as we refreshed our palates, so The Bush refreshed our souls.

Of the many pubs we have been to in Cornwall, all the following thoroughly deserve a visit. Some, like The Pandora Inn, are so well known that a full entry here seems redundant; others, usually as a result of trying to feed the millions, have lost some of their innocence but can still be fun.

★ **THE PANDORA INN**, Restronguet Creek, Cornwall. GAR (F, OP). Roger and Helen Hough.
As others have noted, the Pandora has been 'cleaned up' and is now decidedly up-market. The old fisherman's dive of years ago has gone, but, in fact, cleaned up is all it has been, and the building is still splendid. A steep lane takes you down to the creek, where the pub nestles alongside a long wooden pontoon with plenty of cheap mooring for yachts. The slate floors shine with polish, the danger of flooding means that the fireplaces are high off the ground, and the four bars are still intact. No open-plan here. Food is very much the main game, with a busy restaurant that in the summer will not please purists. Yet the Pandora's delightful situation, the friendly welcome and quiet professionalism of the Houghs make it worth your while. Again, go in winter, when it could be compared to a more sophisticated **CRESSELLY ARMS**, Cresswell Quay (see p. 41).

SECTION TWO

🍺🍺 **ROSELAND INN, Philleigh, Cornwall. LLL.**
Thatched, remote and very unspoilt despite the summer trade it does, The Roseland Inn has a strong local following. It provides good, simple food, sound Devenish beer and welcome hot toddies in cold weather. Roses ramble over the porch. This is the best stopping-point before or after the King Harry ferry.

🍺🍺 **THE NEW INN, Manaccan, St Keverne, Cornwall. LLL (F).**
Quietly situated on the edge of the village off the B3293 near Helford. Homely, civilized, excellent beer from the barrel, unusual food, board games, and a splendid outhouse for the Gents'. Something of an oasis.

🍺🍺 **THE ST KEW INN, St Kew, Cornwall. LLL (F).**
Off the main Camelford road (beware the drinking water), the St Kew has a wonderful old parlour-bar with hanging meat-hooks, an enormous fire, a jumbled yet welcoming atmosphere, not scruffy but not smart, and excellent Devenish cask beer. Unfortunately there is a restaurant which serves a 'secret recipe' steak for which people seem to be prepared to kill. Eat one if you can stand an hour's wait and a dining-room experience, otherwise stick to the parlour-bar and a pint or two.

🍺🍺 **THE TRENGILLY WARTHA, Constantine, Nancenoy (off A394), Cornwall. GAR (I, F, B, M). Tel: 032640332/90631.**
Tucked well away in its own extensive grounds, the Trengilly Wartha proved a haven for one of the authors in a thinly-pubbed area near Falmouth. There is a splendid long bar, with massive fireplace, seriously-tended cask beer, a good mix of local gentry, non-gentry and the usual infiltrators. Perhaps because of its seclusion, conversation comes swiftly here, as though one is in a private house. Good helpings of decent food appear, including local shellfish, and there are clean, adequate bedrooms. Helpful and civilized service make this as decent an overnight stay as anywhere. Regular live music includes folk, jazz and rhythm and blues.

🍺 **THE LEMON ARMS, Mylor Bridge, Cornwall. GLL (FC).**
Only a mile or two from The Pandora Inn, this is the other side

of the coin, a friendly little village local with good conversation and strictly local atmosphere. Soak it up; there isn't much left in these parts.

▤ **THE SEVEN STARS,** Penryn, Cornwall. GLL (E).
Handily situated opposite the chemist, this is an interesting little local, with good Cornish Brewery beer and a landlord who is the oldest in the town. He has an extraordinary collection of brass items, from divers' helmets to bells, which clutter every available inch and make an amusing diversion. He also bears an uncanny resemblance to the columnist and gastronome Jeffrey Bernard, who has been known to enter a public house from time to time. Jeff would like it here, since the regulars are boxing experts who still refer to 'Cassius Clay' and 'Gentleman Henry' and don't reckon much to Mike Tyson, married or not.

▤ **UNION HOTEL (THE ONION),** Chapel St., Penzance, Cornwall. GMTH (B). Tel: 0736-62319.
Recommended by Nice Brian at **THE NEW INN, Tywardreath** (see p. 59), this is a fine old town pub with an authentic local atmosphere. Get the feel of the town here and then venture forth, for Penzance is full of good pubs, and the locals say that it is the best pub crawl in Cornwall; you can do it all on foot as well.

Devon

North-West Devon, the area between Hartland Point and Dartmoor, is a district of hidden villages, lonely farms and scanty population that has escaped the worst ravages of the tourist industry. It is through these hills and valleys that the hard-drinking Poet Laureate Ted Hughes wends his way, pausing between dark thoughts to refresh himself in the dimmer corners of the hostelries.

We set off down the wet lanes expecting to find any number of hidden gems lurking in the dank nooks and crannies of the county. We were sadly disappointed. Most of the old pubs and the cantankerous, bearded old ladies have slipped away into the past – often a past that is tantalizingly recent – leaving only their displaced and confused former customers sandwiched in between the jukebox and space machine where once, only last year, last month, last week, there had stood the servery, the hatch and the proud row of barrels.

It was at this stage of our journey that we began to realize the bitter truth. Our quest for the perfect pub was to be far less fruitful than we had ever imagined. All over the country the big brewers and conglomerates had done their worst, like every vicious and extortionate landlord, forcing up to ever higher levels the rents of their tenants and the targets they are required to meet, until the publican who has for many years provided solace and comfort to his locals has eventually no other recourse but to unwillingly throw in the towel.

From now on we met the occasional criticism of our task – that by writing about these pubs we would help to spoil them – with increasing irritation. For if this book serves no other purpose, it may encourage a few people to visit these wonderful places and so help to preserve them. The continuing desecration of the classic country pub is, on a par with the desecration of a beautiful church, an act of vandalism both architecturally and in terms of the community. And to those who may consider our attitude too traditionalist, too steeped in nostalgia, we would reply that everywhere we travelled we met as many young people as old who felt a sense of loss and outrage at what was happening. Time and time again we would make enquiries as to the best pubs only to be told in reverent tones about Grumpy Bill's place in the next village, or of Old Joan in the Red Lion down the road. Then the pause and the added rider: 'But he/she is not there any more . . . it's been revamped by the brewery . . . it's now a restaurant/holiday home.'

In the case of north-west Devon it was Mark, a local builder in his 20s, who told us categorically 'There *are* no more old pubs in this part of the county.' It was the usual story. 'You're just

THE QUEST FOR THE PERFECT PUB

too late. There was one in Bideford that was the best drinker in the area. But the old couple retired a month ago and now it's unrecognizable.'

However, compared to some areas Devon is a treasure trove of pubs, and we were delighted to be able to award no less than eight stars, more than in any other single county.

We set off south to Hatherleigh where we had been assured we would find a warm welcome at The Tally Ho. Hatherleigh is a market town of charm in central Devon that could just as easily be a village. Although the George Hotel is a fine building dating from the 15th century, as a pub it is currently in serious decline.

★ **THE TALLY HO, Hatherleigh, Devon.**
GGAR (W, F, B, OP). Tel: 0837-810306.
Gianni and Anne-Marie Scoz.
The Tally Ho is everything that a great inn should be. One large room contains a wood-burning stove, several well-spaced handsome tables, a darts board and an accommodating, well-stocked bar. Next door is a smaller and equally attractive dining room.

The atmosphere on any evening in the week is superb. Candles and soft lighting combine to conjure up a perfect glow of ease and content. A reassuring row of barrels contain a range of delicious beers (Huntsman's, Wadworth's, guest beers). The music – anything from pop to opera – is neither unacceptable wallpaper (as in piped) nor lager-offensive (as in jukebox). It is well-chosen and a part of the place. The Tally Ho is packed with people taking their pleasure with the noisy but relaxed enjoyment of a clientele that has absolute confidence in their chosen watering-place.

And confidence is the word. Exuding it from behind the bar is the dashing Gianni Scoz, a Milanese who came to Devon on holiday some years ago, fell in love with the county and the tradition of the English pub, and is now running one of the best houses in the country.

Like every great all-rounder, The Tally Ho caters for all comers. Gianni and his wife Anne-Marie are much-loved by the locals who flock in huge numbers to the darts matches and many other nightly antics. Anne-Marie produces some of the most perfect inn food to be found anywhere, from delicious home-made pasta and pizzas to mouth-watering Italian dishes of more complexity.

The whole place is run with the seamless efficiency that is found only very rarely in this country, where to serve is unaccountably deemed to be demeaning. The staff are enthusiastic, intelligent and sure-footed. They actually *believe* in the enterprise. There is no fuss, no pretension. In his excellent list of Italian wines, Gianni is able to indulge his sense of fun and lack of pomposity. Such-and-such a Barolo is, he is told, better than the one preceding it. Personally he can't tell the difference.

Upstairs there are several comfortable bedrooms furnished with taste and style and available at a reasonable price. Book in and enjoy yourselves. The leaflet that awaits you on the dressing-table sums it up: 'As The Tally Ho is above all a country inn, the locals are likely to become a little boisterous at times, especially on darts nights. If you are finding it difficult to sleep, then why not come downstairs and join in the fun'.

There are other pubs that are worthy of your attention in the area surrounding Hatherleigh. Both the DEVILS STONE at Shebbear, LLL (B), tel: 040928-210, and THE NEW INN at Sampford Courtenay, GLL are justifiably well known, but The Clovelly Inn, hidden away in the pretty whitewashed backwater of Bratton Clovelly, is less so.

🍺🍺 THE CLOVELLY INN, Bratton Clovelly (off A30), Devon. GLL.

George and Elsa Hughes have led entertaining and full lives. They have now retired to this lovely little pub which they run with authority and refinement, to make it everything a village local should be. Photographs of their Devon-trained steeplechasers adorn the fireplace, single cigarettes are sold behind the bar, there is simple food, no jukebox, good local trade and an attentive young barmaid. Look for it.

★ THE DUKE OF YORK, Iddesleigh, Devon. GGAR (W, F, B, OP). Tel. 0837-810253. John Colville.

North of Hatherleigh, in the village of Iddesleigh, is another great establishment, The Duke of York, which with **THE TALLY HO, Hatherleigh** (see above), goes to prove beyond all doubt that it *is* possible, given skill and flair, to combine the serving of (imaginative) food without disturbing the normal flow of a first-class pub. The result is sensational.

The main room at The Duke of York is the loveliest in Devon. A large log fire extends its heat to all corners. Scrubbed tables are set in the right places. The bar is solid and dependable and the array of bottles and barrels a sight for sore eyes. A small and serious selection of vital books nestles between the lemon slices and the angostura bitters. But there is nothing chichi about the Duke. It is first and foremost a pub, as the lively local patronage testifies.

Off the main room is another smaller one, similarly furnished; on the other side lies the tiny and elegant dining room. There are three or four tables and a daily-changing three-course menu to choose from. The food is superb, the landlord's wife relying entirely on fresh ingredients, and it is necessary to book 24 hours in advance. Alternatively eat from the simple but original bar menu – one of the more tempting spied in the course of our travels. There is a winelist to match.

We had been directed to the Duke of York by the Devon-based poet Rob Hartford. He told us that it had until recently been unmissable, run as it was by the eccentric 'Bell', who would throw you out as soon as you entered if your face didn't fit, until his untimely death in a car crash some weeks ago.

The poet's version of events was not entirely accurate. After some awkward detective work we ascertained that the pub had indeed been run in the past by a man of uncertain temperament, but that his name was not Bell but Ball, that he had died not in the last few weeks but all of seven years ago, and that the cause of his death was not in fact a car accident, but the spectre that haunts many a good publican, alcohol poisoning.

The landlord of The Duke of York is currently John Colville, a man of discernment, and while it is in his hands the pub should be visited by hook or by crook. Best of all, book a room.

In residence when we were there were three New Zealanders, researching into artificial sheep embryos or something equally unspeakable, and a silver-haired, safari-suited *Spectator* reader with a nice line in nicknames to compensate for his failure to remember any real ones.

Incidentally, the barmaid, Virginia, provided the best of all compliments to the seductiveness of The Duke of York.

SECTION TWO

'This pub,' she told us, 'is my work and my social life. I would go nowhere else whether I worked here or not.'

Within a few miles of each other, and fulfilling much the same function, The Tally Ho and The Duke of York represent two outstanding, almost faultless examples of how to run an inn in the late 20th century.

September 16th, Thursday
Well set-up by a civilized breakfast at The Tally Ho, we struck off on a south-westerly tack into a maze of flooded lanes. The rain was coursing off Dartmoor and the River Taw was in its autumn spate.

We stopped at the DEVONSHIRE ARMS, Sticklepath, GLL (FC), for elevenses. A flat cap with a mad Devonian face was mopping the floor behind the bar. We ordered cider.

'I'm not the gaffer,' he replied in a thick patois, 'I'm just a bloody old fool.'

Another FC behind us began a high-pitched whinny, subsided into a choking fit and then continued his rambling and inconsequential monologue involving wild mink, death and shovels.

Eventually the landlady appeared, glamorous but hungover. She blamed the brandy. They had obviously made a night of it.

After an hour stuck in a ford with stomachs heaving and churning from the three pints of diesel-like cider we had consumed too quickly, we found ourselves by midday ensconced cosily in The Oxenham Arms, South Zeal.

★ **THE OXENHAM ARMS, South Zeal, Devon. GMTH (F, B). Tel: 0837-840244. James Henry.**
The Oxenham is a lovely, old-fashioned stone inn, built on the site of a Norman monastery, with elegant Stuart fireplaces and fine mullioned windows. Here little has changed over the years. Locals group round the coal fire in the front bar generating a thick fug and making full use of the beers from the cask (St Austell HSD and Tinners).

The thing to do at the Oxenham is to book a room (reasonable rates), try four or five pints of Tinners, spend a couple of hours over lunch (changing three-course menu, good value at £11.50), clamber up to bed, rise again from the dead about six-ish, repeat the performance. And that is exactly what we did.

75

THE QUEST FOR THE PERFECT PUB

September 17th, Friday

★ **THE DREWE ARMS,** Drewsteignton, Devon.
ORD (FC). (Auntie) Mabel Mudge.
The Drewe Arms is one of the most celebrated old pubs in the country and one we had known for some time. Drewsteignton lies off the north-east side of Dartmoor and the pub (formerly the Old Druid Arms until the Drewe family who occupy the nearby Lutyens-built Castle Drogo high-handedly changed the name) can be found at the church end of the enchanting village street.

Inside there is the classic layout. Beer is tapped from the cask and dispensed from the servery. It is drunk in the nicotine-coloured front room, decorated on this occasion by a long string of birthday cards. It was midday and there was an all-pervading smell of cabbage.

No sooner had we drinks in hand than we were taken through to the old kitchen to see Auntie Mabel. Auntie Mabel has been The Drewe Arms for as long as anyone can remember. She had recently celebrated her 93rd birthday. From miles around the people had come to pay her homage. The fiddlers had played, the Morris Men had danced. Now, three days on, she was still wearing her party hat. She nodded and smiled, posed for a photograph like the Queen Mother and said she was hungry.

The Drewe Arms is famous and you will find it in most of the books. It is as good an example as any of a proper pub. It makes little money, but is loved not only by the village people but by a large band of admirers who come from afar to worship at the shrine. It is owned by Whitbreads. If, on the death of Auntie Mabel, the brewery decides to move in and wreck the place in direct opposition to the strong local feeling, and the Drewe Arms does go under, then what hope is there for the other, equally beautiful but less renowned establishments that we feature in this book?

So we issue a direct challenge to Samuel Whitbread: we challenge you to leave alone The Drewe Arms, Drewsteignton and thus show that you still have an ounce of human feeling buried deep in the cold quartz of your corporate heart.

SECTION TWO

★ **THE RUGGLESTONE INN,**
Widecombe-in-the-Moor, Devon. ORD (FC, I, E).
Audrey Lamb.
It is not far from Drewsteignton to Widecombe-in-the-Moor where the fair is still held on the second Tuesday in September. Tourists pour from charabancs in the summer months, but they seldom penetrate the hidden sanctum of The Rugglestone Inn, mercifully hard to find on the edge of town (from the church take the lane signposted Ye Olde Glebe House). A priceless gem of a pub, the Rugglestone is frequented almost entirely by locals and farmers from off the desolate moor.

At lunchtime the form is to congregate in the narrow passage that leads from entrance to servery and drink a great deal of beer (no spirits here) under the stern but forgiving eye of Audrey. When informed by a regular that under the new law there was now twenty minutes of drinking-up time she was quick with her reply: 'Not here there isn't.'

Better still, go at night. The perfect little brown room opposite the barrels then comes into its own. Strange becapped figures smelling strongly of pipesmoke and sheepshit sit round the tables in front of the fire and concoct some of the best jokes to be heard in the West Country on as good a night's drinking as you will find south of Copenhagen. Audrey is the centre of affairs and, if you do not step out of line, will tend to your glass with great devotion until, somewhere towards midnight, you will find that you have been nursed back to health again.

As one of the constant fixtures put it: 'Us be old-fashioned buggers. When we goes out we likes to talk to the landlady.'

After the heady delights of the Drewe and the Rugglestone we spent a depressing rest of the day scouring the 'Devon Riviera' for proper pubs. There are none. In Teignmouth we had hoped for something akin to **THE SEVEN STARS** at **Falmouth** (see p. 63), but no such luck. The nearest to a proper pub is THE TEIGN BREWERY, Teign St., Teignmouth, GLL, a snug little locals' retreat not far from the estuary. Otherwise the Riviera is a must to avoid.

We reach our nadir at Chudleigh where we stop to investigate a fine old building in the High Street once known, after the local family, as The Clifford Arms. Now a John Portley Inn, the Clifford has been renamed The Old Coaching Inn House (the same chain have renamed the nearby Dolphin The Coach and Horses) and is as disgraceful an example of thoughtless reconstruction as we found.

John Portley concentrates on the interior of his buildings (half-wittedly, preservation orders seldom apply indoors) and in the case of the Clifford has quite simply gutted the entire building, installing a hideous bar and a few chip pans, and flogging ill-cooked steaks and badly chosen wine.

This proud old inn, which would once have boasted a labyrinth of panelled and connecting chambers with open fires, various different bars, snugs, smoke rooms, lounges, dining, tap and committee rooms, has been reduced by John Portley Inns to a level of dignity and quality somewhat below that of a Happy Eater.

There was only one straw of comfort at which to grasp. The Old Coaching Inn House was completely empty.

September 18th, Saturday
We prefer to spare the reader details of our nightmarish sojourn in Chudleigh and the violent attack on our integrity and elocution committed by a befuddled Irishman and his son. Suffice to say that after a quick visit to the chemist for sticking-plasters and Savlon we struck north to the fringes of Exmoor in search of comfort and convalescence.

★ **THE MASON'S ARMS, Knowstone, Devon.**
GGAR (W, F, B). Tel: 03984-231.
David and Elizabeth Todd.
The Mason's Arms is situated just south of Exmoor in lovely, hidden country that could still be termed unspoilt were it not for the fact that the road-crazed government saw fit in 1988 to build a new highway directly through this territory in direct opposition to local feeling and across three separate moors listed as Sites of Special Scientific Interest.

An attractive building opposite the church, The Mason's is run with verve and aplomb by the Todds, the longest-serving licensees in the district. With **THE TALLY HO, Hatherleigh** (see p. 72) and **THE DUKE OF YORK, Iddesleigh** (see p. 73), it completes the great triumvirate of Devon inns in which it is a pleasure to eat, drink and sleep.

The main room has a big log fire, a selection of pub games,

pleasing furniture and a delightful bar behind which David tends his gleaming barrels of Wadworth, Boddington and Badger. Off the main room is a smaller one, which features the Best Bar Billiards Table in the West. There is also a charming little dining room where it is possible to eat exceptionally well at sensible prices, and four comfortable bedrooms where you can sleep off the excesses to which the beer will have driven you.

A lively band of locals congregate most nights, mixing happily with discerning drinkers from further afield. We were soon immersed in a fascinating and time-consuming conversation with David about the great pubs of England while Elizabeth mended light fuses, cooked lunch, unloaded the beer lorry and repaired the chilling unit. There is no better pub in Devon.

Unwillingly abandoning David Todd to his endless list of tasks, we motored south to Exeter, in whose environs lie four top-class pubs with very different atmospheres. Our afternoon in these parts proved a triumphant end to the emotional switchback which was our tour of Devon.

★ **THE BRIDGE**, Topsham (off A376), Devon. LLL (E). Norman and Phylis Chefers.
One of the more eccentric pubs in the country is The Bridge at Topsham, a rambling pink-washed establishment overlooking the River Exe just south of Exeter. It is much loved by its many aficionados. Norman's parents ran the pub from 1897. One day in the Seventies they turned to their son and daughter-in-law and asked them if they wanted to take it over. Norman and Phylis decided to try it for three months and have been there ever since though, as Phylis says, 'We're still on probation.'

The Bridge has several rooms including a little snug where you are likely to be put at lunchtimes, a much-coveted inner chamber with chintz-covered benches where favoured locals retreat, and a large bar with river views for bigger occasions. It also has a wonderful list of beers, all served with dedication from the cask.

Phylis, originally a Blackmore of Lorna Doone fame, was a nurse before becoming a licensee and claims that there is no better training. Like other great landladies we have talked to she says that you have to both like people and understand them to make a success of the job, and that if you don't then it is better to plump for something less demanding, like politics or psychoanalysis.

There is nothing she would rather talk about than the good old days, and there is no nicer person or more pleasant place to discuss such matters. It was with great relief that we heard that Norman and Phylis's daughter is herself a nurse and that she views her present occupation as mere training for even greater things to come.

Our next stop is one of the most difficult of all to find, although it is within the city limits of Exeter. From A30 take A377/396 to Exeter, go into Marsh Barton Industrial Estate and follow signs for 'refuse incinerator' and then go over the canal bridge. Persevere, and your rewards will be manifold.

★ **THE DOUBLE LOCKS**, Canalbanks, Alphington, Exeter, Devon. GGAR (W, I, F, M, OP, E).
Jamie Stuart.
Situated on the canal and unpromisingly near the Marsh Barton Industrial Estate and refuse incinerator, The Double Locks is one of the most impressive, individual and best-run operations in the nation. It is another example of how a pub can function superbly in the modern age, providing entertainment and food as well as drink.

The Locks has three large rooms with tables, posters, open fires, a selection of games, newspapers and bar billiards. Behind the bar is a fine array of casks providing a wide range of well-chosen and well-kept beers, up to ten of them. Try them all. The menu offers a good choice of sanely-priced and decently-cooked snacks and meals. At exactly the right volume, a selection of the best pop, jazz and blues provides a constant background to the hum of talk and laughter, and the live music nights are famous. The staff are efficient, relaxed and friendly, none more so than the affable Jamie Stuart, who should be in line for any 'Landlord of the Year' award.

The overall atmosphere at The Locks is more like a club than a pub, and it can be used as such. It is open all day and it would be very possible to base yourself there from breakfast time till closing time with some work, walking, fun, food, drink and conversation all thrown in for good measure.

There have been many attempts in the last few years, especially in towns, to achieve the ambience of The Locks. None can approach the success of this tightest of ships. Training schemes operated by brewers should include a compulsory six-month stint as a deck-hand here under the eye of Captain Jamie. Most of all it is the attention to detail which is remarkable. Even the children's adventure playground is novel and exciting.

The mix of customers is predominantly young, but all types are made to feel at home. On our last visit, at lunch time, a group of businessmen were enjoying the fish pie while, in a corner, a long-haired leftover from 1973 was trying to sell his ambulance – 'a really peaceful machine' – to an Australian nymphomaniac.

THE TURF, Exminster, Devon. GAR (I, B).
Tel: 0392-833128. Kenneth Stuart.
The fact that The Turf is owned by the same family who run **THE DOUBLE LOCKS, Exeter** (see above) speaks for itself. A more traditional establishment, it enjoys a beautiful view across the estuary and provides food and drink of the first order. Beds are on offer as well. Drink here first (it is not open all day) and then canter briskly for a quarter of an hour along the towpath until you reach the sister establishment. Alternatively you can reach The Turf from The Double Locks on the canal boat *Countess Wear*, and make full use of the on-board bar.

The fourth of this group of pubs grouped round Exeter occupied the last evening of our Devon stay.

THE BEER ENGINE, Newton St Cyres (A377),
Devon. LLL (M). Peter Hawksley.
At Exeter Station we boarded the steam train for Newton St Cyres. It is a short journey and the safest way to travel, since near closing time the train will puff you back again to the city where you will have had the foresight to book your billet.

The Beer Engine, an old station, has as its main attraction a thriving home brewery producing Rail Ale, Piston and the powerful Sleeper, which is what it will turn you into if you over-indulge. Often busy, especially on live music nights, the Beer Engine provides simple food, various games and has a self-sufficient and independent attitude which is worth experiencing.

THE QUEST FOR THE PERFECT PUB

Finally, it is worth mentioning one other Devon pub worth knowing about if you are travelling through the West Country.

🍺 THE CASTLE INN, Lydford, Devon. GAR (B). Tel: 082282-242. David and Susan Grey.
The Castle is an old, pink, Tudor inn that has survived well. It is the perfect place to stay if you are exploring the astounding beauty of nearby Lydford Gorge, with its thick woods and gushing rocky streams and waterfalls. Evenings are cosy here around a big fire, with board games of all kinds at hand, reasonable bar food and comfortable old-fashioned bedrooms. Locals and visitors mix well.

Avon and Somerset

September 18th, Saturday evening
The area of Somerset and the new county of Avon is fertile soil for pubs and one we knew well. Confident of a weekend of rich pickings we invited the Gorgeous Blonde Hackette (GBH) and the Fiery Blonde Illustrator (FBI) to join us in our research; they were to travel down by high-speed train and we would pick them up at Bath Spa Station later in the evening.

Bath is an architecturally overrated town in a dank dip, but happily crammed with good pubs, so the first part of the evening could be profitably spent researching these. We kicked off at the best and most traditional of them.

★THE STAR, The Vineyards (A4), Bath, Avon. GLL. Allen Perrett.
The Star is a rare example of a real old-fashioned town pub, with wood panelling, banked-up fires and the classic dun-and-

nicotine colour scheme. Though tiny, it boasts a lobby bar and two other small rooms and a range of beers from the cask almost perfect in flavour and temperature.

The present licensee, a fanatic in a Bass sweatshirt, has altered nothing since the departure of old Sid some years ago, and the place is an old-fashioned delight, much enjoyed by its numerous fans.

'Change? Pah!' exclaims Allen. 'Nothing will change as long as I'm here, and I intend to be here a long time.'

Unable to settle in for the good session that The Star invites, but comforted by his words, we climbed north a few miles to Marshfield, renowned as the coldest village in the West Country.

Other pub books will recommend either of the other two houses in Marshfield, but they are misguided.

🍺🍺 THE CATHERINE WHEEL, Marshfield (off A420), Avon. GLL.

William Hand is now getting on a bit, and no longer serves his consummate Courage Directors from the back room where, he used to say, it kept better (his feet protest at the mileage), but still pours the best bitter from the barrel, and his Guinness is peerless. Beneath his gruff exterior there beats a heart of gold and people come a long way to support this old-style village pub with its dark wood surrounds, powerful stove, machine-free and peaceful atmosphere.

A particularly good session gets under way on Sunday lunchtimes, with a good mix of villagers and others from further afield. Bill is happy with his current level of trade – 'I'm getting old. I can cope with my regulars, but no more.' He will not be drawn on the subject of the future, so pay him your respects while you have the chance.

We drove back through Bath and travelled to the outskirts on the Exeter road to the village of South Stoke.

Tucked away on a terrifyingly steep hill, stands one of the truly great Avon pubs.

★ THE PACK HORSE, South Stoke (off B3110), Avon. LLL. Timothy Brewer.

This year the stone house that is The Pack Horse celebrates its

500th birthday, so count on celebrations. But on any night of the year this is an almost perfect establishment.

The central serving bar is set in the corridor between two rooms, the principal of which sports shuttered windows, quarry-tiled floor, fine furniture, planked ceiling and a huge fireplace. There are no better surroundings in which to drink either the impeccable Courage beer or any one of a range of increasingly lethal ciders. The food is simple, majoring in the best baps – cheese and onion, or ham home-baked in cider – to be found outside **THE COOPER'S TAVERN, Burton-on-Trent** (see p. 106), **THE EARLE ARMS, Heydon** (see p. 192), **THE SARACEN'S HEAD, Saracen's Head** (see p. 179) or **THE WOLSINGTON HOUSE, North Shields** (see p. 154). On Sunday lunchtimes the beautiful chalked slate shove-ha'penny tables are in full clatter and a band of rabid locals jostle with appreciative students and the occasional tourist lost on the way to the American Museum. Miss The Pack Horse and you may live to regret it.

After half a gallon of cider we taxied to Bath Spa Station to collect our female companions. They had made full use of the perfectly adequate TRAVELLERS FARE MOBILE BAR, GITS, on the Inter-City and were in no mood to trifle.

'Food!' they cried, brushing aside our attempts at endearment, so with no more ado we instructed the cabbie to strike off west to Kelston and The Crown, where we had had the foresight to book a table.

★ **THE CROWN, Kelston, Avon. LLL (F, OP).**
Michael Steele.
The Crown at Kelston is a textbook example of how to take over an already excellent pub and improve it out of all recognition. When the present incumbents moved in some years ago, local feelings ran hot. It had, for a long time, been a much-loved and idiosyncratic old-fashioned drinker. There was the old boy, the half-hour wait in the bone-chilling cold while he fiddled about with jug and barrel, dropping bits of fluff and eyebrow into sometimes suspect and murky ale. There was the fact that he had been there for 465 years, and what did we care about the smell of rotting dogs and wet cabbage?

Hands flew up in dread on the fateful day that Michael moved in, repainted the rooms, lit the fire for the first time since 1933, filled the bars with dried flowers and candles, repolished the fine flagged floors and – horror of horrors! – built a kitchen and turned the snug into a tiny restaurant.

The results, of course, are spectacular. More locals than ever before cram the three rooms every night, making free with the Butcombes, Smiles, Marston's Pedigree, Wadworths and good farm cider. Visitors such as ourselves are warmly welcomed and can enjoy a surprisingly romantic dinner at one of the four restaurant tables, dining from a small well-cooked menu, served with style. The energy and precision of the management is reflected in the staff, and long may the 'new' regime continue to flourish.

Our night ended in Bath, with quick visits to THE HAT AND FEATHER, London St., LLL (M) – boisterous, live music, students, THE BEEHIVE, Lansdowne Hill, GLL – small, intimate, eponymously buzzing, and finally The Beaujolais, a restaurant off Queen's Square (genuinely Gallic, lively late at night, where we ate a second dinner). All can be warmly recommended.

Everything seemed sweetness and light as we settled in for a session in a nameless private hotel in the backwaters.

September 19th, Sunday
The following morning the road took us south towards Somerset. Our last stop in Avon and our first of the day was at the recommendation of two local lads we had met in The Crown at Kelston, and bore the same name.

THE CROWN, Churchill (A431), Avon. LLL (W).
The Crown used to be Tim Rogers' local. He knew and loved it so much that when the pub came up for sale he bought it. You can take your pick from Double Dragon, Eldridge Pope, Cotleigh, Fullers, Palmers or other guest beers. The attractive rooms have been altered in very good taste, and the little parlour bar has been kept as it always was. The Crown is up on a hill, close to the hideous scar of the Avon Ski Run and Sports Centre, so the trade here is varied but still has a basis in solid local business. Tim Rogers is an example of the fine new breed of British landlord, who are not in thrall to a brewery, and combine the rest of pub traditions with an understanding of

what people really want from a country pub. He serves a lot of food at weekends, but the menu is sensibly small, the food home-cooked. Alas, no managed chain pub seems able to achieve the personal touch so evident here or at The Crown at Kelston.

This was a very good start to the day, and better was to come. Penetrating deep into Somerset, we passed through Glastonbury, dodging hippies and Drug Squad Officers (indistinguishable) and took the backroad to Langport, and thence the A372 to the prettily-named village of Huish Episcopi.

★ **THE ROSE AND CROWN (ELI'S), Huish Episcopi, Somerset. LLL (FC, W, E). Eileen Pittard.**
There is nowhere *quite* like Eli's. From the outside it looks unpromising. The stonework has been repointed, and one suspects a certain cosmetic touch. Inside, the story is very different.

On entering, glance into the room on your right and behold a marvellous sight: in the firelit crackle of a warm and basic parlour, the older generation of the village are gathered, like faces in an old photograph, and looked after by the landlady, who serves only them; to enter this yellowing and fading enclave, to sit with the in-crowd and talk about the weather is a fine and memorable experience.

The heart of Eli's is the central still room; stand around in the throng and wait your turn. In time a smiling and lissome young attendant will serve you anything from excellent draught Bass to the rough farm cider.

'Watch out for that, it'll make you proper poorly,' she cautioned the FBI, as the latter snatched the glass from her hands and drained it in one. Both she and the GBH had suddenly struck form with a vengeance, for they had noticed the unusual fact that Eli's is run and staffed entirely by women.

On the menu we discovered beans on toast, among other simple delights, and ordered double helpings with toasted cheese on the side. It was delicious, and a finer pub lunch is not to be found. Ploughman's is to be had as well and hot or cold pies, much enjoyed by the local clientele. They are a friendly lot here, and probably grateful that Eli's (after the present landlady's father) has been in the family for 120 years. Longevity of tenure almost invariably indicates a cracking good pub, and this is no exception. We were made most welcome, and urge you to pay a visit.

We will not dwell on the shaming scenes that took place later that long afternoon as we toured the fleshpots of Taunton, Minehead, and Dunster but it was in THE BELL at Watchett, GLL, a lively and attractive fishermen's pub near the harbour, that things came to a head and we decided to take a small break from our increasingly militant research assistants. While they plotted unrest and insurgence among the WI members of Stogumber, we slipped away quietly to the nearby Notley Arms, where we passed a pleasant and uneventful night before returning with some trepidation to collect them the next morning after breakfast.

🏨🏨 THE NOTLEY ARMS, Monksilver (B3188), Somerset. GAR (F, OP).

Monksilver is an attractive village a few miles south of the coastal resorts and a short drive north from Combe Florey, home of the wine bibber and gossip columnist Auberon Waugh. Its chief attraction is The Notley Arms, an old inn in the same category as **THE CROWN** at **Kelston** (see p. 84) and **THE MASON'S ARMS** at **Knowstone** (see p. 78); a bustling village pub run with flair, full of local people but with a leavening of visitors enjoying a well-cooked dinner at candle-lit tables.

Good humour abounds here, and the energetic landlord runs the show with disarming charm and a sure knowledge of his wares; he will produce a bottle of Armagnac with not a second's delay, the Guinness and the bitter (Ruddles and Ushers) are carefully kept and there is a fair winelist. The rooms are more than adequate, and the relaxed feel of The Notley Arms is highly enjoyable.

September 20th, Monday

An ominous silence reigned in the car as we were driven at breakneck speed down a series of tunnel-like lanes and across Somerset by a tight-lipped hackette, her accomplice beside her toying with an open flick-knife. From our position slumped in the back, and regretting the last Armagnac of the night before, they looked not unlike the entire Jesse James gang.

At high noon we drew into Witham Friary, a small ranching

community, and threw back the swing doors of The Seymour Arms.

★ THE SEYMOUR ARMS, Witham Friary, Somerset. ORD (FC, W). Jean Douel

The Seymour Arms is safe, for the time being, in its comfortable old overcoat, for it is a free house, owned and loved by the Douels, who say they will never change it 'or the locals would lynch us.'

The Seymour is painted in fading green and cream and has the classic layout – a central servery between two plain rooms, one with a hatch through which drinks are passed, and another across the passage with bar billiards where the local men billet their women and children. Needless to say the GBH and the FBI marched firmly and unsuitably into the former of these and called peremptorily through the hatch for cider, causing a small stir among the farmers engaged in darts and shove ha'penny. The authors took up a defensive position by the servery and were soon in conversation with the landlord and his wife. They told us the sad tales of two recent pub casualties nearby – the once-classic Lamb at Sneed, not long ago disembowelled by the brewery, and one of the few remaining one-room cider houses at Buckland Dinham, now tragically closed.

Nevertheless, for a time our moods lightened, bathed as we were in the warm glow of the Seymour with its friendly regulars. Even the two suffragettes were losing their mean and dangerous look. Then – disaster.

Into the room stepped a small group of the local landed gentry. They were known to us and we to them. We exchanged cordial but restrained greetings, passed the time of day pleasantly enough for the duration of a pint, and left the Seymour in pursuit of our next goal.

Outside, the cowgirls turned on us and, shooting from both hips let fly a fusillade of abuse. How dare we talk to such people? We were snobs, hypocrites, liars, namby-pambies. It was disgraceful that such stuck-up, toffee-nosed ponces as our 'friends' should darken the door of places like the Seymour and pollute the air with their cocktail brayings. We tried to reason with them. Our friends were after all local people; why should they not be there? Were they not anyway very similar to ourselves in background? And most importantly, was it not all to the good that they should be supporting The Seymour Arms where they were known and liked, and eating its peerless ham sandwiches, rather than spending large sums of money in over-priced restaurants in Bath?

Women, though soft and cuddly little things, are not noted for their grasp of logic or reason, especially when in their cups. The noise in the car on the way to The Tucker's Grave was unbearable, and our prized collection of Tammy Wynette tapes was hurled one by one from the window into a succession of Somerset slurry pits.

★ **THE TUCKER'S GRAVE, near Faulkland, Somerset. ORD (FC, I, E). Ivan and Glenda Swift.**
From the outset of our odyssey across England and Wales we had been longing for this moment: the return to one of our very favourite haunts in the whole world.

The first shock wave hit us as the Tucker's came into view. Where formerly only an old Commer van and a single bicycle would have been visible outside, there were now a couple of dozen smart cars: BMWs, convertible Escort XLs and Japanese 'sports' models.

We almost drove on, but old loyalties coupled with disbelief forced us to pluck up courage and prepare for the worst.

We entered the Grave, hearts aflutter. A quick glance around: thank God! the tiny fire-stoked drinking-den to our right was unaltered, and we could see no changes to the central still room where you stood in line for thick orange cider, cask Butcombe's and Bass. Where were the owners of these cars? Peering through the smoke of shag and Capstan we perceived that the family's living room beyond had been converted into a kind of holding-pen and was hugger-mugger with the kind of upwardly-mobile, wallet-flashing, expense-accounted young clientele for whom the marketing director of a big brewery had already gutted and refurbished 1,235 once thriving and now totally empty pubs. Where were they? They were here at The Tucker's Grave, voting with their feet and their drinking arms.

Within seconds our sense of horror and loss that the Grave had been desecrated was changed to one of mounting celebration. Our point was proven, our position vindicated, our journey and our doctors' bill had not been in vain.

For here, at The Tucker's Grave on a lonely crossroads, deep in rural Somerset, was the final evidence that we, the members of CAMRA and millions of other pub-lovers were right and that the big brewers were wrong; in particular those that CAMRA has so rightly dubbed the 'Voracious Eight': Allied Breweries, Bass Charrington, Courage, Greenall Whitley, Guinness, Scottish and Newcastle, Watney Mann and Truman – and Whitbread.

These are the guilty parties, and though rivals, they are in fact in collusion, partners in the same anti-social crime. They claim that people want the 'modern pub' and back up their argument by pointing to their sales figures, thus fudging the issue. Of course, in an area where there are no proper pubs left, people are forced to drink in their hideous hybrids. But where, as here, and in pockets all over the country, there are still unspoilt gems like The Tucker's and The Seymour, people of all sorts, ages and income-brackets will flock to them in increasingly large numbers. We appeal to the 'Eight' one final time. For everyone's sake, listen to the voice of the people, for it is almost too late.

We set upon the orange cider with relish and abandon. We regarded the GBH and FBI with renewed ardour and fond affection. Yes, we agreed, we were hypocrites, tosspots and namby-pambies, but were we not also men of courage and valour, dragon-slaying knights, debonair boulevardiers, red-blooded buccaneers, handsome, dark and saturnine? All was well in the small room at The Tucker's Grave, God was in his Heaven and by George we were vindicated. We thumped the table till the glasses rattled. The heaving row of cider-bellies glinted mischievously at us in the firelight. We fell into a deep and blissful slumber.

'It's for you.' Mrs Swift was shaking us awake. We were alone in the room; the fire was out, the glasses empty. She shook us again, more roughly this time.

'Telephone.'

It was the FBI filing her copy.

'Bold type: Two barrels. THE GEORGE, Norton St., Philip, Somerset,' she snapped briskly. 'GAR. Wadworth, Bass from the cask and *very good Guinness*. Fascinating old stone building much filmed by cretinous and over-paid TV directors in Phil Collins media suits (see THE EARLE ARMS, Heydon, p. 192). Food good, service friendly and packed with locals and tourists: public, lounge and dungeon bars. Goodbye. We are leaving now for London and may be gone for some time.'

The line went dead.

It was 3.30 pm and The Tucker's was closed. Bleary eyed, we stumbled outside. The afternoon was like a grey shower curtain. The car was gone and our grips deposited by the roadside.

Section Three

The Peak District and the East Midlands

The Peak District and the East Midlands

September 24th, Friday
The autumn sun was warm and the mountain air invigorating as we bowled briskly and with good appetite along the Queen's Highway towards Leek, the capital of the Staffordshire moorlands. We had slunk northwards like old dogs to a lair in the Peak District where we were known, and now, as the leaves began to turn to amber and russet, we felt more chipper. Women!! The luxuriance and finely-chiselled points had returned to our moustaches.

Life stopped in Leek that fateful day in 1960 when Eddie Cochran's sports car skidded on a wet road, snuffing out the life of the rock 'n' roll star who looked like James Dean; that night the inhabitants began drinking, and they still do.

As we descended the main street, the sun was blotted out and the heavens opened. The smell of Brylcreem and the slither of brothel-creepers still infused the dank streets as we did our rounds of the watering-holes. It was 3 o'clock before we realized that we had been there for four hours without spotting a single piece of quiche or a lone king prawn drowning in garlic butter.

Leek is a good drinking town for those of a gloomy disposition and should be visited by anyone with a penchant for simple, honest and unpretentious pubs. Full of little street-corner boozers, the music you hear in Leek tells the story, a shifting soundtrack of Jim Reeves, rockabilly and early heavy metal. Here are our four favourites.

🛢 THE FLYING HORSE, Ashbourne Rd., Leek, Staffordshire. GLL (W).
Solid little local on the main road into town, purveying good Marstons, of which a huge welder was taking maximum advantage. We, he informed us, looked like bloody solicitors (one of

THE QUEST FOR THE PERFECT PUB

us was wearing a tie). He had dined the night before in a converted stately home in Cheshire which was so spick and span 'You could have eaten off bloody toilet floor.' His family traced its history back to before the Conqueror 'but stupid buggers fought on wrong bloody side.' We left The Flying Horse and ventured further into town.

THE SEALION, Russell St., Leek, Staffordshire.
GLL (FC, E).
Rough, friendly; evenings likely to end either in hugs or fisticuffs. An old-fashioned drinker full of froth-flecked moustaches, outsize beer-bellies and deep purple tans. A huge roadgang worker was pouring withering scorn on the Yanks for failing to carve up the 'Chinks' in Vietnam. We thought it best not to argue. Not for a delicate night out.

THE BRITANNIA, West St., Leek, Staffordshire.
GLL (FC).
Another street-corner local, popular, busy, plain and unspoilt. The landlord sports a fun-loving nose. Marston's adequate; a typical Midlands local.

THE MERRIE MONK, Compton St., Leek, Staffordshire. LLL (E).
Good solid pub with Marston's and Burton, the classic Midlands duo, best visited on one of the regular ceilidh nights when behaviour and music get up a good head of steam. Ring first (0538-383624) to check dates. The pub also plays host to the local Frank Muir Appreciation Society meetings. Make of this what you will.

Having restored our self-confidence in Leek, we spent the best part of a week in the Peak District and East Midlands revisiting old haunts and uncovering some first-rate new ones.

We strongly advise our readers to visit the beautiful and romantic Peak District, the lung of the Midlands, within fifty miles of which huddle one-third of the country's population, but preferably to do it out of season. In summer the Peak vies with the Lakes for title of most over-crowded national park and the pubs have suffered accordingly in their scramble to feed the hordes. Our selection is carefully chosen to lead you away from

SECTION THREE

the public lavatories and car parks and into the hidden byways of dales, troutstreams and the old industrial fringe.

The East Midlands, by which we mean Nottinghamshire and Leicestershire, contains less exciting countryside, much of which is covered by the Derby–Nottingham conurbation, ever growing Leicester, Mansfield, Loughborough and minor satellites. It is a less fertile area for pubs, though many of the locals in the mining districts may be approached with some confidence.

Leicestershire at its worst is epitomized by what we have dubbed 'Five-Mile Hell', which occurs along the A5 on the Leicestershire/Warwickshire border. Here, in quick succession, you may enjoy the architectural delights of the following: The Hinckley Island Hotel, a low monolith in red brick near a shellfish farm (in Warwickshire?), no doubt breeding scampi by the million, ready-breaded for the basket; The Carver; The Three Pots and The Hinckley Knight, all paragons of post-Palumbo property speculation. If you want to scare youself, go and look at them. But there is worse to come.

Opposite the slag pyramids near the Sketchley Lane industrial estate stand two buildings which are among the most terrifying in Western Europe: M&B's monstrous Longshoot – a series of function rooms surrounded by a car park, and, to finish you off, The Toby Carvery. In comparison, the pubs we have selected will seem like Paradise.

🍺🍺 THE BOAT, Barford Bridge Lane (off A520), Cheddleton, Staffordshire. GAR (W, F).

This excellent house typifies all that is right with England north of the Trent and all that is so wrong with the dreaded South.

A few miles away from Tunstall, Burslem and Hanley – the now depressed area of the once thriving Potteries – The Boat lies in a dip alongside the River Churnet and its accompanying canal and a stone's throw from a former goods line that until recently was used to haul sand to the Pilkington glassworks. Steam enthusiasts, who abound in these parts, now hope to reopen the line for their own purposes.

Landlord Trevor Woolliscroft provides for all comers, dispensing good beer, decent food at sensible prices and an atmosphere of welcome and charm.

In the South, The Boat would be a place to avoid at all costs, but, being as it is in lovely unfashionable Staffs, there is not a

97

Braying Bengy or Cheerless Caroline in sight – yet – just a lively band of locals and not-so-locals, proving that you don't need a platinum credit card to get a good run for your money.

★ **THE YEW TREE, Cauldon (off A523 and A52), Staffordshire. LLL (M, E). Alan East.**
Hard by the largest stone quarry in Europe, but surrounded by farm, field and moor, The Yew Tree is now one of the most famous and award-winning pubs in the country, a place of great delight and ease, where we have been refreshing ourselves for many years.

The Yew Tree is paying the price of fame, as weekend charabancs of beer-bores with clipboards have, through sheer weight of numbers, forced the landlord, Alan East, to connect his fabled Bass cask, formerly enthroned in the back room, to a handpump like any other beer.

It is still, however, a lovely and unusual place to drink, with its extraordinary collection of Polyphons (early jukeboxes built on the music-box principle), pianolas, bakelite wirelesses, early TV sets and old ladies sipping tea in small, curtained-off parlours. Visit on any night in winter, especially on a Saturday when the mainly local crowd lift up their voices to the strains of Alan's skilful manipulation of the pianola.

THE CAVALIER, Grindon, Staffordshire. GLL (F).
The classic White Peak village of Grindon is the fulcrum of one of the finest pub walks/drives in the area, taking in neighbouring Wetton, Butterton and Hulme End (see below). The Cavalier is at its best in winter, when locals may be spotted. A southern landlady turns out good food, the service is friendly and efficient. The Bass and Marston's perform their celebrated double act, and it is very peaceful.

THE ROYAL OAK, Wetton, Staffordshire.
Nothing happens here, especially in winter. It is ideal.

THE MANIFOLD VALLEY, Hulme End, Staffordshire. GAR (F, B, M). Tel: 029884-537.
Originally The Jolly Carter, this upland pub/hotel caters for locals and tourists, and does a brisk trade. There is occasional live jazz and folk and the charming dining room would be a

SECTION THREE

good place to stage a sex-romp Tupperware party. It is the perfect base for a walking/drinking holiday.

🍺🍺 THE GEORGE, Alstonefield, Staffordshire. GLL.
A fine stone building in an attractive upland village. The George is a simple and snug local best visited on a winter's night when the walkers have departed and the local 'intelligentsia' – infiltrators with beards and funny ideas – stay at home with their New Zealand Chardonnay on account of the cold.

Ashbourne, Derbyshire. The atmosphere of this ancient and peaceful market town, 'The Gateway to Dovedale', has changed little despite the mass invasion of beards, sandals, guidebooks and Dayglo pink spacesuits. The occasional orange-faced woman, laden with heavy and ugly gold bangles, fights for designer clothes in over-priced boutiques; wine bars pollute the 18th-century streets.

However, there are still lovely old shops staffed by the most courteous people you could hope to meet, and Ashbourne vies with Thirsk in Yorkshire as the most pleasant market town in England.

The young drink in THE HORNS, LLL, wear leather jackets and argue about the lyrics to Pretenders' tunes. The flat caps still congregate in SMITH'S TAVERN, GLL (FC), at the bottom of the marketplace or the GEORGE AND DRAGON, LLL (FC), at the top. The beers on offer include Home Ales from Nottingham and fine Marston's Pedigree.

🍺🍺 THE SYCAMORE, Parwich, Derbyshire.
LLL (FC, W, M).
Parwich ('Parrich', or 'Porrich') achieved notoriety in the 1970s and early 1980s when an eccentric actress and her brother acquired a large manor house in its own grounds for the purposes of instructing gullible initiates to their misguided and futile revolutionary party. The locals were unimpressed and continued to take their recreation at The Sycamore, from where the thespian politicos were firmly banned.

The public bar is a pleasure to drink in – flock wallpaper, active piano, be-quiffed, pint-quaffing, C & W singing landlord, fine Peak accents and pool table. Young things are relegated to a side room and there is an inviting little hatch for off-sales. Marston's beer. Worth a visit.

🛢🛢 THE BUTCHER'S ARMS, Reapsmoor (off B5053), Staffordshire. LLL (I, W).

On a lonely backroad on the edge of the moors, young Carl Garnett and his wife run this sympathetic establishment with verve, enthusiasm and the purest White Peak accents you will find. Born and bred here, they insist that drinking their first-rate Marston's is the primary activity but will feed you should you ask them nicely. A big square kitchen table is the thing to lie on when you feel tired. The Butcher's stays open all day, and the locals make good use of the hours. We gave a lift to a ginger-haired man from Leek, who at 11 am had already tarried here too long en route to Longnor Races. He asked us about London:

'Are there any pubs down there?'

We told him no.

'Do you smoke that funny stuff then?' he asked hopefully.

We saw him later that afternoon in the beer tent, clinging to the pole in the centre and winking suggestively at two policemen.

★ THE ROYAL COTTAGE (OLIVE'S), A53 Leek-Buxton Rd., Staffordshire. ORD (FC, I, E).
Olive Prince.

Standing at a remote and lonely moorland crossroads, this self-effacing parlour pub is dwarfed by its neighbour, a garish and vulgar roadhouse, The Winking Man. Do not be fooled. The sign on Olive's wall is faded almost to illegibility, and the hours she keeps are very much subject to her whims but are normally confined to evenings only, except on Sundays when many locals, publicans and drinkers alike, pop in to have a lunchtime pint and pass the time of day with her. On autumn weekends a shooting lunch may be in progress, but otherwise the quiet and the old-world atmosphere, rare in these parts, should be sampled before Olive gets too old.

🛢 THE QUIET WOMAN, Earl Sterndale (off B5053), Staffordshire. GLL (FC).

Unspoilt, fine example of a 19th-century village local, with a good high bar and midday codgers. It was going through a tricky patch at the end of 1988, according to the regulars, but may perk up.

🍺 THE THREE STAGS' HEADS, Wardlow Mires, Derbyshire. ORD (E).
For years Fred and Gwynn Furness ran this beautiful example of a pub within a farm (see also **THE FRENCH HORN, Rodsley**, p. 107 and **THE QUEEN ADELAIDE, Snelston**, p. 107), but age and ill-health forced a sale in late 1988, so sadly we can no longer vouch for the Youngers from the cask which tasted like nectar. We expect the worst – a roadhouse, even a food-factory, God help us all. To add insult to injury, some criminal hooligan has erected a Burmah Oil petrol station directly opposite the pub, which already suffered from an increasingly busy main road. Architects who plan structures like this should have their casual slacks removed, be put in the stocks and publicly pelted with breeze blocks in front of a laughing and joyous multitude. Fred Furness will be fondly remembered as the witty landlord who had 'swallowed ten books and couldn't be beat at words'.

★ THE OLDE GATE INN, Brassington, Derbyshire. GAR (FC, F, OP). Paul and Evie Burlinson.
Like **The Boat** at **Cheddleton** (see p. 97), the Olde Gate would be intolerable were it in Surrey. As it is, it is one of the most enjoyable pubs in the district. Maintained with taste and style by Marston's, the scrubbed tables and immaculately-kept working 17th-century kitchen range immediately inspire confidence and thirst. One bar is firmly marked 'No Children', and in there (beyond which is a fine committee room with Jacobean panelling) locals wearing strange headgear abound, mingling resignedly but good-humouredly with tourists at weekends.

Paul and Evie Burlinson, from Manchester and Connecticut respectively, run the Gate with a sure touch and serve good, inexpensive food.

We ate steak-and-kidney pudding and washed it down with a sound bottle of claret that was lurking on the winelist.

The Olde Gate is in every respect a splendid establishment set in a particularly beautiful village.

THE QUEST FOR THE PERFECT PUB

🍺 **THE HURT ARMS**, Ambergate, Derbyshire. GLL.
For obvious reasons the best pub in the world; frequented in the latter part of the last century by Septimus Le Fowne Alderwasley Hurt, the poet, thinker and author of *Not a Potte to Pisse Inne*, privately printed and published posthumously by The Pisspotte Presse of Wirksworth.

🍺 **THE BLACK LION**, Consall Forge, Staffordshire. LLL (I).
Rough and ready canal/railway-side pub that is best reached by a twenty-minute walk through wooded, tumpy country from Consall Old Hall. Follow footpath signs. Landlady of character, canteen-style food, dogs, walkers. A beautiful situation, where steam trains may be spotted in high season.

🍺 **THE PLOUGH INN**, Kingsley, Staffordshire. GLL (FC).
Furnished in time-bending, 60s brewery plastic woodtrim. Les, the landlord, has several times been the Bass Champion Cellar Keeper, and the quality of his beer reflects this. Open all day Saturday and a good roadside stop on the A52 Ashbourne–Stoke-on-Trent highway.

🍺 **THE SNEYDS ARMS**, Whiston, Staffordshire. GLL (FC).
On the same road as The Plough (see above), this is a good example of an unspoilt Midlands local, with a courteous landlord and two simple rooms to drink in. Surgeries held regularly here by the much-liked local MP David Knox.

🍺🍺 **THE JUG AND GLASS**, (north of Newhaven), Derbyshire. LLL (I, E).
The lonely A515 Ashbourne to Buxton road boasts several good pubs, of which this is the best. At an altitude of 1,100 feet and cut off regularly by bad weather, this would be the perfect place to be snowed up in.

We first visited several years ago, severely dehydrated at five to three in the bad old days of afternoon closing. Observing the undignified haste with which we propelled ourselves to the bar, and the unattractive way our tongues were hanging out, the landlord, John Bryan, merely enquired:

'What's the bloody rush?' We were there until 9 pm.

On our most recent stop the great man was sound asleep at eight of the evening and so we were unable to renew the acquaintance. We did, however, enjoy the company of a holidaymaker who had arrived for a walking tour six weeks previously, but had as yet signally failed to leave the friendly confines of the public bar.

The beer is of exceptional quality, especially the Timothy Taylor Landlord, and due to the pub's isolated position is enjoyed, as the sardonic barman put it, by many regulars but no locals.

It is possible that the emanations from nearby Arbor Low, reputedly the hub of the national leyline grid, were responsible for the dizzy spells and hallucinations which came to possess us in the further reaches of the evening. But it is a remote possibility. The beautifully-kept cellar, visible on the way to the lavatories, held far more magic for us.

🍺 **THE BULL I'TH'THORN**, Hurdlow Town (A515 south of Buxton), Derbyshire. GAR (M).

A hundred feet higher and a little further along the road from The Jug and Glass (see above) towards Buxton is this justifiably famous house. The A515 is an old Roman road and The Bull has been an inn since 1472. It is worth a visit for its Tudor panelling, open fire and many old features, including genuine 17th-century graffiti. On the night of our visit Peak superstars Eric and the Frantics – 'be there or be dead' – were blowing up a storm in the function room in aid of the local Pothole Rescue Association.

🍺 **THE DUKE OF YORK**, Buxton (A515), Derbyshire. GLL (F).

Between The Bull i' th' Thorn (see above) and Buxton, try a glass of Robinson's, carefully nurtured by the old-fashioned and good-natured John Longworth: 'That's proper ale, lads. Four or five pints and you know you've had 'em.'

🍺🍺 **THE BAKER'S ARMS**, West St., Buxton, Derbyshire. LLL.

Steaming all night, this wonderfully reassuring backstreet local is as good a place as any to fritter away the dog-ends of one's

THE QUEST FOR THE PERFECT PUB

life and strike up any number of lively friendships. The local talent in Buxton is not confined to the Opera House. Drink the irreproachable Bass, study the landlord's well-rehearsed stomach, and thank the Lord you're not in Billawonga, Queensland.

🍺 THE RED LION, Litton, Derbyshire. GAR (F, M).

Despite its two barrelled entry, The Red Lion is a borderline case, since these days it functions more as a restaurant than a drinker, and as such is a blow to the locals. However, the goings-on on Tuesday nights fully justify its inclusion here.

The food is simple, English, and of a standard and value rarely encountered these days. In the company of a Sheffield butcher and his wife, we ate the World's Biggest Barnsley Chop with bashed swedes, dumplings and beans from the garden, drank Timothy Taylor's Landlord and were entertained by the county's finest folk musicians, featuring fiddles, mandolins, guitars, flutes, penny-whistles, bodhrans (Irish drums) and a perfectly-formed lady accordion-player.

An assortment of musicians gather at The Red Lion every Tuesday and play for their supper and drinks, attracting a friendly and appreciative crowd from as far away as Manchester. There are two supper sittings; book for the first in advance (tel: 0298-871458) and then head for the bar and the music. These evenings are highly recommended: if you go, you will enjoy yourselves thoroughly.

🍺 THE SWAN, Draycott-in-the-Clay, Staffordshire. GLL (FC, E, W).

It was 11.30 in the morning. We were sitting at the bar of The Swan, listening to the juggernauts roaring past on the Lichfield road, talking to the elderly landlord (whiskers, matching moles and shirtsleeves) and his Moll(y); we were drinking one of the best pints to be found from a row of barrels almost anywhere, and learning the arts of keeping good beer: never put the slops back, sell it quick and don't mess about with it. We were beginning to think that all was well with the world when the door opened.

With a crackle of static electricity, a swish of drip-dry and a whiff of keg Aqua Velva, The Man From Ind Coope oozed in and immediately ruined our day by cursorily informing our host that the beautiful ambrosia currently slipping silkily into our bloodstreams was about to be removed from the market.

The landlord looked pityingly at the youthful thrusting dynamo:

'These three have been drinking your Burton Bitter all morning, and they say it's some of the best they've had. You must be bloody mad.'

Realizing that he was not welcome, and muttering something apologetic about corporate decisions and centralization, the Area Sales Manager slunk out to his Toyota. We finished our drinks and left, but we have no doubt that the publican will find a worthy replacement for the Burton Bitter. After all, his family have kept the pub for 200 years, and have experienced worse hiccups than this.

🍺🍺 THE BURTON BRIDGE BREWERY TAP, High St., Burton-on-Trent, Staffordshire. LLL (FC).

Burton is still the capital of the brewing trade, being the home of Bass, Ind Coope, Marston's and several other outfits, of which one of the smaller is The Burton Bridge Brewery, serving quite a few pubs in the region.

The River Trent is the great divide between North and South; once over the bridge in Burton, you are unmistakably in a different and less flimsy world. It is black-and-white films, a pregnant and barefoot Rachel Roberts, Albert Finney leaning from a window and smoking a Park Drive. The whole town smells irresistibly of malt and hops and there is an abundance of good little pubs in which the beer is taken very seriously. One of the best of these is this tap room of The Burton Bridge Brewery, the sort of establishment that was unaffected by changes in the licensing laws, not because they refuse to open in the afternoons, but because they did anyway.

A garrulous band of regulars gather in the small bar to drink the excellent bitter and strong dark porter in large quantities and to laugh away with derision the landlord's unethical and half-hearted proposal to ruin the place by the introduction of garlic bread, a nasty foreign food found only in the outlandish South and as likely to find usage as a bidet in the Gents'.

THE QUEST FOR THE PERFECT PUB

★ **THE COOPERS TAVERN**, Cross St.,
Burton-on-Trent, Staffordshire. LLL (W).
Helen and Terry Knight.
Dwarfed by the gleaming aluminium vats of the space-age Bass brewery, The Coopers Tavern crouches next door in a backstreet, frequented by friendly Bass employees who know a good drop when they taste one. We tasted several and feasted on The World's Greatest Lunch: seven bacon and black pudding baps, tepid and with a touch of brown sauce.

We were leaving the Midlands, and this was a perfect place to drink a toast to Bates, Finney and Courtenay, wallow in a little nostalgia, shed a small tear for the demise of the winkle-picker and get maudlin on drink.

The best room at The Coopers is the smaller of the two, where the barrels and bottles are at one end and handily adjacent to them, raised on its own dais, is The High Table – two large planks balanced on barrels, where the Chosen Few hold court and play incomprehensible card games. To be included in their circle is a rare and much-coveted privilege.

Towards the end of the lunchtime session, a florid-faced, be-pinstriped director of the brewery entered breezily, acknowledged the muttered greetings of his hirelings and set about the onerous task of checking and sampling his own wares.

'Not a bad morning Tom,' he observed to the barman.

It was 2.55 pm and hailing.

🍺🍺**THE MALT SHOVEL**, Potter St., Spondon,
Derbyshire. LLL.
Spondon (locally 'Spoondon') was once an attractive little village not far from Derby, but is now part of the urban sprawl that blankets the countryside from here to Nottingham. The joy is that in these unpromising surroundings lies The Malt Shovel, a large, old-style, multi-roomed drinker of enormous character, handily situated close to the A52 motorway-feeder road, and packed with an enthusiastic local crowd of all ages. The excellent Bass can be enjoyed in any of the myriad small rooms, each of which offers a different scenario – cards, arguments, jokes, pipe-smoke – or in the friendly and cluttered corridor that leads you to the hatch and bar. More a town pub in a village than a little local, The Malt Shovel retains its own excellent identity.

SECTION THREE

🍺 **THE FRENCH HORN, Rodsley, Derbyshire.**
ORD (FC, W).
The first of two precious rarities (see **THE QUEEN ADELAIDE** below) – pubs that are part of a working farm, where the farmer's wife herself doubles as landlady. Not far from the old Roman road between Ashbourne and Derby, known locally as Long Lane, The French Horn is a simple lino-and-striplight affair within a farmhouse and attracts a staunchly local following. The adjoining farmyard resounds with the hum of electric milking-machines, the landlady has a milkmaid's complexion and a soft, sweet smile, and the pub is hard to beat in the basic, friendly and unassuming stakes. No food.

🍺 **THE QUEEN ADELAIDE, Snelston, Derbyshire.**
ORD (FC, E).
The Adelaide will certainly not be to everybody's taste. It gives the phrase 'no frills' a new meaning. It is set in the middle of a field, and like **THE FRENCH HORN** (see above) it is one room of a farmhouse set aside for public drinking purposes, and is administered by the taciturn landlady who drinks sweet white wine and, rightly, is interested only in her locals.

The bare, high-ceilinged room usually houses three or four elderly farmers with ruddy complexions, silage-coloured jackets and bailer twine for belts. They are what is termed 'characters' and we were surprised to witness the following scene.

Enter normal well-fed couple from Buxton. They go to bar.
Well-fed woman (WFW) to landlady: 'Do you remember us?'
Landlady: 'No.'
WFW: 'Oh. Two halves of bitter, please.'
Well-fed couple sit at table.
WFW (brightly, to flat cap): 'We come here every year to pick damsons.'
Silence.
WFW: 'We come from Buxton.'
Silence.
Well-fed couple finish drinks and leave.
Silence.
Flat cap to crony: 'Bah gum lad, they're characters!'
Despite this, we must confess that this is one of our very

favourite pubs in the world, and if the above has put you off a visit, then so be it; it is hard enough to find as it is, and you will notice that we have skimped on the directions.

🍺 THE RED LION, Birchover, Derbyshire.
LLL (FC, W).

The Popples have run this perfect village local for twenty-two years but will retire at the end of 1990, so hurry, hurry while ye may. Mentioned in the local (1868) classic, *A Walk in the Peak* by James Croston, the spirit and ambience have changed little since. Until recently the main clientele were lead-miners and the old retired boys still get up on the eves of Christmas and New Year to sing lustily, each one having his speciality number which is called for loudly by a howling, table-thumping throng. Each year there are one or two less of them in the bar and, as Mrs Popple puts it, 'One or two more ghosts.'

Any day of the week The Red Lion offers first-class Marston's, a warm and chatty welcome and thick ham sandwiches sliced generously from the huge, home-cooked joint which dominates the kitchen table behind the bar. The Lion is very good for a session.

★ THE BARLEY MOW, Kirk Ireton, Derbyshire.
LLL (W, B). Tel: 0629-825-685. Mary Short.

The Barley Mow is one of the top twenty best pubs in England. A beautiful building with a series of inter-connecting rooms, it was run for many years by Mrs Ford, yet another *grande dame*, and on her retirement thirteen years ago at the age of 89 was luckily bought by the Shorts, who have changed little and operate it with immense taste and charm. The main bar is dominated by a huge open fireplace, and the impeccable Bass, Marston's and Theakston's are tapped from casks and served in enamel jugs. Set aside time for a session, try them all and stay the night.

Take a note, Mr Whitbread, that The Barley Mow, one of the few unspoilt pubs left in Derbyshire, is often packed with young people from the nearby cities of Derby and Nottingham, where most of the pubs are now amusement arcades. They learn how to play dominoes, love the beer and the atmosphere, and revel in the quiet simplicity to be found here. Their grandfathers would be proud of them.

SECTION THREE

◘ **THE SWAN IN THE RUSHES**, The Rushes,
Loughborough, Leicestershire. LLL (M).
The Swan is a thriving town local, with much to offer and good beer, including Marston's Pedigree with a tight northern head, Batesman's, Tetley and Banks's.
　Conversation:
　'Hey up!'
　'How are you Ted?'
　'Lovely!'
　There followed an informed and critical discourse from the first speaker on the subject of Nigel 'Fattie' Lawson.
　Go to The Swan on Wednesday night when Loughborough Slim performs his raw Delta Blues in front of an appreciative crowd.

◘◘ **THE CAP AND STOCKING**, Kegworth, Leicestershire. LLL.
This Victorian brick building, formerly a picturesque hatch-type drinker, has been sympathetically modernized. One of the best pints of Bass we have tasted was drawn from the cask in the adjacent room and served in a jug. It was delicious and nutty, and the M & B Dark Mild was good too. You can choose from a small bar menu – cobs (local for baps), goulash, vegetarian spaghetti – and be sure that everything will be good and fresh.
　There are two good coal fires in the three separate rooms and local businessmen enjoy a robust lunch in front of one of them. At the time of writing, Kegworth had made the national headlines when it narrowly escaped disaster as Flight BD-92 from Heathrow to Belfast missed its rooftops by fifty feet and crashed onto the M1 motorway with considerable loss of life.

◘◘ **THE CROWN**, Old Dalby, Leicestershire. GAR (F).
The village of Old Dalby is best reached by a gated road from the A6006 Melton Mowbray trunk road and is an attractive backwater. The Crown's main feature is its superb central servery opposite the entrance where the choice from the cask is phenomenal and changes constantly.
　You may also eat huge helpings of good but expensive food in any of the series of interconnecting rooms that constitute the interior of this fine old building. In winter, the open fires are

THE QUEST FOR THE PERFECT PUB

ablaze, and in summer you can sit on a terrace outside and gaze upon a well-tended, sloping garden.

The proprietors are trying hard to please here, but would do better to ban the bevy of bearded bicycle bores who talk loudly about clips and gears while you are trying to enjoy your lunch.

🍺 THE BLUEBELL, Belmesthorpe, Leicestershire. LLL.
In the eastern part of the county, and handy if you are contemplating a leap into the dark of Lincolnshire, lies The Bluebell, an old-fashioned establishment with a landlord known for his jesting character and the cheap price he puts on his lunchtime food. He cares about his Marston's and Ruddles as well, and has a solid regular clientele.

🍺 THE STAR (THE PIT HOUSE), West Leake (off A6006), Nottinghamshire. LLL.
The Star is a splendid Bass coaching inn, good for both drink and food, with a firm foothold in the past, and quietly situated down a lane. The public bar is particularly fine.

🍺 THE NEW WHITE BULL, Giltbrook, Eastwood (off B6010), Nottinghamshire. GLL.
The village is known as the birthplace of the bearded and consumptive erotic poet David H. Lawrence, who unwisely left this plain and honest place.

The New White Bull, Giltbrook near the M1 is a friendly, solid, working man's pub with a humming public bar serving Hardy and Hanson's. It is all right, as is THE NEW INN, Newthorpe Common, Eastwood, which serves good Home mild or bitter without any fuss. For lovers of the Midlands local these two will do very nicely.

🍺🍺 THE CROSS KEYS, Epperstone, Nottinghamshire. LLL (M).
The welcome was so warm here, the beer so good (Hardy and Hanson's), the singing and Morris dancing so entertaining (it was Thursday) that we can remember no more details, except that we had a very good time indeed in the company of complete strangers (see THE BLACK COCK, Eaglesfield, p. 132). The Cross Keys is a most lively place, where the accent is on jazz discs, and a continual stream of stories and japes.

110

SECTION THREE

🍺 THE MINERS ARMS, Huthwaite, Nottinghamshire.
GLL.
This was the perfect unspoilt local, run for many years by the same landlady, but her retirement at the time of going to press, and the fact that it is owned by Scottish and Newcastle, puts its future severely in doubt.

🍺 THE WOODLARK, Church St., Lambley,
Nottinghamshire. GLL (FC).
This is another traditional mining village local that has kept much of its character and peaceful atmosphere. The beer is by Home Ales, the locals are friendly enough and play with gusto a wide variety of pub games, from long skittles to the table variety.

Section Four

Cheshire and North Wales

Cheshire and North Wales

September 29th, Wednesday
Leaving the White Peak behind us, we began the north-western leg of our quest. Skirting the 'Five Towns' and the Potteries, we crossed into Cheshire, and a mile from the Staffordshire border, came to rest at evening opening-time in the small village of Barthomley.

🍺🍺 **THE WHITE LION, Barthomley (A500(T) next to M6 Junction 16), Cheshire. GLL.**
Here the landlord, Eric Critchlow, has been in residence for forty years, purveying pasties or baps to the vicar, the occasional toff and locals. The beautiful building, which dates from 1460, features a particularly lovely and unspoilt second room up a couple of steps and a list of all the former landlords of the pub. The Burtonwood Bitter is very palatable.

We travelled on through a Cheshire criss-crossed with railway lines, working canals, and studded with dormitory villages, dairy farms and pockets of industry. Our destination was The Holly Bush at Little Leigh, but at Alpraham we stopped to have a look at an unpretentious place which had been recommended by a man from Stoke-on-Trent.

🍺🍺 **THE TRAVELLERS REST, Alpraham, Cheshire. LLL (FC).**
This turned out to be an unspoilt, well-patronized pub on the A51, only open in the evenings except Saturdays, when they open at 12. The beers are Tetleys and McEwans, the attractions are good conversation and basic fun with a lively lot of singing locals. The pub has a strong reputation in the area, and is well worth a visit.

To the north of Alpraham lay the main attraction of the evening, and it was to sustain us right through what turned out to be a night of bleak and naked horror.

★ THE HOLLY BUSH, Little Leigh, Northwich, Cheshire. ORD (I, W, E). Albert Cowap.

A few miles away from the southern suburbs of Greater Manchester and the manicured stretch of countryside – the Surrey of the Midlands – that surrounds them, lies an urban councillor's paradise of dual carriageway and roundabout, orange street lamps, soft shoulders and conflicting roadsigns.

Albert Cowap has been observing the changing scenery for fifty-four years ever since his father bought The Holly Bush, a sixty-acre farm and pub, near Little Leigh. Albert still works the land as well as being a dedicated and welcoming publican.

He has studied at close quarters how new roads built to deal with the increasing traffic only serve to increase the traffic further, how this pattern has been obvious since the war, and how the planners and local politicians have steadfastly refused to believe the evidence of their own eyes.

'More roads!' they shout. 'More cars! More mayhem, more money! Oh glory hallelulia, how good it is to be alive.'

So sits The Holly Bush, a genuine oasis in a desert of tarmac, unchanged over the years, with its servery and hatch, its three rooms and its coal fires, its beer and its conversation.

'Would you believe it,' muses Mr Cowap. 'We used to listen out for the sound of a motor car. There were only one or two a day when I was a lad and we would rush to look at them. Now we do the same for a horse.'

But Albert is no reactionary. He has been a lover of machines ever since he first saw a tractor and realized he wouldn't have to muck out the stables any more. Now he stages traction engine rallies on his farm, and nothing enthuses him more than the clatter of pistons and camshafts.

Mr and Mrs Cowap keep The Holly Bush immaculately. They produce excellent Greenalls (which *can* be good, despite what the beer-bores tell you) and welcome local and stranger alike with friendliness and good humour.

Albert, a lifelong teetotaller and chocolate addict, talks with wit and relish, punctuating a particularly good sally with an infectious laugh somewhere between a bark and a guffaw.

We loved our stay at The Holly Bush and found it very hard to leave. There was a young couple in the corner. She was a theatre nurse in Manchester. And he? He was an Area Manager for Little Chef. We repeat: an Area Manager for Little Chef.

SECTION FOUR

Why was he at The Holly Bush? Maybe he found it more congenial? It seemed likely, but this illusion was dispelled when in the course of our conversation we let on that we were planning to stay soon in Penrith at The Agricultural Hotel. The Agricultural Hotel? The man from the Little Chef shook his head in disbelief.

'But why on earth would you want to end up in an old dump like The Agricultural Hotel? There's a Little Chef in Penrith! With bedrooms!'

Perhaps it was the Greenalls, perhaps it had just been a long day. We began to feel woozy, unsteady, uncertain.

In the interests of research we drove westish through the dark night to Frodsham and on to Helsby. But our information proved unreliable. The pubs were no good any more.

At 10 pm, tired and hungry, we were forced to beg for food at The Horse and Jockey, a place of indescribable torment.

In the centre of the room, and treated with a mixture of suspicion and resentment by the clientele, lay a large tray of heaped-up old bones. Above it, suspended from the ceiling, hung a giant copper phallus. There was a meaning to it, we felt sure. We surveyed the room for clues. All around us were the people of Helsby, sparks flying between the nylon carpet and their polyester casuals as they traipsed listlessly from green Dralon-covered stools to the bar, which was underlit with a lurid orange glow. Hyped-up on junkfood and keg lager, pasty-faced from years of continuous inhalation of the sulphurous fumes that drift south over the Mersey, they wore expressions of latent aggression, tempered only by a dominant strain of apathy.

Our uncertainty returned, a double dose. What was the copper phallus, why the bones? Whose fault was it that the roads and buildings were still spreading south into the countryside, eating up the hedges and the fields, the birds and the animals? Why did the man from the Little Chef go to drink at the Holly Bush? Did the peoples of Frodsham and Helsby prefer factories to farms, chemical plants to copses? Could they do nothing to stop the desecration? Did they want to? At whose door should the blame be laid? Theirs? Ours? The politicians'?

Later we lay awake in a nearby residential hotel, pondering our fate and that of the people of England. Perhaps it was time

THE QUEST FOR THE PERFECT PUB

to go home and have a rest, time to ring the publishers and return the advance. It was time for a drink, a game of quoits, some sleep, a tray of copper bones, a chemical implant, a factory in a field, a Little Chef in the shape of a phallus. It was time to move on.

September 30th, Thursday
We got out of Helsby fast the following morning, away from the ribbon development and over the border into that northern part of Wales known as Clwyd and Gwynedd, formerly Denbighshire, the two tiny halves of Flint, Caernarvonshire, Merioneth and Montgomery. We spent two days ransacking the area, much of which is spoilt by tourism, and though we uncovered no gems, we present you with the following suggestions, all worthy of your attention when travelling in these parts.

THE HORSESHOE, Llanyblodwel (B4396), Clwyd. GAR (B). Tel: 069181-227.
The Horseshoe is a fine, old, black-and-white, half-timbered building on the River Tanat, and fishing is to be had if you care to spend a couple of nights. It is also known for its weekend singalongs round the piano. The beamed old bar with its collection of knick-knacks is a warm and enjoyable place to drink.

THE SLATERS ARMS, Corris, Gwynedd. GLL (W).
Corris is a remote, former slate-mining village off the A487, and The Slaters Arms is a simple, unspoilt local with two old-fashioned bars, pleasant fires and a piano which often comes into play. The Banks's beer is cheap, and you can fill up (as we did) on good baps and baked potatoes.

Continuing north on the A470, you might try the **TYN-Y-GROES, Ganllwyd, GAR(B), tel: 034140-275**, situated in the middle of the Coed y Brenin Forest, owned by the National Trust and renowned for its salmon and trout fishing, whiskies and comfortable bedrooms, or at the other end of the scale **THE WHITE LION, Trawsfynydd, Gwynedd, GLL (B), tel: 076687-277**, where the atmosphere is unspoilt, the accommodation more basic, but the welcome and the Burtonwood beers much more than adequate.

SECTION FOUR

From here you can rejoin the A487 and make a quick detour to Porthmadog at the beginning of the Lleyn Peninsula, where Welsh-speaking locals can be spotted in large numbers at the busy SHIP, Lombard St., GAR (F). The food is well-cooked here, the choice of beer wide and the ambience typical of the area.

Alternatively, keep on the A470 towards Betsw y Coed, and look for the hamlet of Capel Garmon, where you can pass a pleasant night.

THE WHITE HORSE, Capel Garmon, Gwynedd. GAR (B). Tel: 069-02-271.
In a lovely hilly area, The White Horse offers good home-made food and clean bedrooms without breaking the bank, and you can relax with a drink in the warm bar atmosphere; the regulars may even talk to you if they like the look of you. We stayed here and enjoyed it, before setting off north-east again the following morning, back into Clwyd.

October 1st, Friday
The backroad from Capel Garmon led us up into wild, uninhabited hill country, down into the vale of Clwyd and over the Clwydian range of hills. A few miles inland from the estuary of the River Dee lies the village of Ysceifiog.

THE FOX, Ysceifiog, Clwyd. LLL (FC, M).
Here there are no sophisticated trappings, just a very good old-time feel to the place, which can be savoured best on a Friday evening when, fuelled by the Greenall Whitley beer, the locals lift their Welsh voices in song and try to raise the roof off the old building.

On the way back into England down the A55, there are two excellent unspoilt pubs to visit.

THE WHITE LION INN, Pen-y-Mynydd, Clwyd. GLL (FC).
Another of the unspoilt gems run by a venerable old lady, who pays scant attention to the changes of the last few decades and provides Marston's Border Bitter at the cheapest price in North Wales. We were there, unfortunately, on the one day when the landlady was visiting her doctor, and so did not get a chance to

talk. But even without her the atmosphere is authentic, and a visit there will repay your curiosity well.

🍺 THE KING'S HEAD, Broughton, Clwyd. GLL.

The King's Head lies almost on the boundary of Wales, so before leaving that country, drop in here for a quick pint of Greenall's Mild, admire the traditional feel in the original old rooms, and be thankful that they are still there.

We re-entered Cheshire late on Friday afternoon and headed east. On our way to Manchester we had one important stop to make.

We pulled in briefly to refresh ourselves at a solid and well-preserved local of character.

🍺 THE CHETWODE ARMS, Lower Whitley, Cheshire. GAR.

This is an old-fashioned, large, four-roomed village pub with open fires, function rooms often used for local auctions and sales and, thanks to a Preservation Order, still very unspoilt. The beer is the ubiquitous (in these parts) Greenall Whitley, and the Chetwode remains a thriving, enterprising and efficient establishment which still has a strong feeling of tradition about it.

We now crossed the M6 with mounting excitement; our Welsh trip had been less than riveting and we were looking forward to a great night's entertainment. We were to find it.

★ THE HARRINGTON ARMS, Gawsworth, Cheshire. ORD (FC). Marjorie Bayley.

The Harrington Arms is a large farmhouse with working farm around it. As you enter the house, your nostrils may be assailed by the tantalizing smells of good, plain cooking emanating from the lovely, traditional farm kitchen. Unfortunately, this is meant only for Mrs Bayley's hungry family, but she will happily sell you her home-made chutneys, pickled eggs, jams and even a small bottle of the damson gin which she makes for the local vet.

The chief beauty of this until-recently unspoilt gem is the several numbered rooms which surround the central servery, each designated for a separate purpose. There are one or two into which only Mrs Bayley's most favoured clients may enter, and another where she puts the young from Congleton and Macclesfield who make the trip out at weekends to get away from the clatter of video machines and the loutish urban behaviour patterns.

'You get to know people after thirty years,' observes Mrs Bayley. 'If the youngsters get too rowdy, I flick the lights on and off to let them know I'm keeping an eye on them, and they respect that.'

In fact the youngsters have a very good time; they sit round a large table with a gallon jug of mild or bitter and enjoy the fire and their own conversation.

Unfortunately for all, and for no good reason, Robinsons, the landlords, brutally vandalized the Harrington several years ago, ripping out the beautiful daisy-shaped glass above the old servery (for which they were subsequently successfully prosecuted and fined), dismantling the old wood screens and insisting on the installation of a new bar and handpumps; perhaps the beer tasted too good from the cask.

A bewildered Mrs Bayley remembers:

'On a good night I could sell a gallon of beer from the barrel in the time it takes to pull three pints from the handpump.'

The brewers are obviously lurking in the shadows, counting the days until they can finish the job off properly; perhaps the marketing department should take into account the fiercely protective loyalty of the Harrington's far-flung customers, as witnessed by the impressive collection of postcards from all over the world.

Even if you allow yourself only one good night in a public house each year, make sure (as we did) it is at The Harrington Arms on a Friday, when the fiddlers, accordionists, guitarists and string instrumentalists congregate in one of the rooms and play for free, providing the most perfect pub entertainment to be found anywhere. Drink deep of the ale, and walk back to your bed-and-breakfast billet in the village, at Mrs Worth's, Roughs Hey Farm, Leek Road (tel: 02605-2296). You will arise the next morning and leave refreshed of heart and spirit.

Section Five

Greater Manchester, Lancashire and Cumbria

Greater Manchester

October 3rd, Sunday
Friday night at The Harrington Arms had taken its toll, and the ridicule poured on our attempts at singing 'The Wild Rover' still rankled. We returned for the Saturday night to our safe house in the White Peak and passed a quiet evening. We needed the rest. The next section of our journey was a long and hazardous one.

North of Buxton, the High Peak and the moors began to be studded with industrial outcrops as we drove towards Manchester. The shells of Victorian factories clung to hillsides and mountain streams ran alongside belching chimneys; small, stone-built farming villages nestled in the shadow of the original satanic mills, and it was with some awe that we realized that the whole of this gigantic northern conurbation, now home to some fifteen per cent of the population, was once wild hills. One of the most striking things about Manchester is the continual contrast between city and country, and the views from the surrounding moors provide striking evidence of this. It was here that our business lay, on the fringes of the teeming town.

THE STATION BUFFET, Stalybridge, Greater Manchester. LLL.
At opening time on a bright Sunday morning, we pulled up outside the legendary Station Buffet at Stalybridge. This still serves its original purpose to refresh travellers, but is now privately run as a perfectly-preserved piece of Victoriana, complete with steam days memorabilia, and attracts aficionados from all over the North-West. The beer is reputed to be first-rate and constantly changing, and the landlord is a true enthusiast who has turned a moribund platform bar into a thriving and original public house.

Unfortunately our research had been less than thorough; the Station Buffet was closed. The affable young licensee was, however, topping up his car battery prior to his weekly trip to the Cash-and-Carry. He regretted that he was never open Sunday lunchtimes, but graciously offered us a lift to any of the other pubs in Stalybridge. We declined, promising instead to return at the first opportunity, and took the road again to our next stop where we were not to be disappointed. There have been subsequent rumours of a change of management at Stalybridge, but we had not yet substantiated them as we went to press.

🍺🍺 THE HORSE AND JOCKEY, Stanedge, Delph, Greater Manchester. GLL (FC, I).

On the edge of bleak Saddleworth Moor, whose dark secrets are too fresh in the public mind to need relating here, at a lonely crossroads, stands one of the best and most uncompromising pubs in the area. Hurry in out of the biting wind that swirls around this weathered building. Edge your way through the cluster of flat caps who populate the solid wood central servery that is topped with fine Edwardian stained glass. Order a pint of Mr Kershaw's perfectly kept ale, which changes all the time, but may include Marston's, Timothy Taylors or Everard's; he has been here nearly thirty years and since he does no food can concentrate on looking after his beers. His wife is beside him, smiling at the regulars and treating strangers with honest, blunt, warm, northern manners.

Get right in close to the big coal fire. Enjoy the simple feeling of well-being that will steal over you: the worn, comfortable furniture, the radio which seems to be broadcasting old Light Programme variety shows, the broad accents and local banter about greyhounds, football and pigeons, the relaxed and beautifully-timed service offered by the Kershaws. The overall atmosphere is one of the Macmillan 1950s, unchanged. No jukebox, no fruit machine disturbs the conversation. This is a serious, old-fashioned pub with no concessions to the appalling prospect of the 1990s. In the week it is only open in the evenings, but on weekend lunchtimes there are very lively sessions, well worth attending.

From Delph, take the A640 north to the M62 and travel west. Come off on the spur road at exit 20 (direction Oldham) and take the sign to Middleton. At the roundabout by the industrial estate, turn onto the Castleton Road. If you are lucky, you will spot Thornham Lane on the right; turn here. Continue up the (un-made) road until the houses peter out and you see some ramshackle farm buildings. Park your car.

🍺 **THE TANDLE HILL TAVERN**, Thornham Lane, Slattocks, Middleton, Greater Manchester. LLL (I).

Its extraordinary location is a major reason for the Tandle Hill's inclusion here. It stands halfway along a ridge of farmland that is an island, forgotten in error by the planners, amid a sea of belching smoke and rabbit-hutch housing projects; you can walk for twenty minutes in either direction from the pub in open country, while all around you the Mancunian maelstrom encroaches threateningly. A donkey is tethered outside the pub; a silage-scented farmyard is at the back; sheepdogs slink up with their permanently guilty expression. It is disorienting.

Inside on a weekend lunchtime, friendly disorder reigns; the room is smoky from cigarettes and frying food (it won't appeal to militant non-smokers). Relaxed to the point of slapdash is the motif here, but the locals seem to enjoy it a lot. We ate hot beef-and-onion baps served by willing but inaccurate seven-year-olds. The Gents' proudly displays a 'Now Wash Your Hands' notice, but someone has failed to instal a handbasin. Here they play dominoes and cards and everyone seems to be related; nevertheless, the atmosphere is genuinely friendly to strangers. The Tandle Hill Tavern is a good place to alleviate (or acquire) motorway fatigue, an eccentric, slightly slovenly place – and all the better for it.

Also worth visiting in and around Manchester and Merseyside are the following:

🍺 **THE RAM'S HEAD**, Ripponden Rd., (A6052), Denshaw, Greater Manchester.

Only a couple of miles from **THE HORSE AND JOCKEY, Delph** (see p. 126), this is another moorland pub somewhat battered by the elements. The beer (Theakston's) is particularly good, drawn (unusually for the North) straight from the cask and served in big metal jugs, but the interior has been modernized and there is a certain lack of atmosphere, except when the place really fills up.

THE QUEST FOR THE PERFECT PUB

🍺 **THE SHIP INN**, Cable St., Southport, Merseyside. GLL.
A surviving reminder of what a good northern town pub used to be like, this is a backstreet local of genuine character which has escaped vandalism. There are fine stained-glass windows, extremely good ale, very cheap and simple eats, good local trade and conversation. In its own way, a gem.

🍺🍺 **THE HEATONS BRIDGE**, Heatons Bridge Rd., (B5242), Scarisbrick, Lancashire. GLL.
On the Southport–Ormskirk road, this is an extremely sound, no frills, canalside pub frequented by canal people and not too many others. It has hardly changed at all in the last twenty years, and of its basic style it is a rare example. The welcome is as warm as can be.

🍺🍺 **THE FLEETWOOD ARMS**, Dock St., Fleetwood, Lancashire. LLL.
A proper dockside pub in a working fishing port, reflecting all the character and salty stories you could want. No fake nauticals with jaunty yachting caps from Austin Reed; the company is real, so is the Boddingtons and Higsons ale.

Cumbria and The Lakes

We drove north, eating up miles along the M6. At dusk we pulled off the motorway and into Penrith. Our billet, **THE AGRICULTURAL HOTEL** (see p. 136) set us up for what promised to be an exciting and rewarding voyage of discovery through the fells and lakes. As it turned out, it was the prelude to a journey full of disillusion, bitterness and chagrin.

SECTION FIVE

The old counties of Cumberland and Westmorland, with their long, dark history of bleak, upland farming and bloody border battles between marauding clans and militia, have been transformed into the Leisure Area of Cumbria, complete with clogged roads, tourist information points and mass catering at every turn. The volume of visitors to the Lake District, tourists, walkers and climbers, is quite understandable, given the natural beauty of the area, the literary associations of Wordsworth, Beatrix Potter and others, and the challenge to courage and skill presented by the Cumbrian mountains.

Unfortunately, such activity has all but rid the region of proper pubs. Even, or rather especially, the remotest establishments have developed into mass accommodation and feeding stations. Now there is nothing wrong with this; if you are on a motoring holiday, or a climbing trip, there are many perfectly good inns that will suit you very well. Here are a few of them. Be aware, however, that these are not all pubs in this book's definition, and you may be disappointed.

🍺 **THE WASDALE HEAD INN**, Wasdale Head, Cumbria. GITS (B). Tel: 09406-229.

The Wasdale Head Inn, at the end of wild, solitary Wastwater, England's deepest lake, is the perfect spot if you want a comfortable, fairly expensive night with a decent dinner (between mid-March and October only), in spectacular surroundings. Or, if you're walking the Black Sail Pass then drop into Ritson's bar for a pint of Jennings. But it must be stressed that this is not, in the strictest sense of the word, a pub. The hotel, with its genuinely atmospheric residents' bar, is out of bounds to casual visitors, and Ritson's Bar, which adjoins the main building, has a faintly impersonal feel to it, catering as it does to a mainly transient trade of walkers, daytrippers and so on. Even the fire is gas-log-effect, and the place is so remote that the only locals are the sheep, and in general they are teetotal.

🍺 **THE OLD DUNGEON GHYLL HOTEL**, Langdale, Cumbria. GITS (B). Tel: 09667-272.

In the same category as the above is The Dungeon Ghyll Hotel at Langdale Pikes above Eltwater, although the Climbers' Bar here is decidedly more eccentric. It is a scruffy, barn-like, one-room drinker with a high bar, lots of beams and a big range

129

with a proper fire, around which many serious climbers with beards and jerseys of the same hue cluster, 'singing' hearty songs of Scandinavian origin in deeply unattractive voices. The barman and his girlfriend seem to belong to an early 1970s motorcycle gang, and the room somehow contrives to combine its mountain atmosphere with that of a coffee bar somewhere near Camberley. Again, if you are seeking a good local pub, do not make the effort to come here.

Perhaps the most disappointing experience we had was at The Britannia Inn in Eltwater. This establishment was highly recommended to us, but the recommendation cannot be passed on. It seemed to embody all the pitfalls and compromises that lie in wait when a pub stretches itself too far in too many directions and fails to reach its objective in any of them.

Our night there was spent out of season, but things were badly awry. The bedrooms were comfortable enough, but the bar food was spectacularly indifferent, which made us suspicious of the three-course dinner at a steep £18.00. The tables were unwiped, the beer only average, the wine list a travesty. Even the two fireplaces were cold and bare on a chilly October night.

What made all this so much harder to take was the generally smug attitude adopted by the staff, who seemed unwarrantedly pleased with themselves, indulging in loud private banter and bad self-congratulatory jokes to the extent that we were forced to vacate the bar; obviously most of the locals had done so years ago.

A 45-minute wait to order breakfast the next morning did nothing to improve our view of the Britannia. As we reluctantly paid the bill, we learned that the licensee, a Mr David Fry, was on vacation. It looked to us as though the ship was foundering in his absence, or perhaps just foundering.

These shortcomings seem to be symptomatic of the region; years of catering to all-comers has led inevitably to the lowest common denominator, dressed up as something it isn't, at prices that reflect only the greed of the proprietor.

Happily, there is one country pub (using the word correctly), which manages to pull all these elements together in such an efficient way that it all but redresses the balance.

SECTION FIVE

★ **THE MASON'S ARMS, Strawberry Bank, Cartmel Fell, Cumbria. GAR (F). Helen and Nigel Stephenson.**
Best reached from the village of Bowland Bridge, The Mason's Arms stands halfway up Cartmel Fell and has staggering views, when it is not foggy and raining, that is. There are three small, snug rooms, with a fireplace in the bar. The furniture is old, attractive and well maintained. The bar is small, high and very well stocked. The food is well above the average, featuring Greek specialities and no chips – served unfussily and sensibly-priced.

The main attraction, however, is the astonishing global selection of bottled beers purveyed by the Stephensons. From Germany to Greece, from Belgium to Baltimore, there are nearly 150 of them, imported and wholesaled by the enterprising licensee. For £1.00, you can purchase his 'Beer List', a wittily-annotated catalogue of everything in the cellar, with dissertations on the beer-drinking habits of Czechoslovakia, the beer-stained habits of Belgian monks, and the unlikely hop products of Honduras. If this sounds pretentious, then think again. Nigel Stephenson's enthusiasm sweeps away cant, and the Mason's is a Mecca for beer-bores of all persuasions. A crowd from Yorkshire were in, while we were there, supping and comparing a terrifying range of beers.

'I don't understand them bloody southerners,' vouchsafed one of them to us.

We kept our lips sealed.

'They like their beer bloody flat,' he continued, a baffled look on his face, then he leaned in, dropping his voice and breathing Trappist Chimay Blue Label all over us. 'I once had a pint of Devenish in Cornwall' – and his eyes swivelled round the room in case any stray Cornish were present – 'Flat as a bloody flute it was.' He glared accusingly at us as if we were directors of the brewery in question, and then returned to his Yugoslavian Skopsko (OG 1048).

Luckily, locals still tend to outnumber the beer-bores and the welcome to all is genuine and warm. Yes, of course it gets crowded in the summer, but the clientele are a discerning one, here for the quality of the goods, not the convenience; they know that this is a gem among a lot of dross.

Village pubs in Cumbria have also been forced in the main to

THE QUEST FOR THE PERFECT PUB

expand their activities; here are a few that either do the job properly or haven't changed.

🍺🍺 **THE TOWER BANK ARMS**, Near Sawrey, Cumbria. GAR (F, B, OP). Tel: 09666-334.
The Tower Bank Arms is owned by the National Trust, whose approach to pub preservation bans machines, jukeboxes, prominent beer advertising and so on, and substitutes period furniture, good service and, above all, a landlord who cares (see **THE FLEECE, Bretforton**, (p. 56)). Philip Broadley is the incumbent here, and he runs The Tower Bank Arms with the kind of well-oiled precision of which we make so much, but is a pleasure to encounter.

The bar is spotless, and by the fire a good gaggle of locals are well settled in. Strangers and residents ensconced at the scrubbed pine tables are treated with a friendly courtesy, and served with generous helpings of simple food: steaks, lake trout, gammon, roast chicken. The winelist is better than most around here, too. The flagstones gleam, the service is quietly efficient. Double bedrooms are a reasonable £30.00.

As usual, our advice is: go out of season, when the staff have time to talk. From June to September The Tower Bank, which backs onto the garden of Beatrix Potter's old house, is packed with Puddleduck punters, Tiggywinkle trippers and Bunny bores; but then, that advice applies to the whole of the Lake District.

🍺🍺 **THE BLACK COCK**, Eaglesfield, Cumbria. GLL (FC).
Eaglesfield is a silent village off the A5086 two or three miles south of Cockermouth, birthplace of Wordsworth. It has its own famous son, for here in 1766 was born John Dalton, discoverer of the Atomic Theory. It also contains one of the best examples of an old-fashioned, unpretentious village pub still remaining in this part of the country.

The Black Cock offers little in the way of food, except at lunchtime when you might get some bread and cheese. What it does offer is first-rate beer and a roaring fire around which you will encounter truly local and welcoming company and stimulating conversation. There are two small bars, run firmly by a

SECTION FIVE

landlord who has been many years in the village and is a fund of knowledge. Of our visit to The Black Cock, we remember very little after the first couple of pints; that in itself is a fine recommendation.

▣▣ THE RACEHORSE, Arran Foot, near Ulverston, Cumbria. (ORD, FC, W).

Ulverston is the flat cap capital of the North-West. They swarm in the streets, muttering to themselves as they weave their way from pub to pub; they sit on benches, lifting their knobbled, raw faces to a lowering sky; they dash in front of cars in a stiff-jointed version of kamikaze, clutching a small plastic bag full of rotting swedes. They fill the GLLs of Ulverston with their pipesmoke and steaming tweeds. Drink in THE DEVONSHIRE in Victoria Rd., or THE KING'S HEAD in Queen St. (both LLL, FC), and you will be in the bosom of old Lancashire, though officially it is now Cumbria.

A couple of miles outside town, as you roar past on the new trunk road, cast your eyes to the left. The hamlet of Arran Foot is now completely bypassed and cut-off from the mainstream; this is probably why The Racehorse is one of the last genuine pubs in the county.

Agnes Brocklebank has been the licensee for fifty-four years, and used to farm the land around the pub as well. Property development stripped her of the farm and now old age has robbed her of her eyesight, so her capable and warm-hearted daughter is running The Racehorse. If you look out of her window you can see the new A590 scarring the flats where until the 1930s they used to hold the races which gave the pub its name. Then it was a thriving establishment; after the races the two licensed rooms upstairs were made one by the ingenious raising of a partition wall, and the carousing that ensued is legendary.

'Now there are only three drinkers left in the village,' admits the landlady, pouring bottled beer with the hand that isn't repainting the staircase, 'but we're always happy to see strangers. The old boys still like to come here, and there's never any trouble about cutting you in for dominoes. It gets very cosy in here in the winter.'

And it is easy to picture; the simple room with its benches and small tables would be crowded with more than ten people in it.

133

THE QUEST FOR THE PERFECT PUB

The Racehorse deserves support, for without it the old ways and simple pleasures to be found there will vanish for ever.

🍺🍺 **THE HARE AND HOUNDS,** Talkin (off B6413), Cumbria. GAR (B). Tel: 06977-3456.
At the centre of a quiet village not far from the Scottish border, The Hare and Hounds is a well-known and popular place much feted by other publications. We found it Too Red – red plush, red lights, red gas fire – Too Red in general, and we could not understand why people seem to enthuse about the menu, which struck us as being fairly unimaginative. However, it must be said that the landlord and his wife are pleasant and welcoming, the bedrooms are very good value at £18.00 for single bed and breakfast, and the surrounding countryside is of great beauty. These factors combine to earn The Hare and Hounds its two-barrelled entry.

Here we must return to our first port of call, Penrith, and take up the *real* story of Cumbrian pubs. Put simply, the story is thus. Cumbria's industrial base, in towns like Workington, Whitehaven, Penrith and Barrow, has, like so many places in the North, been eroded until it is almost invisible. Docks lie empty. Whole streets are boarded up. Thrilling 1970s theme disco/fun pubs haven't seen a punter since the works closed down; yet somehow the street-corner boozer survives triumphant. The drinkers may not have the money to buy too many rounds, and they may ration their own intake (we heard of one pub on a housing estate where the unemployed locals used to spend all day drinking pints of orange squash because they were only 50p), but they still bring the pub alive with their conversation, their deals, their plotting, their making-the-best-of-it and their humour. The following cluster of houses we thoroughly enjoyed, and so should you.

🍺**THE GEORGE IV INN,** Stanley St., Workington, Cumbria. GLL (FC).
British Steel finished off Workington when they closed down the big smelting works; the destruction job they had wreaked on Consett had been so enjoyable, why shouldn't they do it here?

Down on the empty quayside, where ragwort grew through

SECTION FIVE

the cracked concrete, and the only vessel in sight was an elderly, rusting dredger, we found The George IV. The landlady, who has been here many years, was eating her breakfast in the company of an elderly FC comfortably into his second pint. They were listening to Jimmy Young, who for some reason was broadcasting from Moscow.

'What's he doing over there?' enquired the landlady with a puzzled look. 'They're Russians; they won't understand him, half of them.'

'They'd do much better,' rejoiced the FC, 'to take Benn and Heffer over there – and leave 'em. They're half bloody Russian as it is.'

And this from a solid working man in a town that has been decimated under a Tory government. We were intrigued. Talk moved on to bemoan the closing of the steelworks and the subsequent decay of the docks.

'Things are getting better though,' offered the landlady bravely. 'We had four ships in last week; quite busy it was – one was unloading coal, there was one with scrap-iron, oh yes and we had an oiltanker as well, and one from Norway with fish.'

We chatted on, had a second half of good Jennings bitter, and left, casting a last sad look at Workington Docks.

The same story is told by Whitehaven down the coast; the same deserted quay, the peeling stucco of The Globe Seamen's Guesthouse, the chimneys that belch no more, the run-down Mecca Social Club. We drank in the public bar of THE CENTRAL, GLL, which was packed with at least ten FCs, lovingly looked after by the landlord, Raymond Stephenson. A pity about the ill-chosen and deafening jukebox selection.

We drove south along the coast, through Egremont towards Barrow-in-Furness. The cooling towers of the Sellafield reactor winked knowingly at us in the hazy afternoon sunshine. We resisted the temptation to throw things at the Visitor Centre, remembering that the locals seemed quite keen on the whole enterprise, despite what the national press will tell you. It does, after all, provide jobs in an unemployment black spot.

In Barrow, a depressing naval and industrial town, where there had recently been ugly scenes at Vickers between the workforce and the management, it began to rain. It continued to rain. We sheltered in an honest working men's pub called THE WHEATSHEAF, GLL, in Anson St., where we drank

THE QUEST FOR THE PERFECT PUB

proper John Smith's from a handpump and over curry and chips (£1.95) speculated on the occupation of Carl Blezard, whose business calendar adorned the otherwise plain walls of the public bar. Was he a small champagne producer, a couturier, a crimper? No, this was Barrow after all, and Mr Blezard turned out to be a 'Bone, Fat and Waste Oil Merchant – weekly collections guaranteed'.

We bade farewell to Barrow and turned inland in the vague direction of Penrith, intending to brave the hazardous inclines and descents of the Hardknott Pass between Eskdale and Elterwater, the most beautiful, spectacular and remote road south of the Scottish border.

We snaked our way up to the top of the pass at 2,000 feet. As we lurched stomach-churningly over the switchback summit in driving rain, our much-loved, Gallic motor car chose this moment to abandon the entente cordiale and withdraw use of the brakes.

Curtains! We looked at each other and shook hands. We had always thought that this book might kill us, but had expected our deaths to occur in a pub or a hospital ward, and not hurtling down a craggy rock face at forty miles an hour. . . .

October 7th, Thursday

THE AGRICULTURAL HOTEL, Cromwell Rd., Penrith, Cumbria. GMTH (F, B). Tel: 0768-62622.
Mrs Hacket, the landlady, smiled sweetly as she cut our delicious steak-and-kidney puddings into bite-sized pieces and fed us gently with a teaspoon. We sucked our Marston's through straws and compared bandages. With one good eye between us, we gazed proudly through the window at the shiny, new, little tourer that gave a touch of class to the car park. It would be a few days before the plaster came off and we could resume our tour, so we were giving our full attention to the delights of Penrith and the Agricultural.

The latter is a solid, stone-built Victorian hotel with six bedrooms and the £12 bed and breakfast is the best value to be had almost anywhere. At its best on market day, it features a big, square, wooden bar dispensing reliable Marston's, much enjoyed by the farmers and members of the North-West Holstein Breeders and the Arran Sweaters clubs who flock there

SECTION FIVE

to hold their meetings. The wholesome food comes from an oil-fired Aga and the busy preparations (beginning at 8 am) for lunch put us in mind of a decent provincial hotel in central France.

Two friendly regulars pushed us around the market-day streets in our wheelchairs and introduced us to the pleasures of Penrith: John and James Graham (established 1793), the thriving grocers, THE MUSEUM INN, LLL, in Castlegate, packed with revellers, and other lively establishments too numerous to mention. Land Rovers lurched hither and thither, full of caps, sheep and carpet off-cuts.

On our last night at the Agricultural, and now sporting merely Elastoplast and bruises, we were intrigued to witness a rare local custom that only survives in staunchly traditional corners like Penrith.

It was closing time. A great deal of ale had been drunk, particularly by a conspiracy of red-faced drovers who had dominated the bar since early afternoon. At ten to eleven precisely, and with no bidding, Mrs Hackett appeared with plate after plate of small triangular sandwiches and five large brown pots of tea. Nothing was said. In silence and with a sense of undeflected purpose, the ten men chomped and slurped their way through the mountain of bread and meat paste and the ocean of tea until, at half-past eleven, they rose unsteadily and all stood to attention.

Their leader, a florid-faced scoundrel, addressed Mrs Hackett formally.

'We thank you, woman, for your good offices. We may now return to the bosoms of our families. Our wives will suspect nothing. May God bless you madam, and save the Queen.'

They left, silently and in single file, like monks returning to their cells after vespers.

Section Six

The North-East

County Durham

October 9th, Saturday. Author's birthday.
In a small pub outside Durham, we first laid hands upon what would prove to be the answer to our prayers: it came in the shape of a large Tanqueray and tonic.

It was October, the leaves had taken on a blueish hue and the buds of what the poets call Spring were blossoming, giving a warm wintry glow to this neglected part of Africa. We began to cry for salvation, a small column in *The Lady*, a packet of lemon sherbets, execution for Sir Dickie, anything, anything . . . Oh the buggers' grips, the tears, the parties, the glug of the women. Oh the drums, the glug of buggers, the women's grips, and Carruthers silhouetted nimbly in the moonlight as we bypassed the Yorkshire Dales and landed nimbly outside the Hotel Des Voyageurs at Gie-sur-Seine. Oh the 4,000 franc menu, oh the bottle of Gruaud-LaRose 1823. . . .

Our companion, nimbly and buoyantly afloat on the last of an Autumn Leaf Soufflé, praised the nimbility of the Attenboroughish Sorbet Oreilles Du Pederaste and then fell nimblisticissiminimally down the chute where 10,000 underpaid, grinning and chanting Africans were waiting nimbly for a Margarita. We soldiered on to the Stanley Baker Pizza served with a coulis of layers and layers and layers and layers and layers. . . .

Later that night, we lay comfortably to rest in a much-used and mercifully cheap small room with superb, if perfunctory service from a multitude of smartly blue-uniformed staff.

October 11th, Monday
The North-east of England, from the North Yorkshire Dales upwards, came as a welcome surprise after the disappointments of the Lake District.

County Durham spread itself around us as we sped through the B-roads on the way to our first destination. From Barnard Castle, we drove through the fiefdom of the Lords Barnard;

here the farmhouses stand starkly white against the skyline like beacons. Since the 18th century, the tenant farmers have been obliged by their feudal lord to whitewash, at their own expense, their dwellings.

One night, returning late from hunting on a foggy moor, the then Lord Barnard became hopelessly lost in his own countryside; the grey stone buildings of his vassals lay shrouded in vapour and no landmarks were to be seen. On his eventual arrival, wet, cold and hungry, the noble lord flew into a towering rage and ordered the whitewashing of all his farmhouses to serve as markers for returning hunters. The practice is still observed.

North of Bishop Auckland and Crook, where the Elvet Ballet School sits nervously next to The Golden Fleece and The Commercial Hotel, the ground rises and suddenly there are panoramic views of wide valleys, carpeted with fields and studded with the thin, dark lines of one-street mining villages like toy trains belching coal-smoke into a blue autumn sky. At Sunniside we stopped at an elderly petrol pump and asked directions from a cheerful girl.

'You going to the Dun Cow?' she asked with interest. 'We go down there. It's an old place, and it's the best pub round here.'

With this heartening news, we covered the remaining mile in a flash.

★ **THE DUN COW, Old White Lea, Billy Row, Crook, (off B6299), County Durham. ORD (FC, I, E).**
Steve Parkin.
The large stone cottage that is The Dun Cow has been a pub since 1740, though it traded without a licence until 1840, when Steve Parkin's ancestor, the first of five generations to keep The Dun Cow, went legit. These days the pub is open only in the evenings, but Steve was chopping wood outside when we arrived at lunchtime and happily took us in for a pint and a natter.

He is a genial, untidy man whose father held the licence here for fifty-nine years ('He didn't make the sixty,' says Steve sadly), and has been heir-apparent for most of his life. He is now as a result, like the Prince of Wales, somewhat eccentric.

The front room is a comfortably shabby parlour or drinking-den, with peeling tables, a couple of benches and a few simple

SECTION SIX

chairs. Dominating the room is a battered but efficient range with a good coalfire and a somewhat ramshackle back boiler that Steve has installed to warm the little rear bar, with its tiny counter, few tables and splendid collection of drinking jugs suspended from the ceiling.

The landlord pulls us good pints of Theakston's and sits down to chat. He tells us that his family came from High House at Easingwold and bought The Dun Cow for £50 at the turn of the 19th century.

These days The Dun Cow, isolated as it is on its little lane, gets well cranked up in the evenings, when locals, miners and their families, and the occasional interloper who can't resist an old-fashioned drinker cram the two rooms and shed their inhibitions and cares with the aid of nothing more than Steve Parkin's good-value beer (80p per pint). He intends to 'go into catering,' but the fare will be plain and simple. He assured us that he has no plans whatever to feature the snails bred by his friend in Bishop Auckland, and this is probably a blessing.

He told us horror stories of a large local hotel, where his regulars occasionally go for dinner, 'when they're washed up and in their best,' which at Christmas fleeces its customers with a three-day £320 all-inclusive binge.

'I'll do the same for £4,' he observed, but his tongue might have been in his cheek.

No visit to County Durham would be complete without a trip to The Dun Cow; it is the last of its kind in this area, a wonderful anachronism supported, thankfully, by a fierce and loyal band of followers.

Reluctantly leaving behind these close-knit, hard-pressed mining communities, we rambled across the moors and swooped down into the dramatic tumble of Weardale, pausing only to refresh ourselves at the very eccentric Rancho Del Rio, where the natives dress in ten-gallon hats, spurs and elaborate shirts, and discuss in thick Wearside accents the relative merits of Tammy Wynette and Loretta Lynn. Sometimes the debate spills out into the car park. We were to lunch at The Cows Hill Hotel, where we had been warned that our reception might not be as effusive as some.

THE QUEST FOR THE PERFECT PUB

★ **THE COWS HILL HOTEL,** Cows Hill, Weardale, (A689), County Durham. GMTH (F, B, E).
Tel: 0388-537236. Walton Siddle.

The patrician Mr Walton Siddle presides over The Cows Hill Hotel and is not a man to be trifled with. Tall and lean, with a sardonic twist to his features, he will not hesitate to exercise his mordant wit upon those who, he considers, do not meet his own exacting standards.

In a small village on a lonely road that clings to the side of Weardale, The Cows Hill has something of the look and smell of a small French country auberge and thus its rating as a GMTH.

Indeed, this was the first place we visited in which we were made to feel like strangers in a strange land, an exciting feeling that returned from time to time during our travels in the North-East, reflecting the remoteness of the area and the untarnished attitudes of its people.

The large, plain and attractive main room was all but empty save for a small clutch of the landlord's cronies.

Mr Siddle eyed us with some distaste. We ordered four half-pints of his excellent beer for ourselves and our female companions. We hesitated for a split-second, noting the two styles of glass into which he versed our refreshments.

'Men's glasses and ladies' glasses!' he barked as though we were mentally deficient. 'Get them off the bar, boy, and sit down without delay. If you require lunch, get on with it. Mrs Thatcher tells me that I may remain open all day. The good lady and I do not agree on the subject.'

It was obvious to us that extended hours applied here only to the inner circle, and so we retreated to the upstairs dining room where Mrs Siddle served us a superb and inexpensive roast lunch, delivered from the depths on an ancient and creaking dumb waiter, an experience not to be missed.

Flushed with food and ale, we committed further foolishnesses. Like eager puppies, we bounded back to the bar.

'Do you have rooms here?' we enquired with keenness.

Siddle gave us an old-fashioned and quizzical look.

'Mm . . .' he volunteered.

'Oh good,' we gushed effusively. 'Well, next time we're in the area . . .'

'Mm . . .' he repeated with less than a smidgen of enthusiasm.

SECTION SIX

We slunk away, our tails between our legs, but feeling that we should have persevered, for The Cows Hill Hotel is a fine and characterful place that would afford a welcome to more likeable personalities than the authors.

🍺 **THE NEWTON CAP**, Bishop Auckland, County Durham. GLL (FC).
Set on the top of the town, with a fine view of terraced houses tumbling into the valley below and a Victorian railway viaduct. A truly old-style joint, where the landlord greeted us with the puzzling observation: 'I've nothing hot, only beer.' It was Cameron's and we enjoyed it in the company of friendly regulars sporting eccentric headwear. No frills.

🍺 **THE FIRTREE**, Cornsay Colliery, (off B6301), County Durham. GLL (FC, I).
Firmly traditional miners' and locals' pub, featuring live music on certain evenings. Spartan interior, but warm welcome. Strongly recommended for those of a cavorting nature.

🍺🍺 **LANGDON BECK HOTEL, Teesdale, (B6282), County Durham. GAR (I, B). Tel: 0833-22267.**
A prankish sort of place, miles from anywhere. On our arrival on a Saturday afternoon, it was obvious from outside that a fine session was in progress. As we tried the door, the bolt was briskly slid into position. Not to be denied, we gained entry through the reception area and joined a frowst of youngish locals in the public bar. Half an hour later we left, with the crisp one-liner, 'Now you can lock the door again, boys.' Gales of friendly laughter followed us out, as the lads realized that their wheeze had not gone unnoticed.

🍺 **THE BLACK SWAN**, Parkgate, Darlington, County Durham. LLL.
A multi-roomed Victorian local of character, full of dedicated drinkers, and featuring a drinking-corridor with finely-engraved, curved and distorting mirrors. Good for a quick one or two before a stagger to the railway station where it all began with Locomotion One.

THE QUEST FOR THE PERFECT PUB

🍺 **THE HIGH FORCE HOTEL,** Teesdale, (B6282), County Durham. **GAR (B)**. Tel: 0833-22222/22264.
Dramatically situated overlooking the splendid waterfall that lends the hotel its name, this is a welcoming and friendly establishment where it is a pleasure to stay and drink in the public bar. Also popular for wedding parties and other local shindigs.

🍺🍺 **THE BRIDGE, Middleton-in-Teesdale,** (off B6282), County Durham. **LLL (FC)**.
Unspoilt, traditional drinker that is unpenetrated by tourists. Simple pleasures enjoyed by locals of all ages and well worth seeking out for its lack of pretention.

🍺 **THE CROSS KEYS,** Gainford, (A67), County Durham. **LLL**.
At the end of a row of pretty terraced cottages, and the best pub in a gem of a village near Barnard Castle. Evenings can get very lively here. Good Vaux beer.

Northumberland

October 14th, Thursday
At opening time in a seamen's dive on the quay in Newcastle-upon-Tyne we waited nervously for the arrival of our two guides to the locality. They were a notoriously mercurial drinking duo, hard-living journalists from a popular northern daily. We shall refer to them as the Gorgeous Blonde Hackette (GBH – see Avon and Somerset) and the Licensing Magistrate Retired (LMR – not to be confused with the old London and Midland Railway). The latter, a lady of a certain age, used to sit

on the Bench, is a prominent member of the community, and should really have known better.

Their performance during the following twenty-four hours was astonishing, and though some of the details have become a little blurred, the essentials will remain with us for years to come. As research companions they were invaluable, steeped as they are in the pub folklore of this wild and savage region.

With the GBH taking the wheel in a determined manner we struck out for the coast, and soon found ourselves in the seaside village of Low Newton.

🍺🍺 THE SHIP, Low Newton-by-Sea, Northumberland. GLL.

Facing the sea, in a quiet, open square of beautifully-restored Victorian fishermen's cottages, The Ship is an unpretentious and friendly local frequented almost entirely by regulars and seemingly untainted by tourism. Originally known as The Smack, and a pub for many generations, it is a fine place to refresh yourself after a bracing walk on the beach or along the clifftop paths. We drank Guinness, the GBH a chaste orange juice, the LMR two large brandies-and-soda.

★ THE OLDE SHIP, Seahouses, Northumberland. GGAR (FC, W, F, B, OP). Tel: 0665-720200. Alan Glen.

Although less than exciting from outside, The Olde Ship is an excellent example of a seaside pub, situated as it is in a working fishing port that doubles as a low-key resort in the short Northumbrian summer. It is still a *real* fishermen's pub but extends a warm welcome to all comers. The food in both dining room and bar is of the first order, the crab sandwiches are *sans pareil*, and the well-appointed bedrooms provide a good night's rest and comfort.

The main bar is decorated with the most comprehensive collection of nautical memorabilia outside the National Maritime Museum: binnacles, sextants, capstans, charts, figureheads, photographs and paintings of salts past and present, all are here, yet the effect is pleasing and not claustrophobic. The conviviality of the customers and the friendly efficiency of the staff make The Olde Ship one of the most pleasant places in which to linger in the North-East.

At the table next to us sat the young bloods of today, the old boys of the future, fishermen all, in 'ganzies' and seaboots.

At closing-time we rolled out of The Olde Ship, praises pouring from our lips, and weaved an erratic course along the strand to Bamburgh.

Under a huge sky, the sun was going down behind the Cheviot Hills which stood like sentinels in the west, guarding the roads from heathen Scotland. Its dying rays cast long shadows over the rolling farmland, fingering the reedy dunes, turning the massive walls of Bamburgh Castle a dusky pink, stretching out to the lonely and puffin-infested Farne Islands, where the myth of Grace Darling still lives, and falling into darkness behind Lindisfarne Abbey, its causeway veiled by the inky-black of the German Ocean.

Or words to that effect.

It was at opening time that we were careering down Coquetdale, through Rothbury and into the maze of lanes that led us to one of Northumberland's true and original gems.

🍺🍺 THE STAR, Netherton, Northumberland.
ORD (FC, I, E).

The Star was built in the early part of the century to cater for the railway. With this in mind, the present licensee's father bought the pub in 1917. But the railway never arrived, and nor, as far as The Star is concerned, did the modern world. A small hatch servery is the centre of operations, and conceals a secret snug or sanctum into which only the landlord's chosen few are granted entry. The GBH and the LMR were content to sit in the public room, perhaps not surprisingly reminiscent, in its Spartan furnishings, of the kind of old-fashioned waiting room to be seen in the 1930s film of 'The Ghost Train'.

The beer, to our southern palates, tasted like nectar – flat, still and nutty. It was Castle Eden Bitter, from County Durham, tapped from the cask (rare in these parts) by Vera, daughter of the ailing landlord, who had returned from her haberdasher's shop in Rothbury to man the helm at The Star.

We were not alone in our appreciation of the ale; standing next to us at the hatch was a bluff businessman, owner of a gleaming red Porsche which was disconcertingly parked outside the pub. A self-made man, he proved a fine drinking companion who had, in his turbo-charged perambulations of the country, become a devotee of good old, flat southern beer.

SECTION SIX

'Bloody waste of time trying to save Scottish and Newcastle Breweries,' he announced. (At the time, several Australian conglomerates were squabbling over this unimpressive company.) 'They've been a lost cause for years. I like to come here when I'm at home and have a chat to Vera, especially after a day like Monday. I set off to a funeral in Surrey, but I arrived twenty-three hours too late, and had to drink my way back up the A1.'

A very quiet place, The Star, and all the better for it. At nine in the evening, the old locals turn up for a couple, but as Vera points out, they tend to spurn her delicious ale, preferring instead McEwans from a can.

There is no accounting for tastes.

At 9 pm we arrived in Alnwick, seat of the Dukes of Northumberland; we were tired, hungry, bad-tempered and liverish. Some dinner and a few hours' sleep seemed like the best option open to us, but the LMR had her fourth wind and insisted on 'trying one or two' in a local that she knew in the town. Feeling that it would be churlish to refuse, we followed her nimble steps down the High Street.

🍺🍺 THE ODDFELLOWS ARMS, Narrowgate, Alnwick, Northumberland. LLL (B). Tel: 0665-602605.

The Oddfellows is a fine sporting pub, run by a fanatical fisherman who decorates the walls of his bar with well-tied flies and nymphs in glass cases and presides over a catch of like-minded and jolly regulars. The Vaux Samson flows like a river here and we all went swimming.

Time passed. After several other stops in Alnwick we entered a premises that shall remain nameless and soon fell into a deep and peaceful slumber at our table. We dreamt of limpid rivers, fast-food outlets, our mother's scent as she bent to kiss us goodnight, the roar of reversing Porches, flat, still, from the cask, the heavy hand of the law on our shoulders, the cold feel of the dock rail in our sweaty palms . . .

The landlord was shaking us awake.

'Can you please control your friends?' he asked. 'We like a bit of fun here, but this is ridiculous.'

We sat up. The noise was deafening. The regulars had

THE QUEST FOR THE PERFECT PUB

arranged themselves into rows as if they were on the terraces at St James's Park. They were chanting, clapping and crying.

'Come on my beauties, let's have it one more time,' they roared.

To our horror and dismay, the kitchen door flew open and like a pair of sleek performing seals, in perfect unison and harmony, the GBH and the LMR made their entrance, not walking, not running, not jumping, but cartwheeling with joyous abandon throughout the length and breadth of the room, scattering before them tables, chairs, glasses, brass bedpans and blunderbusses.

Gingerly we turned to the landlord.

'We are most terribly sorry,' we began, 'but do you realize who that is?' We pointed to the LMR with trembling fingers.

'No,' replied mine host, 'and I would be very interested to find out.'

'She is,' we informed him with the last vestiges of dignity that still clung to us, 'The Licensing Magistrate.'

He regarded us steadily.

'And I'm the Beverley Hills Cop,' he retorted and pointed to the door. 'OUT!'

It had happened at last.

In the full and certain knowledge that any attempt to control our companions would end in bloody and mindless violence, we stealthily extracted the car key from the GBH's abandoned handbag and slunk into the night, friendless, penniless and without a billet. The noise of breaking glass and the keening of sirens followed us down the street.

For those of a quieter and more reflective disposition than our friends, we can also recommend the following Northumbrian establishments.

THE BLACK SWAN, Seahouses, Northumberland. GLL (FC).
Animated local round the corner from The Olde Ship (see p. 147) and a good second choice if the latter is busy. There is a regular shuttle between the two, down a handy alley which serves as an alfresco loo for any of the old boys who cannot quite hold out in transit. Also, lively dominoes and cards, good Vaux beer and company. The ship's sign of the *SS Forfarshire*, to which Grace

Darling rowed out so heroically, was found in the cellar here and now adorns the wall after a long legal battle.

🍺🍺 **THE MASON'S ARMS, Norham-on-Tweed, Northumberland. ORD (FC, B). Tel: 0289-82326.**
Not far from Berwick and hard by Hadrian's Wall and the frontier, the Mason's is well worth a detour; a proper old-fashioned one-bar farmers' pub with a couple of bedrooms and fishing rights on the Tweed. The room is panelled with varnished wood, lit by a good log fire, and is filled in the evenings by villagers and agriculturalists supping up Vaux and Lorimer's ales. There is a kamikaze collie who sleeps most of the day in front of the darts board, and a courteous, though incomprehensible, elderly licensee. 'It's snowing in Scotland,' he said with relish. 'Let them keep it, we don't want it.'
   Scotland is 200 yards away.

From Norham, south to Wooler and Coquetdale, the road skirts the Cheviot foothills, through open, ancient country, wild but well-husbanded, with villages folded into the slopes.
   Rothbury is a fine little market town with its share of tourism, but still retaining its identity.

🍺 **THE TURK'S HEAD, Rothbury, Northumberland. ORD (FC, E).**
This is a primitive establishment, though housed in a fine, grey-stone, town building. The bar is entered through an old coaching arch, and is of the 'neglected minimalist' school, (see **THE RED LION, Llandovery**, p. 47). Regulars here tend not to go in the afternoons, when court is held by The World's Worst Impressionist, who props up the bar and downs Dryburgh's Heavy with intensity.
   He treated us to his entire repertoire, which was long and varied, and flawed only by the fact that all his many voices and impersonations were totally indistinguishable, and delivered in the kind of flat monotone that would make a British Rail announcer sound histrionic. He was apparently invalided out of ENSA, where he had opened shows for Vera Lynn and Anne Shelton, and mysteriously deported to Germany; here he lay low for nine months unaccountably and probably poorly disguised as a Lithuanian terrorist, before returning to his native

sod to bore the local residents out of the public bar. Now he has only strangers left to practise on. Check first if he is there; if he is not, The Turk's Head is the last remaining traditional pub in Rothbury, and worth a visit.

🍺 THE HOLLY BUSH, Tarset, Northumberland. ORD (FC).

Tarset is a tiny hamlet on the Greenhaugh road from Bellingham, or 'out by' as they say in these parts. The Keilder Forest and its attendant reservoir is as fine a piece of wild country as any in the land, and this little-known establishment is the most pure and unchanged place to drink. As you flash through Tarset (unmarked on most road maps) watch out for a row of terraced cottages, one of which is this totally unassuming little drinker with its simple room, plain tables, open fire, tiny bar and warm welcome.

🍺 THE JOLLY FISHERMAN, Craster, Northumberland. GLL (F).

Opposite the kipper-smoking sheds in a well-known fishing village, and with fine sea views, this is a firmly traditional local with a snug. It serves fabled crab and salmon sandwiches, best washed down with decent Tetley's. There are also games, a good salty feel and walks to Dunstanburgh Castle.

★ THE LORD CREWE ARMS, Blanchland, Northumberland. GGAR (W, F, B, M). Tel: 043-475-251. Peter and Pat Gingell, Alex Todd.

The village of Blanchland is inviolate, belonging as it does to the Crewe Estate, which is making sure that its heritage and tradition survive for as long as possible. Ten miles from Hexham, and surrounded by moor, forest and fell, it is an idyllic spot, at the centre of which stands The Lord Crewe Arms.

This imposing stone building was originally the dwelling of the Abbot of the 'white monks' of Blanchland Abbey and retains its medieval feel, with its vaulted Crypt Bar, wide stone staircase, four-poster beds, big, carved stone fireplaces, arched roofs and ancient gardens behind. Run now by the Gingells, escapers from Ilford, and the courtly Alex Todd, it is an excellent place to stay and walk the surrounding hills, eat from the simple and well-cooked menu (three-course dinner £12.50), or just drink in the bar, where the regulars' Northumbrian brogues mingle happily with the relaxed London drawl of the licensees' family and the clipped tones of the occasional nob putting up here during a shoot. Spontaneous sing-songs can break out at the most unexpected moments, and a highly enjoyable time is to be had.

Tyne and Wear

October 15th, Friday
Small Czech cars crammed with maps, fish and chip wrappers, aspirins and a week's worth of dirty socks do not make the ideal sleeping quarters. Or so we agreed when we awoke to find ourselves parked on a wind-lashed headland above Whitley Bay. We had, surely, come to the end of the road.

We gazed at ourselves in the 'vanity' mirror. The haggard, grey faces with haunted eyes that stared back at us seemed unrecognizable. Who were these two mad-looking men with the frightened expressions of pogrom refugees? Surely it was not us. We were poet-adventurers, gifted chroniclers of a nation's leisure habits, bold buccaneers on a voyage of discovery. We deserved better.

Scraping our faces with a penknife and sluicing them with harbour water, we attempted to restore a semblance of normality before setting off in search of some breakfast.

As the clock struck eleven we drove along the headland that overlooks North Shields harbour and staggered thankfully into The Wooden Doll.

THE QUEST FOR THE PERFECT PUB

🏠 **THE WOODEN DOLL**, Hudson St., North Shields, Tyne and Wear. GAR (F, M).
The Wooden Doll looks fairly unprepossessing outside; modern, grey brick, large car park, that sort of thing. Inside, the world is very different. There are two large rooms, both with good fires, and a grand piano, often used for all manner of live music from chamber recitals to modern jazz. There is also a covered verandah, and the windows are huge, giving truly panoramic views. On one side the still-bustling fish quay is directly below you, with porters trundling trolleys of fresh catch to the filleting wifeys in the sheds for packing and despatch. From the other window, cranes, lifting gear and gantries line the harbour sides and long stone jetties as far as the wide mouth, through which huge oilrigs are towed by tugs for maintenance. Inside our deranged cerebella flashed the perfect image of the industrial North-East, where the modern and the traditional exist in well-knit harmony through their common mother, the sea.

A pint of Hall's Harvest Bitter (we could also have chosen Marston's, Tetley's or Burton) and a half-pint jug of local prawns made an unorthodox but vitalizing breakfast, and the extremely friendly staff treated us as rational human beings. Our paranoia subsided, and we made a promise to ourselves to come back here on a musical evening to mingle with the varied company that favours The Wooden Doll.

Half a mile down the quay in a little side road by Smiths Dock sits a large Victorian building which houses the best pub in Tyne and Wear.

★ **THE WOLSINGTON HOUSE**, Burdon Main Row, North Shields, Tyne and Wear. GAR (M). Hugh Price.
The Wolsington is one of those pubs which you enter for the first time with a little leap in your heart, yet you cannot explain why immediately.

It was just before noon, and there were only a couple of old boys in, already involved in a serious relationship with their pints of 'broon'. Yet, as we gazed around the large, high-ceilinged Victorian interior, decorated in lead oxide red and varnished wood, we could sense that Things Happened Here. The bar is a solid mahogany affair down one side of the bare-boarded room. At the door end is a low stage and a

SECTION SIX

blackboard announcing the coming attractions of the next two weeks. Live music features strongly here – everything from folk to country to jazz and blues. The pub music circuit is strong in the North-East and the Wolsington obviously one of its leading venues. The rest of the room is filled with well-spaced tables, and we waited eagerly to see who would fill them.

Ten minutes, a pint of Hartley's SB (rare in these parts) and a streamlined salt beef bap later, our questions were answered. Through the doors streamed as good a cross-section of drinkers as you could ever find, to take their lunchtime pleasure here. Dockworkers young, old and retired; builders with a floury coating of plaster-dust; arthritic oldest inhabitants and reps and businessmen in suits were all suddenly at the bar for refreshment. The din grew to a roar, the air was thick with smoke and talk and the Wolsington humming. The whole transformation had taken less than a quarter of an hour.

The Wolsington is a pub for all seasons, since it is just as packed in the evenings, but with a different, younger, student crowd who come for the jumping music as well as for the good beer and cheap, simple food. Do not miss this one. It will surely, as it did to us, put the roses back in your cheeks.

Just across the river, but approachable only by a long detour round the estuary since they closed the passenger ferry, is South Shields. We made but a quick stop here at another dockside pub, **THE HOLBORN ROSE AND CROWN**, East Holborn, GLL (M), where again harbour life is thriving. The one big bar room is stacked with workers and others at lunchtime, enjoying the traditional atmosphere. Again, live music is a regular feature, and local bobby-soxers and hepcats frug wildly to the syncopated sounds, downing large quantities of Youngers and McEwans (not the stuff in cans).

Another fit of paranoia rocked us. What if the Licensing Magistrate retired (LMR – see **Northumberland**) had turned nasty and alerted the Alnwick Constabulary? What if we just jumped in the car now and floored it out of the county?

That is what we did, and we had nearly cleared the boundary when greed, hunger and duty swung us off the main road (A690) to the village of Houghton-le-Spring, where we ate a delicious lunch in **THE GOLDEN LION, The Broadway,**

GLL (F), which is a fine old three-roomed pub with a very traditional feel, flavoursome Vaux beers and a discreet landlady who asked us no awkward questions. Deservedly popular with ale enthusiasts and eaters, this is a very good place, and, had the hounds of hell not been at our heels, we would have lingered.

We crossed the county line into Cleveland at 4 o'clock.

Section Seven

The Yorkshires, Cleveland and Humberside

The Yorkshires, Cleveland and Humberside

October 15th, Friday Afternoon
Ever since we made the grave mistake of embarking upon this project we have come to treat as an occupational hazard the pub or real ale bore who beards you at the bus stop, drinks party, race meeting or Labour Exchange and tells you about the best boozer in the world at Little Sprocklington-by-Marsh, where Harry, Fred or Freda stands on his/her head and recites the Greek National Anthem in Yiddish before pouring you a pint of Thumpington's New Year Special Dark Triple Brewed Ten Star Willie Wangler, after which, he assures you, you won't be able to remember even your mother's Christian name and will acquire a strong desire to perform acts of sexual heresy with the entire female contingent of Militant Tendency.

The conversation usually goes like this:

Beer bore	(aggressively): I hear you're writing a book about pubs.
Author:	No, you've got the wrong person.
Beer bore:	Have you been to Yorkshire yet, cretin?
Author:	Oh, the pub book, Yes, sorry. Er . . . Yorkshire? Yes. Full of . . . people looking like Harvey Smith and Geoff Boycott and er . . . pubs –
Beer bore:	You're writing a book about pubs, dickhead, and you haven't been to The Monk's at Wilmington.

He pauses for effect and looks pityingly at author.

Author:	Well, when I say we haven't –
Beer bore	(raising his voice and speaking to congregation at large): This idiot is writing a book about pubs and hasn't yet set foot in The Monk's Bellyache at Wallerton. The Monk's is the best pub in the world. Before pouring you a pint, the landlord

THE QUEST FOR THE PERFECT PUB

removes one shoe, hits himself on the head, turns round three times, places a clothes peg over his left nostril . . .

You leave the bus shelter/party/funeral. You have no great desire to go to The Monk's at Willingham but feel that you have to, just in case it is a decent establishment. What you *really* want is a pint of British brewed lager in the nearest Chef and Brewer outlet, washed down copiously with a piece of centrally-fried Drovers Pie with seasonal accompaniments.

What you *really* want is to write: There are no pubs in Yorkshire.

And then go home and have a long, indulgent and uninterrupted sleep. So:

October 15th, Yorkshire. There are no pubs in Yorkshire.

October 15th, Friday–October 17th, Sunday
Well there are actually. Yorkshire is a large and unpleasant county which still greedily takes up much of northern England despite the valiant attempts of Messrs Heath and Walker to cut it down to size.

The best approach to the area is to speed through it on any one of the wide and attractive highways so thoughtfully built by the benign government in a vain effort to put some colour into the otherwise unremitting drabness of the countryside.

If you are mad or happen to live there, then we recommend the following hostelries in the order in which we visited them over the weekend, while en route to our cousin the blacksmith who, we were informed, lived in the middle of a field outside Malton.

★ **THE SUN INN, Knowle St., Stockton-on-Tees, Cleveland. LLL (FC, OP). Megan Walker.**
The Sun is undoubtedly the best pub in Cleveland and probably one of the best ten in the country.

Standing just off the High Street, it is the classic northern town drinker. It goes in for no nonsense or shilly-shallying. There are no food or games, no irrelevancies. A lone TV stands high on a shelf to be switched on only for the big fight. There is a large opened-up room with a fire and the classic interior decoration – dark red oxide and varnish. Any publican who

SECTION SEVEN

thinks he can improve on this particular colour scheme should be sent on a compulsory six-year government training scheme to try out his ideas in Arrowtown, South Island, New Zealand.

The Sun exists simply to provide drink to its clientele with the minimum fuss and the maximum efficiency. By six fifteen the place is filling up fast. The regulars have broken noses and few teeth. A Clark Gable of a barman, enigmatic, moustachioed, pads his territory like a panther, needing only a wink or a nod from a customer to spring into action. In the rare seconds when demand slackens he half-fills a series of pint glasses with ale and lines them up in trays along the counter. His technique is simple. You enter. Within moments he approaches.

'Two?' he enquires.

You both nod.

He dashes the other half of beer into the glasses, producing a beautiful frothing northern pint of Bass, one of the three best pints drunk by your intrepid authors during the course of their researches.

The barman is already back on duty, pacing up and down the long line of imbibers, alert, bright-eyed, brimming with brains. If he thought that anyone had waited more than thirty seconds for a drink he would retire to the cellar with a service revolver and do the decent thing.

You stand your ground at the bar. You watch with increasing adulation a great artist at work, enthralling a hard-bitten northern audience.

You drink half a gallon of beer in The Sun and thank the Lord that there still exists the occasional public house of this integrity and style.

🍺 THE TAN HILL INN, Keld, (off A66), North Yorkshire. GAR (I, B). Tel: 0833-28246.

The Tan Hill is famous as the highest pub in Britain. It stands 1,732 feet up in spectacular moorland, five miles from the nearest neighbour and eleven from the corner shop, and is often cut off for weeks on end in the winter. It was probably at its best during the tenure of Neil Hanson, who should know a thing or two about pubs after his long editorship of the CAMRA *Good Beer Guide*. An oasis for walkers, who in high season make short work of the Theakston's.

THE QUEST FOR THE PERFECT PUB

★ **THE STAR**, Harome, (off A170), North Yorkshire. GAR (F, E). Peter Gascoigne-Mullett.
Peter, once a monk at nearby Ampleforth, and his friend Tim like to play opera and the Mozart 'Mass in C Minor'. They have a pretty dining room where they produce scrumptious, yummy little dishes. They have taste and flair and a liking for port and brandy and gin and cider. They have a fund of funny stories and only visit London once a year when on the way to the airport to put a little burnish on their suntans. They run one of the better and more civilized pubs in North Yorkshire and we strongly recommend booking a table for dinner if you are in the Vale of Pickering.

🍺 **THE MALT SHOVEL**, Oswaldkirk, (off B1363 and B1257), North Yorkshire. GAR (B). Tel: 04393-461.
Ian Pickering ran the show here for eleven years and lent it his own ebullient personality. He was a hard act to follow and The Malt Shovel has not yet recovered from his decision to move on in 1988, much to the regret of his wide circle of admirers. It is now notable only as a building – a superb, early 17th-century pub in an appalling state of repair.

The owners, Sam Smith's, are a rare example of a brewer who can not only produce excellent beer but also care about their buildings, workers and customers. They have plans to restore The Malt Shovel this year and will probably do so with taste. There is reasonable hope that it will soon rise again to its former glory.

🍺 **THE BAY HORSE**, Masham, (off A6106), North Yorkshire. (GLL, OP).
On your way to the entry below, drop into this perfectly formed little pub, a shining example of a good simple pub in a particularly nice little town. It provides good service and conversation, roaring fires, tables set for a good-value lunch and reserved by enthusiastic patrons. Alcohol, too.

🍺🍺 **THE WHITE BEAR**, Masham, (off A6106), North Yorkshire. LLL.
Theakston's, like Sam Smith's, are an exemplary brewery, though now part of the dreaded Scottish and Newcastle combine. The White Bear is hard by the Theakston's offices, was

SECTION SEVEN

once the brewery tap, retains that atmosphere and is as good a place as any in which to have a session, particularly at lunchtime when a throng of Theakston's workers contribute to the happy rumble of ease and contentment.

🍺🍺 **THE BLUE LION, East Witton, (A6106), North Yorkshire. ORD.**
Yes, here's another. Sometimes you wonder where it will all end. In case you're still here, The Blue Lion has all the classic symptoms – a run down exterior, an ancient landlady whose family have been here since 1850, revolting beer, no trade to speak of, a beautiful but numbingly cold sitting room and an atmosphere that is worth travelling hundreds of miles, even to Yorkshire, to savour. The only excitement is provided by a highly strung terrier, the occasional shooting lunch and the twice-yearly Rent Dinner when the local tenants still troop from parlour into den, as though directed by Joseph Losey, to pay their dues to the Factor of the Marquess of Aylesbury (see **THE BRUCE ARMS, Easton Royal**, p. 229) who owns both pub and village and for whom old Bessie Fletcher has nothing but praise.

She shuffles about in The World's Oldest Overcoat, pours her murky liquid in the back and brings it through on trays, tends to her collection of houseplants and flowers from her loyal fans, and adopts a philosophical stance to the brutal modern world.

'I'm not busy any more. My regulars have all died off. The young? I don't have them. They say there's nothing to amuse them here and I say thank goodness for that.'

From The Blue Lion take the enchanting backroad to Caldbergh and the Scraftons across wild dale country alongside Carlton Moor. (Despite the prejudice shown against it by many travel writers, Yorkshire is for the most part devastatingly beautiful and full of modest, charming people!) Stop off at **THE THWAITE ARMS, Horsehouse**, GLL (FC), and experience one of the most unpretentious and enjoyable pubs in the district. There will be you, a fire and five farmers. That's all. Thank your lucky stars. After a suitable interval continue towards Kettlewell, where you turn right onto the B6160 to Starbotton.

THE QUEST FOR THE PERFECT PUB

🛢🛢 THE FOX AND HOUNDS, Starbotton, (B6160), North Yorkshire. GAR (B). Tel: 0756-76269.
The first of a row of three pubs in quick succession along Wharfedale; we cannot vouch for the new regime here, but suspect that it will be an even nicer place to stay than before, due to the addition of bathrooms and a refitted kitchen. The locals like it and so do we.

**★ THE GEORGE, Hubberholme, (off B6160), North Yorkshire. GAR (W, F, B). Tel: 075676-223.
John Frederick and Marjorie Foster.**
That irascible professional Yorkshireman J. B. Priestley used to rest his ample frame in a chair which still sits opposite the fire here. It is said that the sound he liked best was the ticking of the long-case clock, though it is likely that in reality this came a poor second to the sound of his own voice.

The George has a largely unspoilt flagged bar, comfortable bedrooms and an attractive dining room where they serve Aga-cooked, wholesome food. Being in a beautiful spot on the River Wharfe, it tends to be packed out with tourists in the summer months, when the locals desert the place. It is best visited in winter. The George is well run at present, though the character of the landlord is not to everyone's taste and there are vague rumours of a possible sale.

The pub was owned by the Church until 1965 and a candle burns on the bar during opening hours. On the first Monday of the New Year the locals bid for the renting of the surrounding grazing rights, and the last bid taken before the candle goes out is the successful one.

🛢 THE WHITE LION, Cray, (B6160), North Yorkshire. GLL.
The third in the trio of Wharfedale pubs and the highest, The White Lion is a couple of miles from Hubberholme (see above). It has recently suffered from a turnover of four licensees in three years, but is currently being pulled back into shape by the latest incumbent. It provides Goose Eye bitter from Keighley, an ancient, weighted Ring the Bull apparatus, simple food and a good welcome.

SECTION SEVEN

🛢 **THE LEEDS ARMS**, St Mary St., Scarborough, North Yorkshire. GLL.
On the South Cliff Esplanade in Scarborough, home of the popular dramatist Alan Ayckbourn, with a force 9 blowing off the sea and in driving rain, we opened the car doors to take the air and in doing so managed to lose the entire northern section of this book. With mixed feelings we watched it driven by the wind, past the Highlanders Bar and a line of residential hotels until, scattered in all directions, it disappeared into the night and out of our consciousness.

After two or three reviving pints of Bass in The Leeds Arms, an atmospheric, nautical, unspoilt town pub in the old quarter (not to be confused with the nearby Leeds Hotel), our great loss didn't seem to matter so much. It was only a book after all.

★ **THE MOORCOCK**, Langdale End, North Yorkshire. ORD (I, E). Maud Martindale.
We drove through the torrential night to Hackness and on a further two miles to Langdale End where we found this lovely old cottage with its fading sign, its irregular opening hours, its soft-lit parlour, cream walls and simple tables and chairs.

Miss Martindale pours the ale from bottles in the back – there is no draught beer – and proves to be a talkative soul full of wise advice, running as she does a pub as near to perfection as any in these pages.

October 18th, Monday
We began to rewrite the northern section. We had found our cousin outside the horse-racing centre of Malton. He lived on a diet of self-caught cod from Whitby, rabbits from the fields and sloe gin from the hedgerows, and we were happy to follow suit.

October 19th, Tuesday
By 11 am we had completed 240,000 words, and being informed that it was market day in town found ourselves minutes later, in the company of our cousin and his ladyfriend, drinking good Cameron's in the nicely traditional public bar of THE ROYAL OAK, Old Malton, LLL (FC), where they were warming up for the evening's disco featuring Mike 'Mid-Atlantic' Moron.

On Tuesdays and Saturdays there takes place in Malton the

second biggest cattle market in England, on which days it is the best town in Yorkshire for a lunchtime and afternoon pub crawl (followed closely by Thirsk, Beverley, York itself, Richmond and Ripon in that order). We can also recommend with confidence **THE BLUE BALL, LLL** – the snug is the place to drink – and **THE SPOTTED COW, LLL**, right on top of the market, with a particularly good tap room; both are classic and earthy watering troughs and full of character. Sadly the once decent CROWN (SUDDABY'S) and GREEN MAN HOTEL have been recently ruined, though the home-brewed beer at the former is still very good.

Malton is otherwise chiefly of note because Selina Scott's mother runs The Cosy Cupboard knickknack boutique in The Shambles, and there is always the forlorn hope of catching a glimpse of the long-legged television announcer and egghead and, if not, of being allowed to fondle one of her mother's home-knitted tea cosies.

October 20th, Wednesday
For one more day we rested outside Malton, storing energy for a visit to West Yorkshire, a largely built up area that inhabitants of the rest of the county urged us to bypass.

Dedicated truth-seekers that we are, however, we felt compelled to drive there to seek out some country pubs that had been spoken of highly. We endured four hours, our patience dwindling with the petrol, circling the conurbations of Leeds, Bradford, Dewsbury, Halifax, Wakefield and Huddersfield before giving up hope of finding the correct exits for our destinations. We are therefore unable to report first-hand on these establishments, but our information seemed sound enough to make a few bold type entries here, and to encourage you to try them.

🍺 **THE SWAN, Main St., Addington, (A65(T)), West Yorkshire. ORD (FC).**
The Swan is an unspoilt, four-roomed drinker with the traditional servery at its heart and first-class ale, including Draught Bass. Even the Stones is good here.

SECTION SEVEN

🍺 **THE TURKEY, Goose Eye, (off B6143), West Yorkshire. LLL.**
Serves ales from the nearby Goose Eye Brewery and is attractively situated in an old milling community. It was recommended by Lynn of Wilson's Restaurant in London, who is a Keighley girl and brooks no nonsense.

🍺 **THE GRINNING RAT, Church St., Keighley, West Yorkshire. LLL.**
Owned by five CAMRA members, with a central drinking area. It is safe to expect the best.

🍺 **THE BAY HORSE, Market Place, Otley, West Yorkshire. LLL.**
A simple and traditional pub of charm and personality.

★ **THE EAGLE, Skerne, Humberside. GLL (FC, W). Roy and Sylvia Edmond.**
That evening, suffering from motorway madness and bang on opening time, we tried the door of The Eagle at Skerne, a tiny village near Driffield. It opened first time.

There is no more calming establishment than this. Perfect peace enveloped us as we sat down with pints of Cameron's tapped from the cask in the back still room by Sylvia who, with her husband Roy, refused an offer by the brewery to have the place 'done up' and instead bought the pub in order to preserve it.

Two plain rooms, both with roaring fires, face each other across the passage, one with darts and dominoes and one reserved for conversation. There is no food. Sheila says simply, 'I don't like cooking so I don't cater.' The pub fills up later in the evenings with locals from Driffield, but we were happy to enjoy the sole attentions of Sylvia, her beer and her company.

We were beginning to recover from road fever and ordered a second pint. It occurred to us that The Eagle, with its lack of pretensions, was like so many good locals used to be ten or twenty years ago before the breweries ran amok amongst them. At that moment two couples in their late twenties and dressed up to the nines entered the premises. They peeked nervously into the room where we sat, and we witnessed the following exchange.

Girl 1:   'Oh dear, it's just like being in someone's house.'
Girl 2:   'Shall we pass?'
Sylvia: 'Hullo, what can I get you?'
Man 1:   'Is this all there is then?'
Sylvia (politely): 'And the room opposite.'
Girl 2:   'Let's pass.'
Man 2:   'Well . . . I don't know . . .'
Girl 1:   'Come on, let's go somewhere else.'
Man 2:   'Go on then.'
(Exeunt.)

We were still mulling over the implications of this interesting little vignette and failing to reach any specific conclusions when we reached Beverley, where we were to spend the night. Our first stop was at:

🍺 THE ROYAL STANDARD (DOLLY'S), North Bar Within, Beverley, Humberside. LLL.
The Standard has been in the same family for ninety-eight years and is very popular with the town's drinking fraternity. The highly traditional, front public bar is an especially appealing place to refresh yourself and is overseen by the dignified landlord, whose wife runs the more comfortable back lounge which attracts an appreciative crowd of younger drinkers. They were as happy drinking the Thorne's and Ward Darley Dark Mild at Dolly's as their contemporaries had been uncomfortable at **THE EAGLE, Skerne** (see above).

After this we had a predictably dismal experience at the Trust House Forte hotel in the main street, involving bad sandwiches and a gaggle of reps wearing soggy party hats. A once proud establishment, it has been turned into a nylon and teflon Hades. We immediately turned our attentions to one of the most brilliant operations we discovered anywhere, and our faith in the next generation was fully restored.

★ THE WHITE HORSE (NELLIE'S), Hengate, Beverley, Humberside. GAR (M). B. Thurnaby.
Nellie's is a multi-roomed, traditional town pub. It is lit entirely by gas lights, candles and fires. A well-manned central servery (with hatch) dispenses delicious Sam Smith's and there is table service to one or two of the warren-like rooms. Almost any night

SECTION SEVEN

of the week it is crammed with young people revelling in the atmosphere and each other's company, talking animatedly, laughing, joking, starting and ending affairs. Not a boor or lout in sight, they are an attractive assembly of locals, art students and Hullites; the general impression at Nellie's is that of being at a large, lively and well-organized party in a private house.

This impression is reinforced by the fact that upstairs in a long room and free of charge a band is playing on the gaslit rostrum, absorbed in their music, swaying instruments casting rhythmic shadows across a relaxed audience who sit at tables, talk, drink and tap out the beat. We have seen a few bands in our travels, but have not found a better place in which to hear them than Nellie's, and you owe it to yourself to pay a visit, either in the evening or at lunchtime when there are far less people and the excellent roast lunch will only set you back £2.

After a certain time of night the entrance is sensibly and genially manned so as to prevent overcrowding, and the attendance is never allowed to amount to an uncomfortable level.

Pub entertainment in general is a tricky affair, rather like pub food. There is a lot of it, but not all of it is very good and many are the pitfalls for the unwary. Yet sometimes even the most unpromising events turn out to be the most spine-tingling.

It was probably at the Burton Hotel in Kington, Herefordshire, that the lucky few first fell under the spell of 'Dan Cavan and his Radiogram', one of the most original and dynamic acts to grace any stage. Mr Cavan would arrive in a large and derelict station-wagon, execute a few slide turns in the car park and draw to an awesome halt. From the depths of his vehicle he would then begin to unload his precious cargo. First appeared a collection of battered black trap cases containing an immaculately maintained but archaic drumkit. Next, a large piece of furniture was lovingly eased onto a trolley and wheeled into the hall and onto the stage. Finally, a suitcase, decorated with peeling pictures of Torquay and the English Riviera, was deposited by the apparent wardrobe.

It was not until Mr Cavan had set up his drums that the true novelty of his act became clear. For the wardrobe was in reality a magnificent mahogany radiogram, circa 1957 or concurrent with the introduction of the long-playing record, the kind of item in which you could keep a well-stocked bar, several football trophies, a Ford Popular and seventeen racing-pigeons. The suitcase contained a pair of drumsticks and an unparalleled selection of dance-band records, featuring everyone from Henry Hall and Gene Krupa to the mighty Ted Heath Big Band itself.

The lights would dim and the crowd surge forward to the edge of the stage. Smiling beatifically, Dan would place a stack of records on the spindle and, holding the drumsticks in the manner of a man about to inflict permanent damage on a fried plaice, begin to play along with the records, pausing only to acknowledge the tumultuous applause that greeted him every time the platter came to an end and another plopped onto the turntable. Occasionally he would switch to brushes, stirring his snaredrum as though tending a cauldron of porridge. The women would go wild with emotion and even the men, who in those parts are often of the strong, silent type, could not remain unmoved. As entertainment it was *sans pareil* even, and possibly especially, when the needle became stuck in a groove and the Great Drummer, in the middle of a nifty paradiddle, failed to notice.

Alas, such gala events are all too rare nowadays, and while in principle there is nothing wrong with entertainment in pubs, a line should be clearly drawn between what is acceptable and what is not.

In the former category, there is a dramatic variance of taste across the country. North of the Trent, the trend is towards large bucolic comics of the blue variety, with a penchant for breaking into horrendous versions of Tony Bennett standards when the jokes fail, to the delight of the audience and the despondency of the accompanying trio. West of the Severn the hills are alive with the sound of singing cowboys, plumbers by day and Glen Campbells by night.

Very often the performances of both comic and cowboy are side-lined into large and cheerless function rooms, usually situated between the main bar and the lavatories, where their hard core of devotees is swelled sporadically by a passing trade in search of relief.

One of the few redeeming features of the Home Counties is that it is still possible to come across the occasional rhythm and blues band, the drummer of which has a sister whose ex-boyfriend's present wife once went out with one of the Groundhogs' roadies in 1972. Even the well-stocked jukebox is permissible and is still in evidence in roadhouses on the A3(T), frequented by burnt-out and tattooed motor-cyclists. But as a rule of thumb, if the jukebox selection includes 'Feelings' by Morris Albert, leave immediately.

What is unacceptable is the present proliferation of the all-singing, all-dancing, all-catering public house, something to be viewed with the deepest gloom by the serious social drinker. Egged on by recent changes in the licensing laws, the more ambitious landlord is undergoing a frightening metamorphosis into a sort of Frankie Vaughan-like spectre, complete with straw hat, cane, high kicks and gruesome smile, presiding rapaciously over his cavernous mecca of 'entertainment'.

In one corner the lights and bleepings of a thousand games create a dreadful aura that entrances and fleeces the villainous, the slothful and the unwell. On cue, as a metallic voice barks out a number, a bevy of 'hostesses' in Seventies-style satin hotpants and silver moonboots clump heavily across the revolving dance-floor bearing plastic presentation packs of reconstituted carbohydrate, indefinable, inedible.

In the Feature Area loutish youths loiter by the mill wheel and theme-stream, trading insults above the thud and thump of the sound system, while the DJ squawks incomprehensibly into the abyss, Godless, irredeemable.

Close by, where the motif of monochrome and ship's rigging gives way to a pinker, plusher and more feminine design, three women stand uncertainly before a man with side-whiskers and large biceps who climbs clumsily out of his spangled underpants. One of them is sick into her handbag.

Far off in a murky corner, wedged between a display case of condoms and a door designated 'Stags', stands The Man Who Ordered a Pint of Bitter in Funsters. Confused, ostracized, abandoned, he takes a last pull at his LowCal antipodean lager and heads warily for one of the fifteen heavily-guarded exits.

🛏🛏 THE WOODLANDS HOTEL, Great North Rd., Woodlands, South Yorkshire. GAR (B). Tel: 0302-723207.

The best pub in South Yorkshire is The Woodlands Hotel, an enormous, old-fashioned Victorian building in a staunchly traditional mining village. It has more or less everything you could want; cheap and clean beds, good-value, filling food, a comfortable lounge, and as its showpiece a rough and ready but heaving tap room, which is home from home to the locals, who have been using it as their social club for generations.

The Woodlands presents a vibrant and lively microcosm of a mining community and on no account should you fail to visit it, unless you intend to go in and say 'Hello, we're Rupert and Caroline. Could we please have two Spritzers and a couple of quiche and radicchio salads on Mummy's account?'

Other characterful and typical South Yorkshire pubs that merit your patronage include the following:

🍺THE CADEBY INN, Cadeby, South Yorkshire. LLL.
A good village pub that was once a farmhouse; lively, and noted for the quality of its Sam Smith's and Tetley's.

🍺🍺THE TERRACE, Kilnhurst, South Yorkshire. LLL (M).
Another throbbing little mining village local, modernized but still fun despite the Stone's bitter. Occasional live music.

🍺🍺THE WINNING POST, Moorends, South Yorkshire. LLL.
Huge pub that dominates the village. Inside there are many rooms, snooker, and friendly mining locals knocking back the Ward's and Thorne's ales. A centre for gamesmanship.

Section Eight

East Anglia

Lincolnshire and Cambridgeshire

October 21st, Thursday
We crossed the Humber Bridge and travelled through a hinterland of twisting lanes in search of The Green Man at Scamblesby, known locally as Wyn's Place, and one of the last old-fashioned drinkers in a county ravaged by a Stone's Brewery refit job which has turned all the pubs into dull replicas of each other.

Wyn's Place had long been a favourite haunt and what we discovered gave us one of the nastiest shocks of our tour. There on a ladder, bad-temperedly directing a gang of cowboy builders, was the proud new owner who had already stripped out the old interior, built a prefabricated extension and was now putting the finishing touches to his handiwork by smearing a thick coat of purple rendering over the old stone.

Neither of us even had the heart to enquire after old Wyn. Dispiritedly, we turned back to Louth and began an afternoon's listless drinking.

This is a strange outlandish part of Lincolnshire, where the coastal strip of mud and estuary gives way to the undulating Wolds, which is peopled by a strange variety of inhabitants who go about their business undisturbed by the prying eyes of tourists and property developers. Retired miners nurse their ruined lungs in the brisk salt air of Mablethorpe; prosperous 'gentleman' farmers nobly rip out hedgerows in celebration of the sugarbeet plant and the Euro-dollar; louche, one-eyed horse dealers cavort crab-like across ditch, dyke and furrow, their capacious pockets bulging and bloodstained.

At the heart of these badlands, and on the way to nowhere, lies the unspoilt town of Louth (known locally as Low-eth), a lost gem where Time lay down and died in 1962.

In the freezing Georgian marketplace there stands a Salvation Army band, lashed by a vicious wind straight from the Urals. Round the corner, the record shop displays yellowing posters of Billy Fury and Marty Wilde. Quite soon it will take delivery of its first consignment of 8-track cartridges. By the millennium it will be renting videos – Betamax videos. Opposite, in the Ron-dezvous Cafe, the *jeunesse dorée* sit out the dying months of the skiffle boom.

By six o'clock we had given up the idea of serious research for the day, so we hired a taxi and directed the driver to take us to the most typical and unexciting local pub in the area, in order to substantiate the theory that even in the dullest place there lies a hidden and secret half-world which only reveals itself to the dedicated observer.

Examples of The Obscure Local are to be found all over the realm except in the manicured 'countryside' which exists in the environs of Haslemere, Godalming, Pangbourne and other no-go areas. They are very often unremarkable at first sight, and the uninformed traveller may arrive, drink and depart none the wiser. It is only with the benefit of a little inside knowledge that these houses begin to unravel their hidden mysteries and depths. And what mysteries! What depths! It is the regulars – the characters – that lift these places onto a loftier plane. These ordinary men and women become the very protagonists of high drama as they strut and fret their hours upon the stage that is the public bar. Their strengths, lusts, repulsions and weaknesses are nightly played out till the curtain comes down at 11 o'clock (with twenty minutes drinking-up time) and the sound of the takings being counted rattles and thunders in their ears like the roar of a first night audience.

What tragedies, what falls from Grace are here for all to see. With what cavalier flourish will the spurned lover order a half of lager and a packet of cheese snips while, eyes smouldering like furnaces, Sharon, the unashamed Jezebel, moodily flips a Cherry B mat with her little finger and, harlot that she is, flips it again. With what eloquence will the barman mouth 'Sixty-seven p, cock, and you've still got one in from Thursday,' while dismissing from his mind the burning desire to tip the lager over the stupid bastard's bald head for cutting him out of the darts team after one lousy bad throw. With what strange medley of nods, winks and nudges does Roger the Rozzer suggest that

SECTION EIGHT

tonight's an 'off' night and that, for the price of a large scotch and pineapple, or two, he might just choose to forget Sunday's debâcle concerning the foreign bit of fluff, Bill Twilley and the unexplained haunch of venison. With what . . .

Tonight it happened to be at The Stoat and Toothbrush in a small village not far from Louth.

We ordered a perfectly adequate pint of Ruddles, sat near the fire, attuned our ears to the confused local dialect, an imaginative blend of East Anglian, Yorkshire and Romany, and began to observe the evening's strutting and fretting.

Quite soon, and without asking, a heavily-set man joined us at our table. First impressions led us to believe that he was blunt, truculent and drunk. These impressions proved to be accurate, but we persevered; his name was Norman, and in return for a pint he regaled us with unlikely stories of the Travelling People, and after twenty minutes he tried to sell us a horse.

The truth was that he had no horse to sell, though he did live in a caravan, and was bereft of both wife and belongings, since the former left him as a direct result of his selling the latter for a few pounds to a passing stranger. At nine thirty he invited us to his caravan to share his meat, something, he assured us, that he was never short of due to some dark and secret protection racket arranged with the local butchers. We declined the offer.

Norman introduced us to other leading lights assembled at the bar, including a dashing farmer known as Biggles after his flying exploits. Asked not to drive on the roads for quite some time by the local courts, Biggles, after six or seven pints, offered us hazardous and death-defying aerobatics in his light aircraft. It was pitch dark and again we declined the offer.

Attending the air ace was the exotic Fatima, an eastern princess cruelly snatched from her father's minareted palace by a blackguard of a husband who, it turned out, cared more for his EEC subsidies than he did for her. Her dalliance with the intrepid pilot had apparently led in the past to incidents involving her husband, a shotgun and the Cleethorpes constabulary.

Now we were deep into The Stoat's half-life.

The romantic situation was entangled; Biggles loved Fatima, who was worshipped from afar by an eccentric, senile millionaire. This gentleman was the black sheep of a nearby landed family, who was abandoned at the early age of 54 by relatives torn asunder by his libidinous escapades. He now resided at the Elms Private Nursing Home for Distressed Gentlefolk. This monotony was broken only by hopeless and unrequited sorties to The Stoat in pursuit of Fatima, and by disastrous and expensive visits to his private box at Market Rasen racecourse. He was distinguished by his cigar and the intricate filigree patterns of ash and gravy-stains on his waistcoat. Due to his lack of neck, many of his remarks appeared to be addressed to the carpet. This puzzled us at first, but we decided it was probably for the best.

At closing time we were privileged to be invited to sample the sophisticated delights of something called the Air Raid Shelter. We were then driven in an ageing Austin Princess without lights to a bleak and deserted airstrip between fields of rape and curly kale.

In a remote corner of the airfield, buried deep beneath an abandoned clutter of pillboxes, scrub gorse and rusting Nissen huts, a mountainous Neapolitan Signora presided over a ghastly den. Once past the tiny, frightened form of a bouncer, we were presented with a choice of bottled Newcastle Brown or flash-cooled lager that set the tastebuds racing. At a table, two lumpy and bespectacled girls stared desperately into their Pernod and blackcurrant. On the pulsating, strobe-lit dance-floor, the entire gay population of Lincolnshire pounded out its tribal rhythms. Neither of them could dance. In a candlelit corner, the Pilot and Fatima gazed longingly into each other's eyes.

Occasionally a hostile giant of a Welshman, recently expelled from an oilrig for intimidating behaviour, lurched over to the record booth and threatened the disc jockey. He wished to sing. Norman hit him. At the bar, the Signora was deep into the tragic tale of Vittorio. She done all this for him, she wailed, her only son. But Vittorio was not there. He never will be there. He hates Lincolnshire. He likes London. He is living with a Maltese waiter in Earl's Court. She begins to cry.

She guides you onto the dance-floor to comfort her. You feel like a tug pulling the Queen Mary out to sea. You are depressed. You wish to leave. From the constrictions of the Signora's huge embrace, you peer nervously around. Norman is beating up the bouncer in the passage; Fatima and the Red Baron are doing it

SECTION EIGHT

in an alcove; the millionaire has exited, a broken man, in an ambulance.

Five am. Finally, in your room at The King's Head in Louth you long for sleep, but somewhere in the bowels of the hotel an alcoholic woman is crying, and there is no-one to put her or you out of your misery. It is then that you ponder the reasons that brought you here. There are none. You diagnose in yourself the first stirrings of panic. Lincolnshire, you murmur, does not really exist; you are only imagining it in some dark and fevered dream . . . ah, but this is wishful thinking. You are deep in Lincolnshire and you begin to curse bitterly the Dutch cleverdicks who reclaimed it from the sea. You have made a mistake, possibly a series of mistakes. It is time to look for a proper job.

October 22nd, Friday
Under a watery sun that failed to dispel the yellow, gas-like fog rising from the Fens we drove mournfully through Sleaford, where a few minutes stop at THE MARQUIS OF GRANBY, GITS (W) failed to lift the gloom. We had only a few weeks to finish the book and several counties still to cover. We scrutinized the ferry timetables from Harwich to Gothenburg and wondered whether to emigrate or simply go to ground in Stoke Newington.

We drove on through a featureless plain of dyke, spinach and cauliflower. We held out little hope for The Saracen's Head, but how wrong we were.

★ **THE SARACEN'S HEAD, Saracen's Head, Lincolnshire. LLL (FC, W). Joan Moss and Albert Hill.**
From the A17 take the sign to Saracen's Head, just off the main road, and you will find the pub on a bend in the village street. The star has been awarded to the Saracen's Head for being a true oasis in the pub desert of Lincolnshire. Though merely a village local it has everything you need: table skittles, darts, splendid beef or cheese baps (35p and baked specially for the pub), excellent Greene-King and Abbot from the cask, very friendly and talkative locals and an harmonious team – 'I own the half with all the work and she owns the other half' – who know exactly what they are doing. 'We keep it simple and pay no staff.' Drink in the back tap room where the music-loving landlord asked the assembled company which tape they wanted

to hear. This sparked off a heated debate as to the difference between George Formby and Bing Crosby which was finally settled when an old gent in a flat cap pointed out that 'one of them was a bloody window-cleaner, but I can't remember which.'

As we reluctantly took our leave, the company wished us all the best and the landlady said that she hoped to see us again: 'You never know what you're walking into when you come in here.'

A few miles further down the A17 towards King's Lynn is the fossilized market town of Long Sutton where the customers in the Gents' Salon still ask for a half-crown trim and a packet of three for the weekend, Austin A40s and Wolsey Pathfinders line the marketplace and The Bull Hotel presents a perfect time-freeze circa 1927.

★ **THE BULL HOTEL, Long Sutton, Lincolnshire. GMTH (B, VE). Tel: 0406-362258. Mrs Mitchell.**
The 86-year-old Mrs Mitchell remembers when her parents took The Bull in 1921. They employed sixteen staff, including a boots and a bellboy, and sent a car to meet every train at the then thriving station. There were three bars in those days – one for the farmers, one for the 'inferior' smallholders and a cheaper tap room at the back for the labourers. Upstairs were salons, sitting rooms and a dining room with huge, panelled and hinged folding doors.

The extraordinary thing is that, apart from loss of the staff and the back bar, The Bull is almost completely unaltered in 1989, because in the face of increasing pressure for change Mrs Mitchell recently bought the hotel from the brewery and now offers a perfect 1920s atmosphere, including resident's lounge and original fittings. For £12 per night you can take advantage of an atmospheric, if creaky, bedroom and get a good breakfast. Alternatively, drop in at lunchtime, collect your Bass from the hatch/bar and park yourself in the dim red glow of the snug. In the front bar you may glimpse the ramrod figure of a middle-aged Guards officer, sitting over tea and cakes and pondering a world of slipping standards. Pinch yourself; you are not dreaming.

Mrs Mitchell will show you round her living museum with

SECTION EIGHT

glee and delights in the story of the aristocratic, then-chairman of Bass, who arrived at The Bull many years ago to survey it and commented merely: 'Burn it down.'

Mrs Mitchell pauses for dramatic effect: 'Then the stupid man took to the drink, and his beautiful wife followed him, poor thing.'

Mrs Mitchell is teetotal. She and her sister were sent to boarding school locally, where they were led to believe that the station of a publican was 'the lowest of the low,' and so when on holidays at home they used to 'walk past the public bar with our noses stuck up in the air. Nowadays, of course, you can't keep me out of the place.'

Lorries thunder past The Bull most days of the week, there is a little subsidence and the doors don't fit properly any more. A stop here is a unique experience in the modern world. Go now before any harm can come to it.

Our delight in The Bull buoyed us up through our next disappointment when we found the legendary Four Horseshoes at Throckenholt to be boarded up, abandoned, forlorn. We sought solace in the next village at the SWAN INN, Parson Drove, GITS, an old 17th-century inn where the snob, libertine and diarist Samuel Pepys stayed with some cousins, 'poor sad wretches', in 1663, groped the barmaid and got bitten by gnats. Here you may play bar billiards and listen to Ken at the organ on Saturday nights.

Fenland is a foreign country. We decided to return to England and face up to our responsibilities. As dusk gathered we sped through the desolate landscape, where every tree is a landmark, every cottage huddles behind a stunted screen of windbreak, every signpost is unintelligible, and mad old men on bicycles weave and mutter their way homewards for a supper of damp vegetables. The towns and villages came and went; March, Chatteris, Ely, and so to Cambridge, where the afternoon drinking laws were being abused by gangs of shaven, bullet-headed oafs shouting obscenities at each other and diligently pushing up the market value of Carlsberg shares; they were probably reading Classical History or Mediaeval Mandarin. We left them alone, and went to discover the best pub in town.

THE QUEST FOR THE PERFECT PUB

▯▯THE FREE PRESS, Prospect Row, Cambridge. LLL (W).

Chris and Debbie Lloyd are people of taste; they have taken what was a good, old-fashioned, street-corner local and have improved the facilities without disturbing the timeless atmosphere. It is very popular with both Town and Gown, with its two, small, panelled bars and the minute 'Lloyd Room', in fact the old snug, into which they once crammed fifty-nine people for a bet.

Chris Lloyd is a rowing coach and runs his own boat club from the pub; don't let this put you off, since the company is very mixed, and the Greene-King beers of high quality. The food is reputedly good, though simple, and the welcome warm.

On a trip to Sussex some years ago, Chris Lloyd discovered the following inscription on the wall of an old house. Though its origins are unknown, it seemed to him and to us to be such an accurate description of the evils of drink that it must have been written by someone who had been there.

> ### DEGRADATION OF DRUNKENNESS
> *There is no sin which doth more deface GOD'S image than drunkenness. It disguiseth a person and doth even unman him. Drunkenness makes him have the throat of a fish, the belly of a swine and the head of an ass. Drunkenness is the shame of Nature, the extinguisher of reason, the shipwreck of Chastity and the murderer of conscience. Drunkenness is hurtful to the body, the cup kills more than the cannon, it causes dropsies, catarrhs, apoplexies, it fills the eye with fire, and the legs with water and turns the body into an hospital.*

The Lloyds also own **THE CAMBRIDGE BLUE** in Gwydir St., GLL, but found the stress of running two pubs was affecting their sanity. They have now leased The Cambridge to Banks and Taylor, who run it under a manager. It is a similar establishment, tucked away in a backstreet and worth a visit for its solid, old-fashioned feel.

Cambridgeshire, we found, is not a rich pub hunting ground, but places we have enjoyed recently including the following:

SECTION EIGHT

🍺🍺 **THE TICKELL ARMS, Whittlesford, (off A505), Cambridgeshire. GAR (F, E, OP).**
A notice on the door warns that lefties, men in earrings and collarless shirts etc are refused entry, which sets the tone for this most eccentric of establishments, run with a regal petulance by Mr de la Taste Tickell. He is much in evidence, shouting down a portable telephone, feeding the fish in his beautiful garden, and throwing out unwanted customers to the deafening accompaniment of 'The Ride of The Valkyries'.

This rose-covered cottage does not look like a pub, and is easy to miss the first time you go. If you do not conform to the landlord's code it may also be the last time. The food is excellent, though expensive, especially after 2 pm when the prices rise by 33⅓ per cent. The Tickell is not to everyone's taste, but has a wide range of devotees, including undergraduates from the varsity.

🍺 **THE VICTORIA, Ouse Walk, Huntingdon, Cambridgeshire. GLL.**
Good oasis in a town otherwise best avoided by the pub lover.

🍺🍺 **THE QUEEN'S HEAD, Newton, Cambridgeshire. LLL.**
Up the road from The Tickell Arms, Whittlesford (see above) but a very different kettle of fish. It is quiet yet convivial, and attracts a good cross-section of customers. Adnams beers from the cask, simple rooms, games and decent food.

🍺 **THE WHEATSHEAF, Church St., St Neots, Cambridgeshire. GLL.**
A thriving little town local which has a hot darts team and a friendly clientele who make free with the Greene-King beers.

🍺 **THE SHIP, High St., Chatteris, (A141), Cambridgeshire. GLL.**
Pleasant, unpretentious town local with good atmosphere.

183

Norfolk

The way most Norfolk people see it, there is no life outside the boundaries of their beloved county. One of the authors once had a surprising conversation with the mother of a local girl who had recently become engaged.

'What wonderful news,' he commented. 'I expect you're very happy about it.'

'Happy of course, but what a tragedy it is that Tom comes from such a very long way away.'

'I had no idea,' said the author. 'Where does he live? Australia? Addis Ababa? Greenland?'

'No, no. Nowhere like that,' replied the agitated parent. 'Nottinghamshire.'

Sometimes this slightly restricted vision of the world can become mildly exasperating. On a day, for example, when the leaders of the superpowers might be locked in a crucial Summit on disarmament in the Kremlin, the *East Anglian Daily Press*, the only newspaper allowed into any self-respecting Norfolk household, is likely to lead with a story headlined: 'Beet Prices May Rise In Autumn'; and it is this topic that will certainly give rise to the liveliest debate at the Dog and Dwarf that evening.

On the other hand, Norfolk these days has a refreshingly classless society, despite the presence of many old-established and hugely rich landowning families. Both the fathers and sons of such families, quite as in-bred and half-witted as the maddest of their tenants, can often be found sloshing down vast quantities of Norwich Bitter in the public bar with their farm workers. They bark for more beer in the same high-pitched accent that actors employed by the BBC find so hard to imitate. They cross at a tilt from table to bar in the same strange Norfolk gait – a curious, sidestepping, semi-circular movement, legs bowed at the knees as though sitting astride a tractor seat, one foot being dragged a short distance behind the other.

We discovered the reason for this ungainly form of locomotion when invited to a 'party' on the marshes near Morston. As we approached with some apprehension the throng of revellers on the wind-swept wastes, we formed the impression that they were involved in some odd sort of ritualistic dance. Only when near at hand did we realize that each man and woman, as they ate, drank and made merry, were with enormous relish making arc-like, sweeping motions with both feet into the rank and foul-smelling mud, so that he or she, as the hours passed and the bottles were emptied, sank deeper and deeper into the repulsive slime.

This explains a piece of dialogue that may be heard in pubs all over Norfolk – for, failing the marsh, any old ploughed field will do – at any Sunday lunchtime session:

'Looking a big ragged, boy. Good do last night, was it?'

'Bootiful do, boy. Didn't leave till gone three. Right up to the ears I was.'

Since the building of the M11 and other sinister developments, old Norfolk is sadly changing fast and for the worst (see **Gloucestershire:** *Weekend Man is Coming*, pp. 13–14). However, it is still one of the nicest counties in England, with a strong sense of its own identity, and, as we discovered, no shortage of good pubs.

🍺🍺 THE 4.30 pm BR LIVERPOOL STREET–CAMBRIDGE–KING'S LYNN SPECIAL. LLL (E). Fridays only.

Undoubtedly, the finest way to arrive in the locality is by means of the 4.30 from Liverpool Street to King's Lynn on a Friday evening. On one such journey, we were surprised to witness a near-riot when the barman failed to open his shutter at the precise moment that the train left the platform. The regulars, staid and retiring civil servants, sprang from their reserved seats and began battering the grille with their furled umbrellas.

'Show yourself, you bastard,' shouted a senior female employee of the Foreign Office, 'or may God rot you in your horrid little nylon socks!'

For it must be said that the 4.30 from Liverpool Street to Lynn has the finest and most convivial Moving Bar in the country. Particularly stirring is the first leg of the journey, between London and Cambridge, when brilliant and comely female students from the University may be cross-examined at close quarters as to their stance regarding the poetic validity (in the French translation) of the British Rail timetable.

October 26th, Tuesday–October 29th, Friday

★ **THE LORD NELSON**, **Burnham Thorpe, Norfolk. ORD (EE). Les Winter.**
The modest Rectory where Horatio, Admiral Lord Nelson, spent his childhood was demolished in 1802, three years before his death at Trafalgar, and though eight members of the Nelson family are buried in the grounds of All Saints church, and the lectern is made from a piece of *The Victory*, for the hero himself there was no last journey home to the village of Burnham Thorpe. Although Nelson begged in his dying moments to be buried under his native sod, his King and government honoured him with a State funeral and he was laid to rest in St Paul's.

One man alone has kept the great sailor's beacon burning in recent years with a fierce loyalty and an admirable scholarship that belies his ruddy and rough-hewn appearance; he is Les Winter of The Lord Nelson public house, one of the most individual and unusual landlords in the country.

We entered Burnham Thorpe on a blustery noontime with a Force 8 gale blowing in our heads, the result of an eventful but injudicious afternoon's drinking at Fakenham races.

We were looking forward to meeting Mr Winter and perhaps penetrating his reputedly crusty exterior; so our hearts sank when we saw two carloads of unacceptable-looking tourists filing through the door of the pub. All seemed lost; we were too late. However, still curious and anxious to do something drastic to our hangovers, like start work on the next one, we entered The Lord Nelson.

The mood almost immediately brightened; though we stood in a dark corridor, from inside we could hear the braying tones of people demanding bar snacks and exotic cocktails, and a quiet but firm Norfolk-tinged voice explaining that though he did not, regrettably, supply these items himself, they were to be had in abundance at The Captain Sir William Hoste in Burnham Market, if his visitors cared to turn left at the end of the village. We shrank back against the wall as the disgruntled

SECTION EIGHT

motorists left the premises, muttering darkly about the primitive standards prevalent along the eastern coast, and when we entered the room a few seconds later our change of mood from sullen apathy to one of pure delight was complete.

It is a small, square, brown room with a sink and rows of beer glasses under a window. At the rear is a door which leads to the back cellar where Les keeps the Greene-King beer he is so proud of. Two high-backed settles form a screen between the sink and the rest of the room. There is no bar. There are plain wooden chairs and three or four small tables with, instead of ashtrays, hand-written notices requesting No Smoking; to one of these the landlord had returned and resumed the interrupted game of dominoes he was playing with his small granddaughter. No-one else was in the room.

The walls are completely covered from cornice to skirting board with all manner of Nelson memorabilia: oils, watercolours, etchings, prints, press cuttings, contemporary drawings; an astonishing collection of items, of which Les is justifiably proud, some acquired by the publican and many donated by other Nelson buffs, and examples of which are reproduced in his scholarly and entertaining book *Hero's Country: Nelson and the Norfolk He Knew* (five editions), available on application to the author.

Showing due respect, we timidly requested a pint from the burly, weatherbeaten figure in the fisherman's jersey, upon which he disappeared into the cellar to tap our beer from his cask. Once our courage was restored, we began to ask him about his collection. Slowly his demeanour softened as he told us about the correspondents worldwide who had contributed, the pieces he himself had discovered, something about the life of the village at the turn of the 19th century, and the dangerous concoction of spiced rum known as 'Nelson's Blood' which he occasionally inflicts on favoured visitors.

Over the second drink, in which Les joined us, he relaxed and became a fascinating companion in a long and wide-ranging conversation interrupted only by the high-pitched ravings of an insane, but harmless gamekeeper from a nearby stately home who had strange obsessions with the Russo-Japanese War of 1904/5, quadrophonic sound and country-and-western, in no particular order, and who entered shouting for rum-and-black just as proceedings were hotting up.

THE QUEST FOR THE PERFECT PUB

When Les Winter and his wife took over the Lord Nelson some twenty years ago, along with the adjoining Post Office and Stores, it was with a vision in mind. Being a far-sighted man, Les was ready for the inevitable modernization and rationalization attitude of the breweries to their tied pubs. So when he was offered the expected deal – 'move out or modernize' – he had his answer. He bought the pub. It is now safely in the hands of an inspired English eccentric. Not only does the Nelson sell few spirits, its beer is quite superb, crystal-clear yet with a deep, mature, nutty flavour. There is no particular secret. 'I try to keep the cask for three months before I sell it,' Mr Winter admits freely. 'There's people say you can't keep bitter, it goes off. That's nonsense if you look after it properly; it's a living substance, like wine, and it goes on maturing.'

It must be said that Les Winter is no *faux naif* or phony primitive. He has appeared on radio and TV several times and has been frequently interviewed, notably by fellow Nelson scholar and pub connoisseur Tom Pocock; yet he has not become a pompous, 'professional Norfolkian', puffed up with his own importance. He is a genuinely interesting and good-hearted man running a minute but perfect jewel of an enterprise, and a visit to his little Empire and Shrine cannot be recommended too highly.

Les Winter was a wise man to hock himself to the hilt in order to secure his pub, and he is all too aware of what may lie in store for a large number of pubs in Norfolk, which were bought in 1988 from Watneys Norwich Brewery by a consortium known as Brent Walker Leisure. Brent Walker are not even a brewery, but a 'leisure group' with no proven feel for the needs of a community, and fingers in a great many pies.

The coast road from Hunstanton to Cromer is full of bowdlerized Innes. But inland, in the intricate network of lanes which is one of Norfolk's great surprises (you can cross from one side of the county to the other hardly seeing a main road), there are still a few untouched houses, sometimes presided over by a landlady with second-generation credentials, an old tradition and customers who have been regulars for fifty years or more. How long will they resist the 21st century tactics of the marketing yobbos with their Costa del Scampi ideals and their rhyming slang culled from 'East Enders' and 'Minder'?

SECTION EIGHT

From The Lord Nelson we made our way to the rural retreat of a well-known local farmer and bon viveur. While he spent four days and nights dancing alone in the flicker of a strobe light adorned in a series of brightly-coloured and increasingly improbable wigs, we quietly motored around his county gleaning the information which we present for you below.

🍺🍺 THE ANCHOR, Morston, Norfolk. GLL (FC).

Doris Temple has run The Anchor at Morston since the death of her mother Anne, who was landlady since her husband took the pub over ninety years ago. Morston does happen to be on the coast road, but Doris makes no concessions to that. In fact the brewery built her a nice new lounge bar extension a few years ago, but she refuses to use it except under duress. 'It doesn't have the same atmosphere somehow,' she says, and prefers to operate her tiny public bar with its simple fittings and open fireplace, where in winter the old regulars can warm their bones, talk, drink and generate a fug that you would need a Stanley knife to cut.

She loves to chat, but the ship she runs is a tight one; she'd rather tell someone to leave than make money out of them if she doesn't think they'll fit in. Les Winter of **THE LORD NELSON, Burnham Thorpe** (see above) likes to tell the story of two sophisticated young things turning up in a roadster not so long ago, entering The Anchor and asking for gins and tonics; naturally Doris left her seat by the fire, came behind the bar and served the drinks.

'I say,' came a plaintive voice. 'Have you got a slice of lemon?'

Doris gave the customer a look mildly described as old-fashioned, and replied that they were in a pub, not a green-grocers. The young things drank their drink quickly and quietly and left.

🍺🍺 THE CHEQUERS, Gresham, Norfolk. GLL (FC).

There is a well-known and ancient boys' public school at Gresham, but the village is delightfully rural, and in The Chequers boasts one of the simplest yet most enchanting locals in East Anglia. Arriving as your intrepid reporters did at 11 am on a monsoon of an autumn day, soaked to the skin between car and bar, it seemed like a true haven, the kind of place you could spend a wonderful lost day of beer and conversation.

THE QUEST FOR THE PERFECT PUB

The lights are on in the tiny front bar, and through a doorway to the side can be seen another room, dim yet hugely inviting, with a large square table taking up most of the space, next to a promising-looking fireplace. On the counter are two baskets of blackberries, picked that morning by Winnie Lawes' daughter and still wet with rain and dew. Behind the bar Mrs Lawes is giggling to herself as she tries vainly to pour lager from a tap that won't work.

'Just don't want to oblige me,' she mutters, shaking her head.

Eventually, after much discussion, it is agreed that the beer would flow more easily were she to turn on the gas tap; more laughter, and we concur that if it needs gas it's not proper beer, settling instead for a very decent pint of Courage Directors, a maligned but generally consistent beverage.

There are two regulars in the bar this morning (and probably every morning from about 10.30); a red-faced man is chasing Scotches with half-pints, still recovering from the trauma of last night's exploding TV set.

His companion, an interesting looking greybeard with a healthy thirst for Directors and a sharp tongue, suggests that it was his own fault for watching stupid, daft quiz shows when he should be in The Chequers making conversation. There is a moment's silence of solemn agreement, and then the talk passes on.

This is a quite excellent establishment, where you will not find the hot basket lunch that you may desire (though we doubt that if you did you would have persevered thus far with this book), but you will find the warmest of welcomes, very good beer and entertaining company.

★ **THE BELL**, Brisley, Norfolk. GLL (FC, E).
Ada Griggs.
The third, and possibly the greatest, of these venerable *grandes dames* is 88-year-old Ada Gricks, who keeps what must be the finest of all unspoilt village pubs in Norfolk, The Bell at Brisley.

Ada's father held the licence before her, and the ancient building was the birthplace of the Reverend Richard Taverner, the 16th-century translator of the Bible, who fell foul of Elizabeth I and spent the customary uncomfortable spell at Her Majesty's Pleasure in the Tower of London.

Once there were four pubs, a shop and a Post Office in

SECTION EIGHT

Brisley. Now there is just The Bell. Overlooking a large tract (170 acres) of common land on the edge of the village, the pub sign faded, not a car in the forecourt, with three old-fashioned rooms passed over by the years, The Bell represents a perfect time-capsule of the 1930s. It is a reminder of what the average Norfolk pub must have been like two generations ago.

Hurry there quickly while you can, for sadly the modern world is encroaching apace. Ada's husband is none too well, and the ubiquitous Brent Walker have got their hands on the freehold.

The Bell is doomed, and with it a way of Norfolk life. The Griggs are the most charming people to talk to and know all there is to know about the area. They remain stalwart and unmoved by the demands of current taste.

'I don't encourage the young,' Ada says. 'I don't want 'em. I've got no phone, no food, no entertainment at all, so there's nothing for 'em here.'

But there Ada is wrong. For The Bell offers sanctuary to anybody, young or old, who wishes to drink quietly and unmolested by the fripperies and irrelevancies of the ghastly 'leisure industry', in a pub where the only distraction from the glass is the art of gentle conversation.

THE BULL, Shire Hall Plain, Great Walsingham, (B1388), Norfolk. GAR (W). Tel: 0328-701340.
This is a friendly and relaxed establishment in a village of shrines and pilgrims, run with a flair and warmth that makes you want to stay all night. We were amazed to find on entering the small back room (recommended: striplights, lino, easy access to the well-stocked bar) a clutch of five fat and well-watered gay clerics, hemming in at a table a twittering and obviously senile old lady. We watched, fascinated, as one of the priests guided, oh so gently, her pen hand towards a cheque book which was lying open in front of her. This would be a good place to put up for the night, be you religious, light-footed, both, or neither.

THE OLD BREWERY HOUSE, Market Square, Reepham, (B1145), Norfolk. GMTH (B). Tel: 0603-870881.
The Brewery House is an outwardly beautiful old hotel in this miniature market town where, were it not for the litter of cars in

the square, it would still be possible to imagine the butcher, the baker and the candlestick-maker going about their business before the days of Dewhursts, Mother's Pride and the Central Electricity Generating Board.

Arrive on a Wednesday morning – market day – when you can buy excellent local produce and fish from Lowestoft. After these exertions, slip quietly into The Old Brewery House for a taste of the Rapier Pale Ale, brewed in the town. Take note of the untrustworthy-looking character who will be lurking in the darkest corner of the already dark Brewhouse bar.

This character can be seen on market day in any town in England and Wales, but is particularly visible in East Anglia, the Welsh Marches (see THE BLUE BOAR, Haye-on-Wye, p. 55), the West Country and Cumberland. He has instant recall for which day is market day in every town in a fifty-mile radius and is thus effectively active, or inactive, from 11 am till 11 pm six days a week.

Whether he is spied in Monmouth or Carlisle he is to all intents and purposes the same man. He is between 30 and 40, dark-haired, good-looking in a shifty sort of way, and wears an old blue corduroy jacket, patches at the elbows, a red-spotted neckerchief and a ring in one ear. He has an eye for the girls. He drives a battered old Minivan and lives in a corrugated iron-roofed cottage full of other people's shotguns, fishing rods and tools. His constant companion is a disreputable mongrel, with corkscrew tail, that has fathered many an unwanted litter. He slips lithely into the scruffier 'antique' shops, hoping for a piece of the action, any action – a dodgy deal or two, a possible piece of thieving, the chance of getting a bit lucky with the owner's wife. Then it's back to the Old Brewery House for an innuendo, a joke or two and another pint of Rapier.

THE EARLE ARMS, Heydon, Norfolk. LLL (FC).
A perfect example of an unpretentious, well-patronized local, featuring striplighting, lino, and some of the best baps and cask beer (Adnams and Greene-King) in Norfolk. Heydon is an unusual village, which sits at the gates of a big house and is unsuitably pillaged with monotonous regularity by many a charmless BBC TV producer for expensive and badly-made costume dramas which are scandalously financed from the

public purse and which no one in their right mind would ever consider watching.

🍺 **THE WALPOLE ARMS**, Itteringham, Norfolk. LLL (FC).
The locals may not welcome you with open arms here, but persevere, for it is worth it. The public bar is as snug a room as any on a winter's night, the landlady is not as fierce as she pretends, and from the pool-room comes the faint thud of a jukebox that features expertly chosen and ancient rock 'n roll, much appreciated by the local youth.

🍺🍺 **THE HARE AND HOUNDS**, Baconsthorpe, Norfolk. LLL (F).
A successfully de-modernized, well-run local with good beer and food, patronized both by flat caps and marauding bands of Simple Simons (see **THE BUCKINGHAMSHIRE ARMS** below). The walls are stripped back to the brickwork, and good country furniture sits on the flagstones. The Woodford's Hobson's Choice bitter is brewed especially for the pub by the nearby Spread Eagle Brewery at Erpingham.

🍺🍺 **THE BUCKINGHAMSHIRE ARMS**, Blickling, (B1354), Norfolk. GAR (F, B). Tel: 0263-732-233.
The Bucks is a handsome and substantial building owned by the National Trust and opposite Blickling Hall, the fine Jacobean property. It offers excellent beer, decent bar food, an overpriced restaurant, and a few charming rooms, which do not come cheaply but are a pleasure to stay in. The ample figure of Nigel Elliott runs the place with skill and taste, and if you happen to need to get married in a hurry near the premises he will lend you a stiff collar and studs.

Infested on summer weekends by tourists, The Bucks is also the HQ of the thriving Norfolk branch of the 'Prancing Peter and Drawling Damian Self-Appreciation Society'. It is best visited on a winter's night in the week, when either of the attractive bars are good for a session.

🍺 **THE KING'S ARMS**, Blakeney, Norfolk. LLL (F).
A lovely pub on a quiet evening in winter. In the summer months and at weekends The King's Arms, due to the volume

THE QUEST FOR THE PERFECT PUB

of trippers, turns itself into an uncomfortable fast-food factory.

🍺 **THE BLUEBELL,** Langham, (B1388), Norfolk. GLL (FC).
The Bluebell is a first-class, well-run little local that has been in the same hands for a long time and draws a lively local trade. The licensees are shoe fetishists.

🍺 **THE LIFEBOAT,** Thornham, (off A149), Norfolk. GAR (F, B). Tel: 048526-236.
Lying apart from the village at the edge of a salt marsh, this is a well-documented pub, a nice place to stay, with huge fires in winter, Adnams, Rayments and Greene-King beers. It also boasts a decent restaurant which is packed in summer. You may find that the courtyard and garden feature too many children.

🍺 **THE JOLLY SAILORS,** Brancaster, Staithe, (off A149), Norfolk. GAR (F).
Once a brilliant waterside pub, The Sailors is now mainly of interest to anthropologists for the fine parade of Jumped-up Jonathans and Vamping Vanessas who unfortunately take it over at weekends and make displays at each other. Go there under sail and on a weekday. The food can be excellent and Greene-King beers make their usual solid showing. You can play tennis on their hard court or walk restoratively along the dunes and flats to Holkham.

🍺 **THE OSTRICH,** Castleacre, (off A1065), Norfolk. GLL (F, B, M). Tel: 07605-398.
Note the street-corner loiterers in a village with a reputation. The pub itself is on the green, has enterprising food, Greene-King beers, two working fireplaces and occasional live folk, jazz and blues.

★ **THE HORSESHOES,** Warham, (between A149 and B1105), Norfolk. LLL (F, M). Iain Salmon.
A small, unspoilt, attractive village local, serving excellent Woodforde's and Abbot from the cask and with a loyal band of regulars. The food is unpretentious, honest and reliable. There are two rooms to drink in and the further one, on the last

SECTION EIGHT

Thursday in every month, is taken over by a changing line-up of folk musicians (fiddles, pipes, drums and strings) featuring a girl who sings like an angel. Visit also on a Saturday evening when the piano takes over and the heaving crowd threatens to burst out of the walls. A convivial evening's entertainment is assured.

🛏 **THE CHEQUERS, Binham, (B1388), Norfolk. LLL (B, M). Tel: 032875-297.**
Cosy, simple village local offering decent food, comfortable beds, good fires and Bateman's and Woodforde's beers. Quite a good crowd takes advantage of the weekly jazz and folk features.

🍴🍴 **THE GREYHOUND, Tibenham, (off B1134), Norfolk. LLL.**
Tucked away in a tiny village in South Norfolk, this is a well-run, well patronized and idiosyncratic establishment with two rooms, fires, Woodforde's K9 and a lot of character. It is well worth a visit except at lunchtimes Mondays to Fridays when it is closed.

🍴🍴 **THE CHERRY TREE, Harleston, (A143), Norfolk. LLL (FC).**
A stone's throw from the Suffolk border, as the Adnams beer testifies, this is the best pub in the area and is sympathetically run. The lounge bar caters for all comers, but it is the separate public bar that should be visited, packed as it is with jocular locals necking back the pints like there was no tomorrow.

Suffolk

Suffolk is still by the skin of its teeth hanging on to its identity and unspoilt image. The atmosphere is relaxed and unhurried, and the indigenous farmers remain very tolerant towards the large number of immigrant drop-outs whose buses, ambulances and caravans all broke down outside Bury in 1973 and haven't moved since. The pub tradition has absorbed and embraced them as well, and they mingle, long-haired and toothless, with the old boys in the country pubs, playing Irish jigs and Bob Dylan tunes on battered old guitars, unembarrassed about their ignorance of local songs.

It must be said that as we approach the 1990s Suffolk is still a good hunting ground for proper pubs.

Indeed it was in this county that we finally found the answer to our quest: The Perfect Pub. We do not name it here, but refer you instead to the very end of the book.

Despite this great discovery, Suffolk is beginning to go the way of so much of England. Huge highways scar the rolling fields, the A45 divides the county like the Berlin Wall, and insatiable commuters clamour in town halls for more feeder-roads on which they can sit patiently in ten-mile tailbacks of their own creation, drumming their fingers on the wheel to the sound of the John Dunn Show.

October 30th, Saturday–November 2nd, Tuesday
We slipped quietly into Suffolk through the backroads and made our way without fuss to the old coastal town of Southwold, off which in 1672 James, Duke of York fought the Dutch under De Ruyter in the inconclusive Battle of Sole Bay.

🍺 **THE CROWN**, High St., Southwold, Suffolk.
GAR (F, B). Tel: 0502-722275.
This handsome old building is the flagship of Adnams, who brew in the town and set standards matched only by a few other

SECTION EIGHT

independent breweries. We are on the borderline of our brief here since The Crown functions mostly as a restaurant, but it is still possible to drink, and the food is of a very high standard, though with a price to match. The winelist is full of enticing bottles chosen carefully by Simon Loftus, Adnams' managing director, who, as well as being the author of *Abe's Sardines and Other Stories*, can tell a Cru Bourgeois from a banana milkshake.

★ THE HARBOUR INN, Blackshore Quay, Southwold, Suffolk. LLL. Ron Westwood.

Southwold is a good drinking town and this short excursion across the golf course and past the water tower is essential. Standing on a creek amid a jumble of fishing-smacks and huts, The Harbour is a simple and friendly place which is still a kind of fishermen's social club.

Home-cooked fish and chips and pies are provided with no fuss, and the Adnams beer stands up to close scrutiny. Characters and good stories abound, and here can be had one of the most relaxed and entertaining evenings on the East Anglian coast. We have many fond memories of days and nights spent sloshing around in gum boots at The Harbour unable to return to our billet, while flood waters lapped hungrily at the window-sills. The talk was of ghosts at Walberswick and the beautiful twin sisters from the sixth form at nearby St Felix's, and happily the bar service continued unimpeded.

⊟ THE LORD NELSON, East St., Southwold, Suffolk. LLL (B). Tel: 0502-722381.

At the top of East Street, and almost on the seafront, The Nelson is a cheerful little local with tasty Adnams, cheap beds, good barlife and 100-proof, rum-drinking regulars. Very handy before or after a swim or beach walk.

⊟⊟ THE BELL, Walberswick, (B1387), Suffolk. LLL (B). Tel: 0502-723109.

Across the River Blythe from Southwold, Walberswick was a busy port in the 16th century. The ruins in the churchyard are best avoided on nights of the full moon when shadows walk and dead men talk. Instead, drink in The Bell, a pretty, flagged village pub with rambling rooms, a friendly atmosphere and good beer, spoilt only by an area known as The Salad Bar. In summer sit outside and soak up the Suffolk theme of flint cottages and boats. You can also stay, though the bedrooms are not given away at £40.00 per double.

🍺🍺 THE PICKEREL, Ixworth, (off A143), Suffolk. GAR (F, OP).

The building is beautiful, an 18th-century coaching inn with an astounding Elizabethan timbered barn across the yard. Quieter at lunchtimes, The Pickerel is packed in the evenings as people swarm in from the surrounding countryside to eat the excellent seafood available in bar and restaurant. The service is exemplary and an object lesson. Locals still use the bars as a drinking and social centre, and it is for this reason as much as for the food that it merits its bold type entry.

★ THE KING'S HEAD (THE LOW HOUSE), Laxfield, (B1117), Suffolk. ORD (W, E). Janet Parsons.

The front room at The Low House has a large table beside the blazing fire which is surrounded by old high-backed settles. Here, as you enter, you will encounter the wits and mischief-makers of the village, among whom can be counted the landlady's husband. They will insist, though they may not know you from Adnam, that you join their conversation while your pint is tapped from the cask and delivered to you with style from the back still room.

The talk is prankish and full of fantasy, as a friend discovered one evening. After a long and liquid Sunday lunch featuring several bottles of port, he arrived at The Low House at opening time, and soon was engrossed in conversation with the vicar. Recently separated from his wife, he felt the need to unburden his woes. Constantly refreshing both his own and the parson's glass, he railed against womanhood and went into confessional detail about the physical and spiritual incompatibilities of the failed partnership. The vicar drank deeply, murmured comforting words, said good night and left.

'What a marvellous man,' wept the deserted husband, 'if only all churchmen were like that!'

'Churchman?' exclaimed a local. 'That's no churchman! He's just the local piss artist!'

We were looking forward to meeting this gentleman. We were in luck. After a few minutes of hilarious debate with a

SECTION EIGHT

hyperactive local businessman, we watched as the landlord approached the other occupant of the table, a foxy-faced individual with spectacles and a laugh like a reversing Morris Minor.

'Will you be taking the other pint, Vicar, or will you be late for evensong?'

'There's always time for another,' replied Reynard. 'Fill it up, as fast as you like.'

We said nothing, but could discern a certain expectancy in their faces as the regulars studied our reactions. Ten minutes later the charade was repeated.

'Vicar, I must tell you that you are ten minutes late for the service. Shall I be having your glass?'

'Bugger evensong,' shouted Foxface. 'Slosh it in and keep 'em coming.'

Again the moment's silence as they scrutinized the strangers; by now they were indulging in surreptitious winks and nudges. Little did they know that our foreknowledge meant that the joke this time was on them. But what a good joke it is! And what fun they must have playing it on unsuspecting newcomers who fall unwittingly into their snare.

By any standards The Low House is a great pub and now offers a wider range of attractions than it did previously, including mulled cider and a small menu. Some die-hard purists complain about this, but in our opinion the expansion has done nothing but good.

★ **THE VICTORIA,** Earl Soham, (A1120), Suffolk. LLL (F, M). Clare and John Bjornson.
The Victoria could be described as the perfect local, and it is almost worth selling your house to go and live nearby. It brews its own mild, bitter and winter special and provides a good corned beef hash among other simple victuals. Locals abound from opening time onwards. They play cards, the piano and anything else they can lay their hands on. Fires and handsome furniture ease the way for good conversation, in true Suffolk accents, about whether a rat will take an egg or not. The answer is it won't, but it will take a chicken.

🍽 **THE OYSTER,** Butley, (B1084), Suffolk. GLL (M).
The Oyster had recently changed hands when we visited and

earns its entry for its potential under a good licensee. There are two rooms, one smarter with an often-used piano and a scruffier bar with lino, wooden tables and chairs. We shall watch its progress with interest, since the atmosphere will be very good indeed once the regulars unite behind the new tenants.

🍺 **THE JOLLY SAILOR**, Orford, (B1084), Suffolk. GAR (B). Tel: 0394-450243.
A delightful family of Jack Russells dominate the main bar here, an attractive room with the most effective wood-burning stove in East Anglia. The food is reasonable in price and quality and the accommodation is basic. Orford is a very unspoilt little harbour town and The Jolly Sailor is potentially as nice a pub as you could want. It is only let down by the surliness of the licensee, who carried off-handedness to its extreme, not deigning to acknowledge our presence, despite our having drank, dined and slept in his establishment.

★ **THE BUTT AND OYSTER**, Pin Mill, near Chelmondiston, (off B1456), Suffolk. GAR (F, OP). **Dick Mainwaring.**
Commanding a view over the estuary of the River Orwell and three or four (rare) working sailing barges, The Butt is another justifiably famous house, well-patronized for its beautiful position, its excellent food and the Tolly Cobbold from the cask. The landlord watches operations with an eagle eye from his reserved eyrie at the end of the bar, but seldom has to intervene. With one large coop sensibly set aside for families, serious drinkers congregate in the main bar, a lovely room from which it is a delight to watch the tide rising almost to the walls of the pub itself.

As usual, The Butt is best avoided on high days and holidays when hairsprayed, jauntily yacht-capped, bebangled would-be mariners swamp the best room in their Docksiders and talk loudly and inaccurately about binnacles and bowlines. Otherwise, drink deep and enjoy.

🍺🍺 **THE BENNET ARMS**, Rougham, (off A45(T)), Suffolk. LLL (FC, W).
At the simpler, more rural end of the scale, The Bennet Arms is a very good, little local village inn, where, whether you are

staying in the area or merely passing through, you will receive a warm welcome and be served a decent pint of Greene-King and a steak if you want one. The regulars are friendly and colourful, good jokes fly about and the atmosphere is genuine and unponcified.

★ **THE BLACK FOX,** Thurston, (off A45(T)), Suffolk. ORD (FC). Joyce Ong.
At the time of writing, the fabled Fox had been closed for six months while the owners took a US sabbatical. It is scheduled to reopen in the early summer of 1989, but we cannot vouchsafe that its simple, untarnished pleasures will remain intact. In the past, The Fox has been one of the most lovely pubs in Suffolk – beer from the back room, lively talk, the odd sing-song – and let us pray that it will remain so and continue to justify its star.

🍺🍺 **THE NUTSHELL,** The Traverse, Bury St Edmunds, Suffolk. ORD.
One of several pubs in England that claims to be the smallest in the world, The Nutshell is the nicest place to drink in this charming Georgian town, especially on market days (Wednesday and Saturday). Conversation and the extraordinary collection of *objets d'art* are the main attractions in this tiny room. Spontaneous and dangerous sessions can occur on feast days when it is sardine-like with excitable townspeople.

Essex

November 3rd, Wednesday–November 5th, Friday
Essex is a schizophrenic county. In its more rural reaches there are perfect, gem-like, stiflingly dull villages where, sheltering

THE QUEST FOR THE PERFECT PUB

behind the walls of weatherboarded or half-timbered cottages crouch hordes of blue-haired spinsters and widows. They emerge twice a week, once on pension day and again on Sundays when they arrange the flowers in the 900-year-old, fortified Saxon church before matins and take sweet South African sherry with the vicar afterwards.

Nearer London, in the marshy areas around the River Blackwater, psychotic villains in car coats, brought up on a diet of irresponsible and violent television programmes, blast away noisily and incessantly with sawn-off shotguns outside restaurants called The Thatched Barn not far from Braintree, or feed selected pieces of their wives to their Pit Bull terriers in deserted hangars and pillboxes.

As a consequence there are almost no pubs left in Essex. They masquerade either as olde tea shoppes for the little olde ladies, or have been brutalized by failed petty criminals in love with mirror-tiles, lager and malodorous, barn-like, L-shaped layouts.

We spent a dispiriting couple of days dodging Ford Escorts with raised suspensions and GoFast stripes attempting to uncover a couple of proper pubs, and a couple was about all there was.

THE GREEN MAN, Little Braxted, near Witham, Essex. GLL.
Mr Macgregor is not a villain, simply one of the longest serving licensees in the area. He has been here twenty years and runs a proper pub with a decent tiled public bar and a separate games room. His Ridley's beers are well looked after, the setting quiet, and in winter the lounge boasts a fine log fire.

THE WHITE HARTE, Burnham-on-Crouch, Essex. GAR (B). Tel: 0621-782106.
This is a place of some interest and atmosphere, with a private jetty and wonderful views from the front bar which overlooks the Crouch estuary. We passed a pleasant night here, eating local fish washed down with Adnams and Tolly Cobbold, sleeping in the comfortable bedrooms and paying the usual inflated Home Counties prices.

SECTION EIGHT

🛢🛢 THE CROOKED BILLET, High St., Old Leigh-on-Sea, Essex. LLL (M).

The Crooked Billet is probably the best and most atmospheric pub in Essex. There are two rooms: the public bar (lino, games, log fire) and lounge (stove, cockleboat pictures), and a big terrace which overlooks the old cockle sheds and working harbour. Decent, simple pub food is provided as blotting-paper for the range of beers which includes Tetley, Burton and Young's from London. The famous jellied-eel stall of Ivy Osborne is within shrimp-throwing distance, and if you go on a Tuesday you can heckle the finger-in-the-ear folk fanciers upstairs.

🛢 THE VIPER, Mill Green, Essex. GLL.

The Viper has a comforting cottagey feel which extends to its garden in summer. The wood-floored tap room, with its old wall seats, hasn't changed much over the years, and there are three other rooms to drink in, including a darts room and a lounge with log fire. Walkers in the oak and beech woods which surround the pub enjoy the simple bar snacks and Ruddles and Trumans beers.

🛢 THE MOLE TRAP, Stapleford, Tawney, Essex. GLL.

Once this was a remote pub but recent events, such as the building of the useless and dangerous M25, have conspired to entrap it and ruin its isolation. There are still good views if you look for them, and the McMullens mild slips down well in what has miraculously remained an unspoilt atmosphere.

Coming out of The Mole Trap we heard a series of loud reports like pistol shots coming from somewhere close behind us. We panicked, flung open the doors of the three-wheeler (the Lada had failed us in Suffolk) and headed at top speed for the old ferry port of Felixstowe.

Shaking with fear, we pulled off the road some thirty minutes later and downed large medicinal brandies at THE RISING SUN, Duton Hill, GITS, until the noise of further shots propelled us back into the vehicle and keeping our heads well down we gunned the powerful motor across the Suffolk border.

In Felixstowe that evening, disguised as professional Badminton players, we spent three hours in THE FERRY BOAT,

Old Felixstowe, GITS. Paranoia had us in its grip. Why were we being hounded? What had we done? And for that matter, how could we make amends?

Outside the sporadic sputter of machine-gun fire was such that we expected any minute an ITN reporter to appeal in canvas shirt and trousers and sign off in classic television style '. . .Tarquin Tumpfish, News at Ten, in war-scarred Felixstowe.'

When the firing died down for a moment we regained the car and drove quickly past Manning's Amusement Park, The Rattan Restaurant and Carvery and advance hoardings for Humpty Dumpty at the Spa Pavilion. We thought of begging for sanctuary at the Alice Kirkland Nursing Clinic, or even at the Fankirk Retirement Home. No. We bought two tickets for Rotterdam and boarded the ferry. The sky was lit up with streams of tracers, and the crump of mortar fire boomed across the harbour.

It was not until shortly before midnight in THE WHEELHOUSE BAR, GITS, that we discovered from the purser that tonight was Bonfire Night.

November 12th, Friday
We have been here in Rotterdam for a week. At 4 pm we telephone the Mesmerizing Brunette Editor (MBE) at the publishers.

'We're in Rotterdam.'

'What the hell do you mean?'

'Researching a substitute book.'

'Have you taken leave of your senses?'

'*The Hundred Best Stripjoints in Rotterdam.* It'll sell like hot cakes.'

'Listen, laddie. If the pub book isn't on my desk by Christmas Eve, we sue.'

'But I tell you, we can't go on. We're all washed up. If we have to look another pint of beer in the face we'll go crazy. You must understand, and it'll be all your fault. Please, please . . .'

She hung up.

Section Nine

Middle England

East Shropshire and the West Midlands

November 15th, Monday
One of the great charms of Shropshire is the variety of its landscape. From the wild and woolly western hills of the Clun Forest and Offa's Dyke, so different from the flatlands of Holland, you drive east through the civilized farmland of Ludlow and the Teme Valley to the fascinating area around the Ironbridge Gorge and Coalport, the 18th-century crucible of the Industrial Revolution, now beautifully preserved but still untamed. Here you would scarcely believe that it is only a stone's throw from the planning madness and cultural wasteland of Telford, a 'new town' second only to Milton Keynes in its wretchedness.

Shropshire is rich in home-brew houses which help to preserve the county's pub identity. The closure of the Davenports Wem brewery in 1987 has left Wood's at Wistanstow as the only brewer of any size.

West Shropshire has **THE THREE TUNS** at **BISHOP'S CASTLE** (see p. 28), and East Shropshire borders on the Black Country where home brewing is an old tradition. We set out one morning to investigate, sensibly taking a teetotal chauffeur with us; we had no intention of stinting ourselves and knew that some of the beers we were to taste are what the French call *traître*, that is, they come at you with a winning smile and one hand behind their backs wielding a piece of iron piping with which to clobber you.

The history of Ironbridge is now legend, and the Industrial Museum there is a most interesting place in which to while away an hour or so, afterwards refreshing yourself in the recreated Victorian ambience of THE NEW, ORD, actually inside the museum itself, or at THE BIRD IN HAND, GLL, with its open fires and views of the gorge and original Brunel bridge. We

THE QUEST FOR THE PERFECT PUB

eschewed both these choices, taking instead the Coalport road and skirting the terrifying suburbs of Telford until we came to our goal.

★ **THE ALL NATIONS**, Coalport Rd., Madeley, Shropshire. ORD (FC, I, E). Keith Lewis.
The twisting road between Ironbridge and Coalport is an amazing patchwork of wooded valley, river, derelict factories with square chimneys and tiny villages. Keep alert, for it is easy to miss The All Nations. A sharp turning is signposted 'To the Pheasant Inn', and you have to take this. But do not go as far as the Pheasant, a mediocre establishment. Immediately before it there is an alarmingly steep driveway, at the top of which sits a small square house with a discreet sign that advertises The All Nations.

The building itself, though plain, is listed and adjoins the old iron rail bridge which used to take the coal away from Coalport to road transport depots nearby, and the pub was purpose-built to cater for the workers at the turn of the 19th century. It has been brewing its own beers nearly as long and is an institution in the area, quite content to look after its own lively local trade, though it has become over the years a place of pilgrimage for real ale enthusiasts.

Behind the pub is a clutter of outhouses, a hencoop and the brewery itself. Inside, the one bar is reassuringly plain and simple: lino floor, hard chairs, formica-top tables, darts board, domino league fixtures up on the noticeboard, cribbage boards neatly stacked. Behind the bar Keith Lewis, son of the respected late landlady, is pulling the first pint of the day. He is recovering from a hard night, he tells us, and there is brewing to be done this afternoon.

'We only get the locals in the winter,' he says, 'and I brew once a fortnight. In the summer, though, we get visitors and I have to do it every ten days, sometimes once a week.'

We congratulate him on the delicious All Nations Pale Ale, refill our glasses, and watch as the first of the regulars comes in with his ancient dog. Half an hour later things are warming up, and a better or more friendly crowd of all ages would be hard to find. We tear ourselves away with reluctance, cheeks glowing from sheer pleasure.

The All Nations is genuinely unpretentious, and in its

strange idyllic location is unique. No food is served, the comforts are basic, the welcome restrainedly warm. We urge you to pay it a visit.

Ten miles down the Severn from Madeley lies the attractive, steeply-streeted town of Bridgnorth. Here is a genuine curiosity of a public house, a must for all followers of time-warps.

🍺🍺 THE RAILWAYMAN'S ARMS, Platform of Severn Valley Railway Station, Bridgnorth, Shropshire. ORD (W, E).

Bridgnorth is the northern terminus of the Severn Valley Steam Railway, a thriving and much patronized enterprise which from March to September puffs busily between here and Bewdley and Stourport to the south. Enter the station; admire the immaculate, 1940s British Railways' rolling stock gleaming along the platform; sniff the exotic scents of steam and coal hissing out of the superbly preserved locomotive that will pull them down the track. Spot the welcoming doors of the Railwayman's Arms alongside on the platform. Enter – and step back forty years.

The big black and gilt fireplace is blazing away, heaped with coal; the paintwork is old but shining. The benches and tables are original, the bar all mahogany and soft lighting. Behind it Derek the barman is pulling pints of excellent Bass, Holden's Black Country Bitter or Courage Directors, chatting to his customers and serving them with a hot pie or pasty (the only food here). And who are those two in the corner, close together, he with a handkerchief, she gazing into his eyes? Could it be – yes, it just might be Trevor Howard removing that fateful piece of grit from Celia Johnson's eye.

Half an hour later we were back in the late 1980s and swinging our way down country lanes to our next destination some ten miles south by south west, to another of Shropshire's collection of brewery-pubs.

🍺🍺 THE FOX AND HOUNDS, Stottesdon, (off B4363), Shropshire. GLL (FC).

The Fox and Hounds was for a long time under the stewardship of the idiosyncratic 'Dasher' Downing, who brewed the hoppy mixture he christened 'Dashers' and was a well-known local character. Two weeks before our visit he had finally retired to a bungalow in Bewdley, and the pub had been taken over by the Woodwards.

Normally this would have put us off a visit so soon after change-over, but by a happy coincidence Derek, the barman at **THE RAILWAYMAN'S ARMS** (see above) lives not only in Stottesdon but right next door to The Fox and Hounds, and he was able to speak up for the Woodwards. So, local information being the basis of our research, here we were, sampling not only the last brew made by Dasher before his exit, but comparing it to the first batch of Dashers brewed by Glen Woodward. He has learned his lesson well, for the quality has not suffered, and so enthusiastic is the new incumbent that he has added his own brew, 'Woodie's', to the roster of ales.

The Fox and Hounds is a quiet, unspoilt village pub with two small bars and the usual repertoire of regulars and reprobates who treat it very much as a gentleman's club, although women would not feel uncomfortable here. Mrs Woodward breeds an extraordinary species of Italian hound and is a lively figure who brings to the public bar the femininity that was perhaps lacking in Dasher's day. The couple plan to keep the pub as it was, and the simple food they intend to offer will be eaten in a converted back portion of the building, so as not to interfere with bar life. All in all, the future looks promising for The Fox and Hounds, a rare thing these days.

From Stottesdon we ventured east into the fringes of the West Midlands, a new euphemism for the proud old name of the Black Country. Here the tradition of lively working-men's pubs and small breweries is still alive, and in the outer reaches of the conurbation there are good places to be found. We ducked and dove around ring roads, estates and shopping malls, looking for the old village and town centres where real life still goes on. The following is a distillation of what we found, and it must be said that for the true pub lover, the rewards to be won here are worth the horrors of most of the landscape.

🍺 THE OLD SWAN (MA PARDOE'S), Halesowen Rd., Netherton, West Midlands. LLL.

Doris Pardoe, landlady for twenty-five years and home-brewing pioneer, is dead now, but the pub is still known as Ma Pardoe's.

Hoskins now own the pub, but the beer is still brewed on the premises, and though refurbishment in 1987 has knocked the two bars together, the locals still hide away in the back half, shielded by a big pillar from the more casual visitor in the front, and this is the place to drink.

On our most recent visit we arrived late after traffic hold-ups to see the depressing sight of towels draping the pumps. At first we pleaded with an unyielding barmaid for a swift half, but her icy heart would not melt. We explained that we had come miles to sample the beer. She gazed stonily back at us. It was not until the gang of hard-core locals behind the pillar put up a vociferous lobby in our favour – 'Come on luv, don't be such a ratbag, give 'em a drink' – that she relented, and we spent a happy hour in conversation with her and the die-hards, who of course got their reward for helping us out. Still staunchly traditional despite the refit, the home brew is light and flowery and The Old Swan is a good place to kick off your Black Country tour.

🍺 THE LITTLE DRY DOCK, Windmill End, Netherton, West Midlands. LLL (E).

Round the corner, tucked away in Bumble Hole, is Netherton's other good pub. Owned by the same people as **O'ROURKE'S PIE FACTORY** (see below), the ambience is a jumble of canalside memorabilia, including the servery which is actually a narrowboat somehow crammed into the building. Novelty and kitsch are the motifs here, though well done and not in any way annoying. The pub's own Little Lumphammer ale goes down well and the thing to eat is the enormous Desperate Dan Pie which comes crowned with a pair of horns in true *Beano* style. The Little Dry Dock is not easy to find, but worth the effort for the colourful characters who frequent it as well as for the decor.

🍺 O'ROURKE'S PIE FACTORY, Hurst Lane, Tipton, West Midlands. LLL (E).

This is another eccentric establishment, housed in a converted butcher's shop with the old slicing and processing equipment still intact, as is the hanging room, complete with hooks and pulleys. A large pig sits in the foreman's office presiding over the goings-on, and the beer and food are identical to that served in its sister pub, **THE LITTLE DRY DOCK** (see above). An amusing place with a good sense of humour well in evidence.

THE QUEST FOR THE PERFECT PUB

🍺🍺 **THE VINE (BULL & BLADDER), Delph Rd., Brierley Hill, West Midlands. LLL (F, M).**
The Vine remains a classic Black Country pub, adjoining as it does Batham's Brewery, whose wonderful full mild has to be sampled as an example of a taste that is all but extinct. In winter try the Delph Strong, eat the hefty cobs (local baps) or fresh seafood, and go on Friday nights for the jazz or Sunday lunchtimes for rollicking Irish folk music. The crowd here know how to enjoy themselves, and unless you are a dismal, dim, stick-in-the-mud so will you.

🍺 **THE WAGGON AND HORSES, Reddal Hill Rd., Cradley Heath, West Midlands. LLL.**
The Waggon and Horses is an extremely lively and friendly town pub in the centre of Cradley Heath, serving mild and bitter from Banks's, yet another of the good Midlands' brewers. The landlord is a great enthusiast of that most courageous and dignified of dogs, the Staffordshire Bull Terrier, and they and associated memorabilia are much in evidence. This is the place to stop if you are driving through.

🍺🍺 **THE BREWERY INN, Station Rd., Langley, West Midlands. LLL (W).**
The other side of the M5 from Cradley Heath, nestling cosily by the canal and a stone's throw from the station, is this well-liked local with the Holt, Plant and Deakin brewery behind (an encouraging bijou branch of the appalling Allied Breweries). Bargees, railway workers, young people from the surrounding area and canal holiday-makers cram in here in the summer to make inroads into the HP & D Mild, the Bitter, the Entire and the aptly-named Deakin's Downfall. The redecoration is based around local artefacts and very well done in both tap and parlour, the welcome is genuine and the great chunky doorstep sandwiches of hot beef or lamb are quite delicious. Proximity to the BR station enables safe homeward journeys to be undertaken – leave the car behind!

🍺 **THE STRUGGLING MAN, Salop St., Dudley, West Midlands. GLL (FC).**
Leave the centre of Dudley on the B4588 and a mile or so out of town you will come across the converted farmhouse that is The

SECTION NINE

Struggling Man, where the pleasures are old-style and simple, the atmosphere quiet and the Hanson's Mild the thing to drink, following the example of most of the regulars. The only struggle we encountered here was the internal one of whether to have just one more or not.

🍺 THE CROOKED HOUSE (GLYNNE ARMS), Himley (off B4176), West Midlands, Staffordshire. LLL (E).
The Crooked House is actually just in Staffordshire, but is associated so much with the West Midlands historically and geographically that it fits well into this section. It gains its (E) rating because of the extraordinary state of the building. Years of mining the substrata here has caused massive subsidence, and the whole building sags and slopes alarmingly in every direction. You will find it hard even to open the front doors, and once you are inside will feel as if you have ingested about fifteen pints or several ounces of small native mushrooms, so disconcerting are the sight lines. The *trompe l'oeil* is most effective on one slanting table, where a pint sleever laid sideways on the surface will appear to actually roll uphill. This is all highly diverting, and the Banks's beers are perfectly good, but a new extension at the back and an intrusion of machines serve to dampen one's enthusiasm a little. Still, for novelty value alone, The Crooked House merits your attention for half an hour or so.

Warwickshire, Northamptonshire, Bedfordshire and Hertfordshire

Emerging from the tangled chaos of Birmingham was a relief, but we were not looking forward to the next section of our progress. Most of our informants in these four counties had warned us not to expect a string of pearls, and unfortunately they were right. Nothing that we found proved to be eligible for top honours, but here follows a list of the least mediocre establishments. The fact that neither Warwickshire nor Northamptonshire can boast a real ale brewer between them is perhaps comment enough on the state of their pubs.

THE MAID OF THE MILL, Coleshill Rd., Atherstone, (B4116), Warwickshire. GLL (W).
The future of the beer here is now in doubt since Greenall-Whitley brutally closed the remaining (and award-winning) Davenports brewery in Brum at the beginning of 1989. The cluttered charm of this basic boozer will, we hope, survive.

THE CASE IS ALTERED, Five Ways, Haseley Knob, Warwickshire. LLL (FC).
This is one of the best pubs in the region and for that reason the most famous. It is a quiet, three-roomed, traditional house, still frequented by farmers enjoying the Flowers Original produced from the cask by means of unusual gravity pumps. The timeless atmosphere so carefully nurtured by the long-standing former landlady, Mercedes Griffiths, has not been spoilt by the current licensees. No food at all.

SECTION NINE

🍺 THE DURHAM OX, Shrewley, (B4439), Warwickshire. LLL.

The Durham Ox was recommended to us by a former Warwickshire native, who had wisely removed himself to the richer pastures of Devon. It is an island in a sea of transport lines – canal, railway, and the lovely new M40 gouging its sewer-like way through the country against the express wishes of the inhabitants. The M & B beers are extremely cheap, so are the basic snacks. The landlord reputedly turned down a huge offer for the site, and his regulars have much to thank him for.

🍺 THE SHOULDER OF MUTTON, Stretton-on-Dunsmore, Warwickshire. GLL.

A characterful old pub, built in Regency times but added to in 1952. This extension still bears the telltale signs of austerity and The New Look. The other bar is snug and small. Concentrate on the M & B mild and getting out of Warwickshire.

On our way out, we decided not to shirk our duty and entered Rugby. We had no pointers here, so instead followed the recommendations of the generally reliable CAMRA *Good Beer Guide*. They suggested THE ENGINE, Bridget St., LLL, THE RAGLAN ARMS, Dunchurch Rd., LLL and THE SQUIRREL, Church St., LLL. All proved to be well-run, traditional places with appreciative followings, in any of which 'Flashy' Flashman would have felt quite at home. Rugby is obviously the best drinking town in the county.

🍺 THE DUN COW, Brook St., Daventry, Northamptonshire. GLL.

Feeling that perhaps towns might yield more treasure than the countryside round here, we soldiered on to Daventry where we walked the streets for a while until we found The Dun Cow. If for some strange reason you are forced to go to Daventry, then console yourself in this, the only real pub left in the town. It is also a Davenport pub, so God knows what will happen to the beer, but the snug, so discreet as to be almost concealed, is a delight, and the fire blazes.

🍺 **THE GEORGE AND DRAGON,** Chacombe, Northamptonshire. GAR (F).
This fine old building is famed mainly for its trencherman's food and the landlord's ebullient personality. People fight for tables at dinnertime and reserving can be like trying to get tickets for one of Mr Lloyd Webber's undergraduate musical reviews. We found, however, that it is quite possible to drink a quiet pint of Bass or Donnington's without getting caught in the melee.

🍺🍺**THE MARSTON INN,** Marston St Lawrence, Northamptonshire. GLL.
One of the authors has known this pub since the early 1970s as 'The 14p Pub', reflecting the price of a pint in those days before inflation. The Hook Norton from the cask is still cheap, appears from a back room and is served through a hatch into the public bar with its fire and good darts crowd.

🍺 **THE SWAN,** Newton Bromswold, Northamptonshire. GLL.
A decent village local with good Greene-King IPA and Abbot Ale and a local variant on the game of skittles.

🍺 **THE SOW AND PIGS,** Toddington, Bedfordshire. LLL (M).
Toddington is best known for its M1 services, but proves to be a nicer village than you would expect. Opposite the green stands The Sow and Pigs, something of a local institution, an enterprising, welcoming place with good fires and a lively trade. The front tap room features a harmonium and the larger back room a piano. Both are preferable to the video games which lurk in corners. Live music happens here on certain evenings.

🍺 **THE MUSGRAVE ARMS,** Shillington, Bedfordshire. GLL.
Richard Jepps returned recently from the wilds of Lincolnshire to take the reins at this comparatively unspoilt village pub which has been in his family for nearly a hundred years. He has plans to enlarge it – 'but not much'. The Greene-King IPA is served from a cask behind the bar, but he is hoping the brewery will build him a temperature-controlled cellar.

SECTION NINE

🍺 **THE COCK**, Broom, Bedfordshire. GLL.
The main pleasure here is the big central cellar, from where your pint of ubiquitous Greene-King is dished out from a cask. There are several small rooms to drink in, but somehow the place lacks an identity despite the efforts of the friendly licensees. They are strong on cheese here.

Bedfordshire begins where the Chilterns stop, and its scrubby landscape, spotted with new towns, airports and car works, peters out into Hertfordshire which, despite some attractive rolling farm country in its northern reaches, yields little of note to the student of public houses. The south of the county is a lost cause, being mostly covered by Watford.

There are only two proper pubs in the county. These are they.

🍺 **THE PLOUGH**, Ley Green, King's Walden, Hertfordshire. GLL (FC).
This was the nearest thing that we found to a country pub in Hertfordshire and indeed we even managed to overhear the last three local accents left in the county. They came from three old boys who had no doubt become used to the noise from nearby Luton Airport and did not let it disturb their dominoes. On the edge of the village, this is an unassuming little place surrounded by fields, and the Greene-King (surprise, surprise) is drinkable. This part of the 'countryside' is where tractors are outnumbered ten to one by company cars and gem-encrusted Lamborghinis driven by the former wives of golfing ex-popstars.

🍺 **THE SWAN**, Park Rd., Bushey, Hertfordshire. GLL (W).
Bushey? Yes, Bushey. Where is Bushey? Nowhere – somewhere near Watford. Where is Watford? Somewhere in the Fourth Division. Fourth Division of what? Publand.

But there is always The Swan, a commendable and proper pub with simple pleasures, good wooden interior, open fire and decent Benskins and Burton beer. Bacon or fried egg sandwiches appear swiftly and the landlord, a friendly type, stays open in the afternoons for as long as it takes to slake the thirst of the regulars.

Section Ten

Buckinghamshire, Oxfordshire, Berkshire and Wiltshire

Buckinghamshire

November 20th, Saturday
We crossed into Buckinghamshire and came to the small Thames-side town of Marlow in search of an old, unspoilt pub that we had heard of.

As we drove down the High Street looking out for landmarks an old lady dashed out from the side of the road and leaped in front of the Reliant, forcing us to slam on the powerful air brakes. We feared she was dead, but she was up in a flash, tearing open the passenger door and throwing herself in.

'Follow that cab,' she cried, pointing at a telephone box on the corner. 'You've got to get me to Salzburg by dawn. The Prince is in great danger and David Niven is his double!'

Ever gallant, we prepared for a dash across Europe, but at that moment two nurses appeared at either door and kindly but firmly removed our new companion to the safety of an ambulance.

'Terribly sorry,' said the younger one brightly. 'It's only Mrs Fitzhugh. She often escapes on Saturday mornings.'

THE CLAYTON ARMS, Quoiting Square, Marlow, Buckinghamshire. LLL (W).
The Clayton Arms is one of a breed that is fast disappearing, especially in the Home Counties. It is the archetypal, little, town local in a town where the brewery (Wethered) has been closed down by Whitbread and all the other pubs have undergone brain surgery.

The Clayton Arms is lucky for two reasons; firstly it belongs to Brakspear's of Henley, and secondly the licensee is the long-serving Mr Page. He presides over the one small bar and tiny snug next door, both in the classic colour scheme and the former with a good fire. From opening time onwards the best faces in Marlow cluster here to drink the bitter, mild and old, swap stories and nurture a good frowst. The windows are often steamed up from 12.30 onwards.

Mr Page knows his drinkers; there is a good supply of chocolate bars to keep the blood-sugar level stabilized and no other food. It is the last proper pub in Marlow and good for a quiet drink in the snug or a more boisterous session with the boys in the bar.

THE STAG AND HUNTSMAN, Hambleden, Buckinghamshire. GAR (F, B). Tel: 0491-571 227.
New licensees have arrived here in the last year, but the pub remains the enjoyable heart of a pretty and much-photographed flint village. The car park is huge and at weekends the usual hordes descend (there are good walks in the hills beyond). There is also a large garden and a variety of real ales (Brakspear's, Huntsman and others). Too many Volvos and gins-and-tonic for our liking though, unless you go early in the evening during the week and frequent the public bar, when the locals come out of hiding.

THE OLD CROWN, Skirmett, Buckinghamshire. GAR (F).
This is an old Brakspear's house, formerly run by an elderly couple who had changed nothing, and was thus a delight. Now there are carpets on the tiled floors, a huge menu and a lot of dressed-up weekenders in high heels and expensive jumpers eating from it. The beer still comes from the cask, and the fire still roars; these are the two attractions nowadays. It serves its purpose, but is only half the pub it used to be.

THE BULL AND BUTCHER, Turville, (off B480), Buckinghamshire. GAR (F, M).
One of the first, and best, of the food pubs that have sprung up in this area over the last ten years. Ex-racing driver Peter Wright has been here for a long time and it shows in the assurance of the service, the quality of the food and the friendly atmosphere. In the summer the garden is a fine place to eat and drink (Brakspear's again). If you're looking for a good bar lunch then this is the place to go for it. Live jazz on Thursdays.

SECTION TEN

⊟⊟ **THE OLD SHIP**, Cadmore End, Buckinghamshire. **LLL (FC).**
Only half a mile from the M40 (junctions 4 or 5) and sunk away from the road (B482) down a dip so that only its roof shows, this is a true little oasis a mere thirty miles or so from London. There is one tiny bar and a minute snug beyond, both crackling with good log fires on a dank November day.

The Brakspear's is kept in a deep cellar and the barmaid disappears to fill your glasses; her family have been here since 1919 and have learned how to keep beer properly.

You couldn't swing a hamster, let alone a cat, in the bar, so it is not long before it fills up with a merry band of locals in jocular mood. Beyond in the snug, some serious cribbage is going on, and the ambience is decidedly sporty.

⊟ **THE RED LION**, Twyford, (off A421), Buckinghamshire. **GLL.**
Up in the sparsely populated flatlands of North Bucks lie small, desolate villages full of four-wheel-drive Toyotas and former colonial businessmen, now retired from pushing nurses off balconies at home-brew parties in dry Middle Eastern states. They live in West London during the week and think Buckinghamshire is incredibly remote. That they are eight miles from Milton Keynes does not seem to have occurred to them.

Most of them congregate at The Red Lion on weekend lunchtimes. The pub itself is small and fairly unspoilt, standing at the end of the village by the church, and has two small bars with open fires. The local Aylesbury bitter (brewed in Burton-on-Trent) is not bad for an Allied Breweries product.

There was a small restaurant here, much appreciated by the regulars, but domestic upheavals sadly led to the departure of the landlord's wife and closure of the kitchen. 'And I haven't found a suitable replacement yet,' he admits gloomily.

On Sundays he still closes at two, thus forcing the ex-tea-planters and civil engineers to go home for lunch and watch the Pro-Celeb Golf or mow the lawn.

⊟⊟ **THE LIONS OF BLEDLOW**, Bledlow, Buckinghamshire. **LLL.**
Our last stop in Bucks was at this famous and popular local on the Oxfordshire border. Beamed, rambling, inglenooked, vil-

THE QUEST FOR THE PERFECT PUB

lage greened and reputedly haunted, The Lions has everything a tourist could desire, including a lot of tourists. Nonetheless, there are a good number of pub games to play and the beer (Wadworths, Courage and so on) pleases connoisseurs. Again, don't go at weekends.

Oxfordshire

There are five breweries in Oxfordshire, of which Brakspear's at Henley and Hook Norton at Hook Norton are the best. They control between them enough of the tied houses to ensure that Oxfordshire is still a fairly good drinking county. We have known the region for years and refer you here to half a dozen of our favourites.

★ **THE PEYTON ARMS**, Stoke Lyne, Oxfordshire. ORD (FC, W). N. Oxlade.

The Peyton Arms is everything that an old-fashioned village pub should be. Up in this northern part of Oxfordshire, the villages are muddy and unmanicured. Stoke Lyne is one of them. Opposite a fine old church stands The Peyton Arms. Half of it used to be the village shop and a window still bears the old Brooke Bond sign. Enter with confidence.

There is one room, a tiny bar-counter and a couple of tables, at one of which a local is sitting in front of a game of solitaire. Table skittles take up the surface of another. Packs of cards lie on a windowsill. The walls are covered with old photographs of village teams and personalities. Order your pint of Hook Norton from the friendly young barmaid. She will fill it from the barrel in the back, and you will drain it quickly as you chat

224

to the red-faced band of villagers with mud-spattered trousers flapping round their calves.

The Peyton Arms is a delightful surprise; the relentless road schemes that gash the countryside as they force the M40 extension through rural Oxfordshire have made you despair of ever finding something like this. Yet in the bar at The Peyton you could be anywhere, from the Welsh Borders to Widecombe. It is one of the best pubs in the country.

★ **THE DUN COW, Northmoor, Oxfordshire. ORD (W). J. Douglas.**
The Dun Cow shouldn't be where it is, only a few miles west of Oxford and in an area sprouting high-tech business parks making useless items which no one wants, but happily for all of us it is.

At the end of the commuter village of Northmoor it sits, a long white building, run with energy and charm by Joyce Douglas, following in her mother's footsteps. There are two rooms, with fires and flock wallpaper, on either side of the passage which leads to the still room at the back. Sitting in either of them is a little like being in your aunt's parlour on Christmas Day. Joyce passes from table to table, sitting down at each for a few moment's chat while keeping a beady eye open for approaching customers. As soon as she spots one she darts out to greet him in the corridor and escorts him to the row of barrels, where he may choose from Morland's good, dry bitter or their mild, which the brewery now perversely insists is kept under CO_2.

'I don't understand why everybody wants to go back,' she says in disbelief. 'All the young want to do is the things we've been doing for years – candles, eating outside, beer from the barrel – I don't know.'

We suggest that it is the unsatisfactory nature of modern life that brings on this affliction, and there are plenty of sufferers it would seem, looking round Joyce's two rooms, packed with locals with Oxford burrs, rugby fiends from Merseyside, old, young, blonde, ginger, stranger and friend, all enjoying the timeless atmosphere. This is the kind of place in which to spend all day, make several new friends and forget your way home.

THE QUEST FOR THE PERFECT PUB

🍺🍺 THE LAMB, Rotherfield Greys, Oxfordshire. LLL.
The Lamb has recently changed hands after the departure of the popular husband-and-wife team who ran it with gusto for many years. Luckily it doesn't seem to have changed much. A huge log fire divides the two rooms, one where the Brakspear's is tapped from barrels, and the other set aside for darts and bar billiards. It attracts an enthusiastic and mainly local band of admirers, never seems to get too crowded for comfort and remains the most satisfying place to drink in near Henley.

🍺 THE CROWN, Nuffield, Oxfordshire. GLL.
Set just off the A423, The Crown is easy to flash past as you thunder out of Nettlebed towards Wallingford. Fred Duke has given up drinking these days and now pours your libation with a resignation bordering on the lachrymose, yet he has for many years been delighting his regulars and visitors with a mordant sense of humour and decidedly eccentric outlook. Sadly, he will be retired shortly on reaching 65 (Brakspear's policy), but this unpretentious, warm and fairly comfortable establishment is unlikely to be ruined by his successor.

🍺🍺 THE CROOKED BILLET, Stoke Row, (off B481), Oxfordshire. LLL (M).
Die-hard locals deserted in droves to **THE BLACK HORSE** (see below), when Ben Salter had the temerity to tamper with the classic layout at The Crooked Billet on the retirement of Nobby Harris. In fact, all he has done is to knock out a couple of walls so that you no longer have to stand pressed into the passage, and introduce some simple, edible food to the proceedings. It is still a very good, unspoilt pub with Brakspear's from the cask, a villagey atmosphere and no pretensions whatever. Musicians gather on Wednesday's and Sundays.

🍺🍺 THE BLACK HORSE, Checkendon, (off A4019), Oxfordshire. GLL (E).
The elderly sisters Mrs Saunders and Mrs Textor live here, outside the village, in the middle of a wood and next to their farm at the end of a track. It is a splendid place, and has been in the same family for eighty-five years (they also used to own **THE CROOKED BILLET** [see above]). There are three rooms, inter-connecting but each with a different and timeless

collection of items: octagonal card table, piano, dried flowers, worn sofa. The bar room is square, with a good fireplace and solid counter. Next door in the cellar they keep a barrel of Brakspear's, and will talk all day about the area, its changes, its inhabitants and their escapades.

🍺 **THE FOX AND HOUNDS, Christmas Common, Oxfordshire. GLL.**
This is another pub where nothing much has changed in the fifteen years that we have known it. Simplicity is the key: two simple rooms, fires, simple food, Brakspear's from the cask, small garden, quiet and sylvan situation.

Berkshire

The parts of Berkshire that are not Reading contain some decent countryside, particularly the horse-racing area on the downs near Newbury and Lambourn.

🍺🍺**THE OLD HATCH GATE, Cockpole Green, (off A423), Berkshire. ORD (E).**
Entering the county from Oxfordshire, this was the first pub we fell upon, and a joy it was. Only just across the Thames from Henley, and on the way to Maidenhead, this is another time-warp close to London. Untidy, slapdash and erratic in its hours, The Old Hatch Gate is nevertheless a good country pub, with its old tap room (the other bar never seems to be open), Brakspear's beers, and enjoyable atmosphere. Don't miss it.

THE QUEST FOR THE PERFECT PUB

🍺 THE POT KILN, Frilsham, (off A4), Berkshire. LLL (M).

The Kiln is at its best on Sunday evenings when you are liable to find folk musicians performing to a packed house, but is enjoyable any night of the week, providing a pleasing combination of simple food, Arkells and Theakstons from the pump and a good range of the usual pub games. If you go in the daytime and it is not pouring with rain, give yourself time to explore the surrounding countryside, which may be near the M4, but borders on the spread of racing country which centres around the Lambourn Downs.

🍺 THE IBEX, Chaddleworth, (off A338), Berkshire. LLL (F).

Shortly before his recent retirement, Colin Brown achieved fame in racing circles as rider of the great Desert Orchid. Having hung up his boots he now runs The Ibex, which has been renowned for years as a friendly and well-run joint. He is maintaining that tradition. Most people come here to eat the good, if pricey, food, but locals settle into the bar for a good session as well.

🍺 THE CROWN AND HORNS, East Ilsley, (A34T)), Berkshire. LLL.

East Ilsley is in the heart of Berkshire's racing downland, and this first-class pub in the quiet village is full of speculation as to what will win the 3.30. The food is varied and *soigné*, as is the beer – a wide range from both handpump and cask.

Wiltshire

It was in **THE LAMB**, Marlborough, GITS (B), tel: 0672-52668, over a good pint of cask Wadworths, that we first learned of the legendary Bruce Arms, on the road to Pewsey, just west of the village of Easton Royal on the B3087, and we immediately hastened there for the lunchtime session.

★ **THE BRUCE ARMS, Easton Royal, Wiltshire. ORD (FC). Ellen Raisey.**
Opposite the present building, there was for many hundreds of years a thatched coaching inn which served the needs of travellers using the old Roman-built Wessex Way.

By the early 19th century, the Wessex Way had outlived its usefulness, and was supplemented by a new stone road built by the Marquess of Aylesbury (see **THE BLUE LION, East Witton**, p. 163), who also erected the current Bruce Arms when the coaching inn burnt to the ground in 1836.

Continuity of tenure is the theme here, but sadly Mrs Raisey, whose father held the licence before her, is now 83 and has no one to follow in her carpet slippers, so it is only a matter of time before the Bruce falls prey to Whitbreads and their whims.

Ellen Raisey used to relish her standing as Whitbread's oldest tenant, until she read of the 93rd birthday of 'Auntie' Mabel Mudge of **THE DREWE ARMS, Drewsteignton** (see p. 76), but she is still able to point out that, though Auntie Mabel may be older, she herself has been a licensee for considerably longer.

The Bruce Arms no longer does the business it used to, being isolated from the village, and Mrs Raisey blames the advent of the drink-drive laws, which she considers to be inflexible and unfair.

'Some men can stand six pints and drive from here to the Isle of Skye,' she points out, 'and after all, when Strong's Brewery had the pub, the draymen's morning ration, before setting out

THE QUEST FOR THE PERFECT PUB

on first delivery, was two pints of their choice – and the barrels was twice as heavy in them days.'

The Bruce is a charming, little, cottage-style local, with two numbered rooms, a cosy, boxed-in bar, fireplaces, two long tables with benches, and decent Whitbread from the cask. Hasten there while you may, for Mrs Raisey will not be there for ever. No lover of the modern world, she is all too aware of the latest trends in pub design.

'Soon they'll all be complexes covering an acre of ground,' she opines wisely, 'where you'll be able to get everything from a needle to a coffin.'

Her favourite story is how her mother once served tea to four officers from the Lancers, one of whom, younger than the others, turned to shake her hand and thank her on leaving. Later, when a sergeant arrived to pay the bill and refresh himself, he revealed that the polite subaltern was none other than Prince Henry, Duke of Gloucester.

Saying farewell to Mrs Raisey, we struck across country to a real enthusiasts' pub, run by Tony Coultiss, a fully-paid up member of the clumsily-named Society for the Preservation of Beers from the Wood.

🍺🍺 THE NEW INN, Coate, (off A342), Wiltshire. LLL (W).

Best visited for an evening session, The New Inn provides little in the way of food – 'It's a proper drinking pub' – but everything in the way of good beer and games: cribbage, dominoes, darts, an angling club, skittles in the new alley, brewery trips and jovial evenings around the fire in the bar. If you get desperate for blotting paper, they can produce a chunky cheese or ham sandwich.

🍺🍺 THE BECKFORD ARMS, Fonthill Gifford, Wiltshire. LLL (B). Tel: 0747-870385.

On our way to Dorset we had two important stops to make in the southern reaches of Wiltshire. The first was here, at The Beckford Arms, much recommended to us by local contacts. This old stone-built house, dating from the 1600s, is a delightful place to put up for the night though you will need to forage

SECTION TEN

further afield for your dinner (see **THE HORSESHOE INN** below). Formerly owned by the Beckford family, the estate on which the pub is built is full of lovely walks and the high-ceilinged bars with their blazing fires are the perfect places to refresh yourself afterwards with good Wadworths from the cask.

⊟⊟THE HORSESHOE INN, Ebbesbourne Wake, Wiltshire. GAR (B). Tel: 0722-780474.
Mr and Mrs Bath have retired, but their son is now in charge preserving the continuity and charm of this simple, pleasurable inn. Attractive surroundings, both inside and out, decent and good-value food, excellent Wadworths from the cask and a well-stoked fire provide the perfect framework for a lengthy and indulgent session.

Section Eleven

The Southern Counties

Dorset

December 1st, Wednesday
The old county of Dorsetshire is one of the most pastoral and unspoilt in England, with its limited base in manufacturing and accent on dairy farming, sheep and maritime pursuits.

Despite the strident attempts of the Thomas Hardy industry to transform the county into a living museum and its inhabitants into smock-wearing, straw-chewing yokels, Dorset remains a land of pleasing contrasts, from the chalk hills that cross the centre to the coastline of cliffs, farms and small settlements.

The only major blot on the landscape is the agglomeration of geriatric Bournemouth and arriviste Poole, self-consciously jaunty in its yachting casuals despite the unremitting drabness of its underbelly. The nearest thing to a flat cap here is an elasticated pork-pie hat driving a gleaming Allegro very slowly over the middle of an experimental roundabout. We avoided all this and drove deep into the heart of the Isle of Purbeck. Here in its southernmost hamlet lies one of the finest public houses in the country.

★ **THE SQUARE AND COMPASS,** Worth Matravers, (B3069), Dorset. ORD (W). Ray Charles Newman.
It was a crisp and sunny December morning when we arrived spot on opening time at The Compass. The view over the farmland, with its old strip system still in evidence, to the cliffs and a sparkling sea beyond, was little short of breathtaking, and the salt air made us yearn for the first pint of Pompey Royal. We entered the low-ceilinged corridor, and surveyed with relief the row of casks behind the servery hatch.

We sat down in the smaller of the two rooms – a concerto of scrubbed table and nicotine – though we could have made use of the grander and more stately second room, with its fine oak panelling below rough stone walls. The fires are banked up at all times. We were hungry, and to our delight we found that on offer was nothing less than the classic triumvirate of pub fodder – baps, pasties and local crab sandwiches. We ate our fill.

The Newman family have been here for eighty years and are used to the summer weekend onslaught of tourists. The usual caution applies. On a quiet morning, however, there was just the landlord, grey-bearded and long-haired like an Old Testament prophet, reading *The Sun* at one of his tables, and a bobble-hatted hippy armed with battered Zippo lighter, cider and *The Independent*. The Square and Compass is one of the 7,654 pubs in which the once-fashionable sketch artist Augustus John is said to have seduced the barmaid with one hand while daubing a canvas with the other, but we found no evidence of this. There is, however, a magnificent skyline view of Corfe Castle as you leave this marvellous haven and head back inland.

★ **THE FOX**, Corfe Castle, Dorset. GLL (FC).
G. White.
For as long as we have known it, the timeless front bar at The Fox has remained unchanged despite the massive tourist trade that descends on the town in the summer months. It is one of the nicest places to drink in England, with its huge fire, enormous oval oak table, round which it is just possible to squeeze, and hatch from where appears your splendid pint of Fremlin's straight from the cask. Alternatively, do what the locals do and stand and jaw in the passageway outside the still room which leads to a comfortable lounge.

Today The Fox was closed at noon. Aghast, we peered through the window. The fire was blazing in the hearth. Not knowing what to make of this, we looked around for enlightenment. On the corner a couple of elderly and forlorn FCs stood in anticipation of a return to normal service. There was a funeral, they informed us, the licensees were attending it. But they'd be open before the end of the midday session. Unable to wait, we reluctantly struck north-west.

The village names in Dorset are marvellously evocative and unlikely and might have been invented by P. G. Wodehouse himself. Pick your own favourite from the following: Piddletrenthide, Plush, Mappowder, Melbury Bubb, Affpuddle, Beer Hackett and, best of all, Ryme Intrinseca, perhaps a haven for local poets, possibly Hardy himself, whose fine verse is infinitely preferable to his overrated novels.

🍽🍽 THE TIGER'S HEAD, Rampisham, (off A356), Dorset. LLL (W, F, B, E). Tel: 093583-244.

Halfway between Dorchester and Crewkerne lies the pretty village of Rampisham, with a fine church and this eccentric, welcoming public house.

Pat Austin and her husband Mike have been here for four years and have put their mark on the place. A breeder of prize-winning Arab horses, whose many rosettes adorn the back of the bar, Pat loves to talk, preferably about them. There is a sweet little dining room where you can eat excellent, home-cooked food (rabbit pie, pigeon, venison etc) and the Butcombe's from the cask is preferable to the handpumped Bass. The Austins take every Tuesday off to fetch fresh fish from wherever it is cheapest, even as far away as Plymouth, so Wednesdays are good eating days here.

She told us about a Turkish gentleman who spent two hours photographing The Tiger's Head to get ideas for his latest project – an interesting marriage between doner kebab joint and traditional English pub. He had come a long way to find his premises in a suburb of Poole, he confided. When pressed to reveal his origin, he admitted that it was as far away as Basingstoke.

🍽🍽 THE FOX, Corscombe, (off A356), Dorset. LLL.

Two miles up the road towards Crewkerne lies Corscombe, at the centre of which is this delightful old thatched inn with its dark, wood-panelled, fire-warmed bar full of talkative horsey ladies in jodphurs and spurs. Bring your own whip. The Eldridge Pope beers come straight from the cask and the welcome seems warm enough. The Fox had just undergone a change of ownership on our last visit and some refurbishment was going on, but it looked to be in safe hands.

🍽🍽 THE FIDDLEFORD INN, Fiddleford, (A357), Dorset. GAR (B). Tel: 0258-72489.

Our last Dorset pub is a handsome, stone building in the flag-floored bar of which it is a pleasure to drink the fine Bateman's and Wadworths. The food used to be the downside of the operation, but the newish regime are said to be making great efforts in this direction, though on this visit we had time only to grab a packet of crisps. It is also an enjoyable place to stay but look out for spiders under the bed.

Hampshire

December 12th, Sunday
Until the 1960s much of Hampshire was either rolling farmland intersected by deep lanes or untouched 1,000-year-old forest. Then someone discovered Basingstoke, a small market town, and decided to import, or 'relocate' as they loved to call it, many hundreds of thousands of people from London, who were perfectly happy where they were. Every street was renamed Pall Mall or Piccadilly, multi-national corporations built huge skyscrapers, and every self-respecting resident abandoned the area.

Now every Hampshire village is like any in Surrey: a neat line of Queen Anne redbrick cottages with cosmetic carriage-lamps, painted cartwheels and hanging baskets, his and hers Toyotas, and sauna baths in the old dovecote.

It is a county that we used to know and love, having been partly brought up in Rotherwick, where old Mr Franklin ran The Coach and Horses and spent his time writing letters to the Prime Minister in between serving up jugs of ale to the few customers he allowed to set foot in the place. If you were favoured, he would brandish well-thumbed scraps of Downing Street headed paper.

'You see!' he would shout. 'The PM knows I'm right. Look at this letter. He agrees with every word I say.'

On the piece of paper was the standard printed and somewhat

SECTION ELEVEN

curt official reply: 'The Prime Minister thanks you for your comments, which have been brought to his attention.' It was signed by an Assistant Parliamentary Under-Secretary.

Now, predictably, The Coach and Horses, like a thousand other pubs in Hampshire, is a food-infested no-go area and we will not dwell further on the subject. Trust us instead to lead you to the only five pubs in the county worthy of your patronage.

🍺 THE ROYAL OAK, Fritham, (off B3078), Hampshire. GLL.

The Royal Oak is in the heart of the New Forest and the last remaining unspoilt pub there. It has been run by the Taylor family for over eighty years. The Flowers and Strongs from the cask are good, and there is one beautiful snug room with the archetypal high-backed settles and huge open hearth. The other room has been fitted with tongue-and-groove planking and a bar, but is still a traditional room. Unfortunately, the winter trade seems so slack here that on our visit early in the evening, neither of the fires was lit, and we detected a certain world-weariness in the welcome we received. A pity, because with a bit more effort this could be a humming little joint.

🍺 THE BUNCH OF GRAPES, Bishops Waltham, Hampshire. LLL.

Pub lovers in this small town ignore the several barn-like theme pubs dotted around the ring road and congregate here to drink Courage from the cask in simple and honest surroundings that have been tended enthusiastically by the same family for three generations. At 7 pm it was jumping with drinkers and the keen barman's immediate and only question – 'Bitter or Best, sir?' – with sleever at the ready, inspired great confidence and put us in mind of the noble 'Clark Gable' (see **THE SUN INN, Stockton-on-Tees**, p. 160).

🍺🍺 THE WHITE HORSE (THE PUB WITH NO NAME), Priors Dean, Petersfield, Hampshire. LLL (I).

Without doubt this is the most famous pub in Hampshire and was bought sixteen years ago by the landlord, an ex-Hampshire cricketer, in order to preserve it. Preserve it he has, and the machine-free, old-fashioned atmosphere, warmed by good log fires, is hard to fault. The range of beers is good and the feel relaxed, but we consider that its fame exceeds its merits, perhaps because it sticks out noticeably in the pub barrenness of the region. We even had the feeling that the regime is resting gently on its laurels. Worth a visit, certainly, but a little Too Orange.

We left The Pub With No Name a little dissatisfied, but a treat was in store. By a mixture of dedicated research and pure chance, we had booked rooms for the night at the best pub in Hampshire, in one of the few remaining villages still worthy of the name.

★ **THE FLOWER POTS, Cheriton, (B3046), Hampshire. GLL (W, B). Tel: 096279-318. Patricia Bartlett.**
The Flower Pots is one of the more modest and unassuming stars in this book, and anyone expecting a riotous night out should pass it by. For lovers of the proper pub, however, it is perfect, with two rooms – a plain public with benches, lino and a fruit machine and a more comfortable little lounge with carpet, pot plants and an old chintz-covered sofa where you can sit in front of the fire. Here it is something like your granny's front parlour, except that your granny would not necessarily have five or six gleaming barrels containing immaculate Flowers and Strongs.

The charming and attentive Mrs Bartlett is one of our very favourite landladies, and staying in her old-fashioned (and cheap) bedrooms with solid furniture and comfortable beds cannot be recommended too strongly. It is typical of her that she finds time to ring round the locality to find you a table for dinner (she only does toasted sandwiches), and to nip upstairs during the evening session to turn on your electric blankets. The breakfast is guaranteed 100 per cent grease free.

🍺 **THE NEW INN, Stratfield Saye, (off A33), Hampshire. GLL (W).**
Once the authors' favoured lair, The New Inn is a friendly, tidy establishment with a rare traditional smoke room and bar billiards. It is as off the beaten track as you can get in this beleaguered part of the county and worth taking a ganders at.

Sussex

December 14th, Tuesday
We had harboured hostile preconceptions about Sussex, having experienced first-hand the destruction of Hampshire. So it came as little less than a revelation to discover that much of Sussex is still charmingly unspoilt and in fact contains two of the best pubs we found on our journey. The only problem is that you need to be a millionaire to live there.

It is also worth mentioning to our London readers that all these pubs, most of which have good walks nearby, are within easy driving distance from the capital and are perfect for chasing away the claustrophobic weekend blues which can descend so rapidly in the Smoke.

🍺 **THE THREE HORSESHOES, Elsted, West Sussex. LLL (F).**
The first comforting thing we noticed was the 'Sorry, No Children' sign on the door. We entered with confidence in the knowledge that the large goat-ridden garden, quacking with ducks, was large enough to contain the little dears and their tiny psychodramas. Inside, two attractive food-pens at either end of the building are separated by two pleasant and rustic bars, where Ballard's and Harveys among other beers are available from the cask. The food is important here, the menu original and someone can obviously cook. Fresh fish is a speciality, though the prices are Sussexish. Bar life does go on though, as cribbage boards and domino sets bear witness. Local eggs are sold on the bar. A civilized establishment all round.

★ **THE DUKE OF CUMBERLAND, Henley, West Sussex. LLL (F, W). R. Seaman.**
This is a little-chronicled establishment, tucked away off the road between Fernhurst and Midhurst (look for the signs to ICI

THE QUEST FOR THE PERFECT PUB

up a track and keep going). Sitting above the lane, the pub has a trout pool, fed with running water, just outside the door. At a price (£7.25), you can select your lunch live, and it will be plainly cooked and delivered curiously through the front door rather than over the bar. Mr Seaman is a Norfolk man, son of a corn merchant, and still returns there every year to his native trout stream to fish.

The two bars are almost mirror-images of each other, with matching fireplaces and scrubbed tables. Although when we first knew The Duke it was famous more for its cider than its ale, in the last few years the Seamans have introduced Ballards and King and Barnes which they tap skilfully from the cask. Food is available at all times except Sunday lunch, and there is no better place to eat either before or after a walk on nearby Black Down. At 919 feet, the latter is famous for its views over the South Downs and as the home of the writer of doggerel and light verse, Alfred, Lord Tennyson.

THE BLACK HORSE, Byworth, West Sussex. GAR (F, OP).
Byworth is one of those annoyingly pretty and well-kept villages that it would be petulant and childish to criticize, so we won't bother. The Black Horse is a handsome building in the capable hands of a dedicated couple of licensees who know their market, which tends to be of the Puffa and pearls, Barbour and Hunter ilk so prevalent in these parts.

Despite the worrying length of the menu (twenty starters alone), the food is very good and some effort is made to separate the eaters from those who wish merely to drink and play darts in the bar. A versatile sort of place where you could get quietly sozzled one night and then take your mother to lunch there the next day.

★ **THE BLUE SHIP**, The Haven, Billingshurst, West Sussex. LLL (W, I). J. R. Davie.
The Blue Ship is a splendid, timeless public house that would be very hard to top, no matter where you travel in this country. We were utterly taken with it. Arriving at 3 pm after a frantic dash across country, we found only the landlord and a couple of cronies settling in for a good afternoon session. Without hesitation he rose, went behind his tiny servery, lovingly produced

perfect pints of King and Barnes from the cask, and more or less invited us to join in the conversation.

The best room in the pub has the servery, a massive hearth, simple tables and chairs and an indefinably warm and friendly atmosphere. There are two other rooms, one with a bar billards table, and one set aside for those who wish to eat the simple bar food. At weekends the young give The Blue Ship their patronage, and who can blame them?

Our visit this time was all too brief, but Mr Davie and his pals regaled us with the story of one of their number who, on New Year's Eve, started off with half a bottle of sherry, then downed four large whiskies, moved on to nine pints of lager and rounded it all off with a cup of coffee. Feeling distinctly unwell the next morning he attributed his acute malaise to the Nescafe.

🍺🍺 THE PALACE BARS (PIGS IN PARADISE), White Rock, Hastings, East Sussex. GAR (M).

Resort towns out of season are an acquired taste, but five years of hell in a boarding school on the tip of the Isle of Thanet has seasoned us to withstand all but the gloomiest aspects. Yet even our own hardened sensibilities received a severe jolt when, amid the tattered hoardings left over from the summer shows on the Pier Pavilion, we espied a gaudy and ill-designed flyposter advertising 'Jack and The Beanstalk', starring one of those odious, toad-like, overweight little TV presenters. Who could it be? Take your pick. Answers please under a plain wrapper to The Nell Gwynne Revue-Bar, Cleethorpes, including a cheque or postal order made out to Hurt Bros, Cayman Islands a/c for twenty five guineas (£26.25).

Certainly no one in Hastings knew or cared, since the queue outside the theatre was conspicuous by its absence.

The theatre fans of Hastings were, to their eternal credit, instead ensconced in several of the town's public houses, the best of which is The Palace Bars. This cavernous building siphons off the lively student element of the town, offering all-day service, food of all sorts from pasta to marmite sandwiches, mulled wine served bizarrely in coffee cups, beer and spirits, and in the evenings has regular live rock music.

The building is splendid, situated directly on the seafront near the pier and is a good attempt at a contemporary club/pub (see **THE DOUBLE LOCKS, Alphington**, p. 80), but it

THE QUEST FOR THE PERFECT PUB

suffers in comparison to The Locks due to its somewhat gloomy decor and its less sure, though well-meaning, service. Nevertheless when the band is on the stand and the place is packed, a very good time can be had.

🛢🛢 **THE DORSET ARMS, Withyham, (B2110), East Sussex. LLL (FC).**
On the edge of Ashdown Forest and opposite W. Welfare, Draper and Grocer, The Dorset Arms is a classic country pub which caters for all types and could be situated anywhere in rural England. While the restaurant provides solid English cooking for those who require it, the public bar houses the locals, and this is where the rubicund landlord and his consort choose to spend their time. At any weekend session it might be compared to the very wonderful **NAGS HEAD, Abercych** (see p. 45), packed as it is with all sorts, from Barboured beauties to fag-rolling farm workers, all getting along famously and slurping up the local brew (Harveys from Lewes) in front of a roaring fire.

Kent

December 16th, Thursday
The cabbage fields of the Isle of Thanet and their wild, vegetal aroma are imprinted on our minds like Calais on the heart of Mary Tudor, and we would not recommend our worst enemy and his dog to visit Margate, except that there are two sound drinking houses to help you forget your surroundings. THE ORB, Ramsgate Rd., GLL, is a CAMRA stalwart, plain and relying on the excellence of its Shepherd Neame beers for its well-deserved reputation, while THE SPREADEAGLE,

Victoria Rd., LLL, a fine and perfectly-run operation, offers a wide range of thirst-slakers, from Brakspear's to Burton Bridge bitter. Either of these places is perfect for doting parents to get stinking in, while their children are thrown from the heights of the Space Mountain Disco Dipper Water Slide at the nearby theme park, which used to be a perfectly good funfair called Dreamland.

Avoid Broadstairs, where never a house was better named than Bleak House and where mad ex-Indian Army colonels wield swishing canes in cheerless common rooms. Move on to the town of Minster outside Ramsgate, where you will find a welcome and a good pint of Fremlin's at THE BELL, LLL, in the High Street. This is the most popular dive in town, and the atmosphere and character are as inviting as the prices. On your way to our next near-perfect pub in Romney Marsh, travel via Folkestone where, in the Sandgate area near the front, you will find THE CLARENDON, Brewers Lane, LLL, which need not delay you long but is well worth a visit for its old-fashioned feel, lively and friendly throng and well-cooked, inexpensive food.

★ **THE RED LION**, Snargate, (B2080), Kent.
ORD (I, E). Doris George.
Apart from childhood visits to the miniature railway which runs from the sinister silos of Dungeness Power Station to the minor resort of Hythe, we had not before visited Romney and Walland Marshes. We were pleased and surprised by their flat, remote and faintly villainous aspect. Outside hidden farms, men in sheepskin coats were loading unidentified polythene-wrapped objects into the backs of Transit vans, smallholders polished their vegetables in fields surrounded by slimy dykes, and the rank and seductive stench of salt ribboned the cloud-streaked air.

At five to eleven on a Saturday morning we pitched up outside this isolated old building which stands in the middle of the marsh on the road between Tenterden and New Romney. Already parked outside was a rusting Hillman Avenger. The driver of this, a stocky individual with a nice smile but bad teeth, was hammering on the door.

'Open up Doris, we're thirsty,' he implored.

In time Mrs George, rather the worse for wear after a night on the cherry brandy, slid back the bolt to her enticing enclave. The Red Lion consists of two unadorned and unchanged rooms. The bar room has a marble-topped counter, bare floorboards, glinting barrels of Goacher's from Maidstone (light and redolent of local hops), a roaring fire and the basic pub games, including Toad-in-the-Hole. The second room, similar in style, has an equally good fire and a bar billiards table.

Our fellow drinker ordered a pint of Shepherd Neame Master Brew – 'An acquired taste and I've acquired it' – and three gins and orange. He left the room with the latter, returned a minute later without them, summarily despatched his pint and ordered another round.

This ritual was repeated thrice during the next twenty minutes. We were too polite to make enquiries as to the destination of the stream of gins and orange, and it was not until we left, sometime later, that the full implications of this astonishing performance were revealed to us.

There, squeezed into the back seat of the Avenger and surrounded by useless tack purchased that morning at a boot sale, sat the women in our fellow bar-propper's life: wife, mother-in-law and grandmother. Corralled unwillingly in the motor while the man of the house made merry within the comforting confines of the Lion, they were by now somewhat the worse for wear and glared viciously and accusingly at our female companion who had had the temerity to enter the male precincts of a public house.

The authors kicked each other savagely about the shins to make sure they were not dreaming. This was not Pembrokeshire, nor Northumberland and certainly not Cape Wrath on the northern tip of Sutherland. This was Kent, the cosy Garden of England, a mere seventy miles from London, yet a wilder, woollier or more enjoyable place would be hard to find. No food.

From the Red Lion we drove north through the county making several quick stops to verify the current status of a few well-known watering-holes. We found **THE THREE CHIMNEYS, Biddenden, GAR**, in fine fettle, still retaining its public bar alongside its smarter food operation. There is nothing wrong with **THE BELL, Smarden, GAR (B), tel: 023-377-283**, except for their insistence on holding vintage car rallies as often as possible, and despite some locals' misgivings about the change of licensee at **THE DUCK, Pett Bottom, GAR**, we enjoyed the beer and the atmosphere.

The second best pub in Kent was our next stop.

★ **THE QUEEN'S HEAD, Cowden Cross, Kent.**
GLL (W, M). Elsie Maynard.
The elderly but spry Elsie Maynard runs this simple and unchanged establishment on a quiet crossroads. Beware that on Sunday lunchtimes she closes at 2 pm, mainly because the local wives got fed up with their husbands being late for lunch and also to prevent teachers at the local convent from arriving at vespers late, drunk and blasphemous.

In the small public bar Mrs Maynard makes lively talk in a pure Kentish accent while locals tend the fire and ogle the pictures in last Sunday's *Sunday Sport* – 'Blimey, I bet her shoulders blades are as big as her front'. When it is time to go home they are informed politely and wordlessly by means of a hand-printed sign placed on the bar by Elsie and reading simply: 'Time Ladies and Gentlemen Please'.

The larger second bar plays host every first Tuesday to the best singers in the neighbourhood, and these evenings have become local legend. Elsie orchestrates the proceedings like Von Karajan conducting a cocktail party, and while the choir harmonize lustily she moves among the throng introducing strangers to regulars and making sure everyone feels part of the occasion.

Such is the loyalty of Elsie's regulars that last New Year's Eve, fearful that the drink-drive laws would minimize her custom, they dragged out their old push-bikes, unused for years, and cycled in convoy to drink copiously of her deep-cellared Whitbread and see in the last year of this depressing decade. Later that night they lay for hours in ditches along the Kent/Sussex border.

The last two country pubs in Kent lie south of the River Swale and just east of Sittingbourne. They are nowhere near Dartford, birthplace of the discredited Glimmer Twins, Jagger and Richard.

🍺🍺 THE MOUNTED RIFLEMAN, Luddenham, (off A2), Kent. ORD (W).

The Rifleman has almost everything you could hope for in a good pub: quiet surroundings, Fremlin's brought to you on a tray from the cellar, old country-kitchen atmosphere, traditional games, and sandwiches if you ask for them. There are two simple floorboarded rooms and that's about it, except that it's very hard to find. If you come across the railway crossing at Stone, then you're almost there.

🍺🍺 THE SHIPWRIGHT'S ARMS, Ham St., Oare, Kent. GLL (I, M, E).

This is the only pub we know of where the lighting is by generator and the water from a well. The bulbs flicker atmospherically as a result and, forearmed with this knowledge, you need not consult your cardiograph. There are three small rooms where you can drink your cask-tapped Adnams, Shepherd Neame and Youngers. Stay clear of the Looney Juice. The pub is set above a boat-filled creek that flows into the River Swale, across which you could swim to the Isle of Sheppey if you fancied, as we did, taking the ferry from Sheerness to Flushing and thus avoiding the sea-shanty manglers who insist on drinking the bar dry every Monday night.

Section Twelve

Surrey and The Perfect Pub

Surrey

December 23rd, Thursday
Second only to the Highlands of Scotland for sheer, natural, mind-bending beauty, Surrey is so full of traditional, simple alehouses that it was hard to know where to begin. We had spent several happy days tramping the old drovers' paths that connect the isolated hamlets between Croydon and Guildford, settlements with such evocative names as Caterham, Surbiton, Purley and Virginia Water.

Spoilt for choice as we were, we decided after much agonizing to feature none of them, but we can assure our reader that in almost any of the roadhouses along the Hog's Back or the A3(T) he or she will be immediately transported back to a purer and altogether more glorious era.

Between Weybridge and Egham there is an old coaching inn called The Dick Turpin Motel and Conference Centre. It was here that we came across one of the indigenous tribesmen (*homo Surreyanus*) who populate this area. They are a primitive and aloof people who still wear with pride their decorous regional costume – a vertically-striped tunic with matching collar, all but concealed by a two- or three-piece overgarment of sombre hue. Around the Christmas period they add an arcane piece of headgear to this ensemble – a brightly coloured paper hat worn at a rakish angle, giving them a fierce and warlike aspect.

We were half-way through a delicious and fizzing pale local concoction, interestingly tapped through a cylinder of gas. He detached himself from a noisy group of village elders and approached us with the stumbling gait associated with this kind of pow-wow.

'Are you with the Wholesale Welders and Associated Trades Christmas Party?' he demanded brusquely.

Oh how we would have loved to say yes and join their revelling throng! But, honest as we are, we shook our heads sadly.

'Then fuck off out of here you bloody gatecrashers, this is a private party,' he confided.

Before we could reach for our notebooks and record this interesting example of the local vernacular, he unceremoniously struck the older of the authors on the left ear and then downed with a 'rugby tackle' the younger, who had almost gained the exit in a neatly executed demonstration of fast footwork.

The Perfect Pub

December 24th, Friday, Christmas Eve: Suffolk

★ **THE PERFECT PUB, Somewhere in Suffolk.
GGAR (FC, I, W, F, B, M, OP, VE). A. Genius.**
The manuscript was delivered, our wounds dressed. Our sticks were lying beside us, and good tweed caps disguised the unpleasant contusions that marred our otherwise perfect and finely-chiselled features.

We were mulling over our final problem: which other nine apart from this would we include in our definitive list of the Ten Best Pubs in England and Wales?

The Perfect Pub is paradise.

It has two simply furnished rooms, both administered from one central servery. Fires leap high into the chimneys of the old hearths. There is a cast of colourful and incomprehensible characters playing the gamut of pub games and lapping up the ambrosial Greene-King bitter from a cask. The pub is named after a farmyard animal and is situated somewhere east of the main Sudbury–Bury St Edmunds road. The present licensee is steeped in pub lore and follows the fine tradition set here by his

SECTION TWELVE

forerunners – Ivy's father from 1900, followed by Ivy herself and then old Sam, who still comes to drink here. He refuses to change a molecule and serves no food, but there are often unshelled peanuts freely available on the counter.

He told us how after a career in the hotel trade he had taken the tenancy here in his early retirement and, not needing the money, was determined to lead a quiet and unmolested life with only his family, regulars and close friends for company.

Then, with uncanny instinct, and knowing nothing of our quest, he made the following statement.

'You are welcome here my friends, and I will be delighted to see you any time you pass by. But please, please, please don't tell anybody else about us or where we are.'

We respect his wishes.

Over several pints of beer and with heated argument we hammered out our ultimate list. It is as follows:

1. THE PERFECT PUB, Somewhere, Suffolk.
2. THE CRESSELLY ARMS, Cresswell Quay, Pembrokeshire.
3. THE KING'S HEAD (THE LOW HOUSE), Laxfield, Suffolk.
4. THE TALLY HO, Hatherleigh, Devon.
5. THE TUCKER'S GRAVE, Faulkland, Somerset.
6. THE OLDE SHIP, Seahouses, Northumberland.
7. THE BARLEY MOW, Kirk Ireton, Derbyshire.
8. THE DOUBLE LOCKS, Alphington, Devon.
9. THE WHITE HORSE (NELLIE'S), Beverley, Humberside.
10. THE SUN INN, Stockton-on-Tees, Cleveland.

It was the end. At last we had completed our quest. Exhausted and happy, feeling old beyond our years, we ordered the last pint of the book, sank back into our seats, pulled our caps down over our eyes and began mumbling incoherent snatches of the shipping forecast to the tabletop.

It was then that the door opened and in waltzed a bright young couple from Lavenham. They ordered spritzers, served with resignation by the landlord.

'I say, James, this is a totally weird sort of place.'

'Oh, I dunno. Rather brill, really. Look at those two marvellous old flat caps in the corner.'

We looked around. There appeared to be no one in the room apart from them, the two of us and our host.

The landlord regarded us and began to laugh.

We looked around again. Where were these wonderful old dodderers? The landlord's shoulders were heaving, his face suffused. Soon he slid from view behind the bar and began to drum his heels on the barrels.

We left The Perfect Pub and went home. We never did get the joke.

Index

Abbey Hotel, Llanthony xviii, 22
Abercych, Pembs xii, 45–6, 244
Addington, West Yorks xvi, 166
Adnam's ales 5, 19, 183, 192, 194, 195, 196–7, 202, 248
Agricultural Hotel, Penrith xv, 117, 128, 136–7
Aldridge, Jeff 30
All Nations, Madeley xii, 208–9
Alnwick, Northumbria xvi, 149–50
Alphington, Exeter xii, 80–1, 252
Alpraham, Cheshire xv, 115
Alstonefield, Staffs xv, 99
Ambergate, Derbyshire xix, 102
Anchor, Morston xvi, 189
Anchor, Newcastle-on-Clun xviii, 30
Angel Hotel, Helston xviii, 64
Angle Bay, Pembs xiv, 38–9
Archer's ales 19
Arran Foot, Cumbria xv, 133–4
Ashbourne, Derbyshire xix, 99
Ashley, April 55
Atherstone, Warwicks xx, 214
Austin, Pat and Mike 237
Avon xii, xiv, 83–6
Aylesbury bitter 223

Baconsthorpe, Norfolk xvi, 193
Badger ales 79
Baker's Arms, Buxton xv, 103–4
Ballard's ales 241, 242
Banks and Taylor's ales 182
Banks's ales 109, 118, 212, 213
Barley Mow, Kirk Ireton xiii, 108, 253
Barley Mow, Presteigne xviii, 26
Barrow-in-Furness, Cumbria xix, 135–6
Barthomley, Cheshire xv, 115
Bartlett, Patricia xiii, 240
Baskerville Arms, Clyro 26
Bass ales 44, 53, 59, 60, 63, 89, 98, 102, 104, 105, 106, 108, 109, 110, 161, 166, 180–1, 209, 216, 237
Bateman's ales 109, 195, 237

Bath, Avon xii, 82–3, 85
Batham's brewery 212
Bay Horse, Masham xx, 162
Bay Horse, Otley xvi, 167
Bayley, Marjorie xiii, 120–1
Beaumont, Francis 3
Beckford Arms, Fonthill Gifford xvii, 230–1
Bedfordshire xx, 216–17
Beehive, Bath, Avon 85
Beer Engine, Newton St Cyres xiv, 81
Bell, Brisley xiii, 190–1
Bell, Minster 245
Bell, Smarden xvii, 246–7
Bell, Walberswick xvii, 197–8
Bell, Watchet xix, 87
Belmesthorpe, Leics xix, 110
Bennet Arms, Rougham xvii, 200–1
Bennetts, J. Barrington xii, 63–4
Benskins ales 217
Berkshire 227–8
Bernard, Jeffrey 70
Beverley, Humberside xiii, xvi, 168–9, 252
Biddenden, Kent xvii, 246
Billingshurst, Sussex xiii, 242–3
Billy Row, Co Durham xiii, 142–3
Bingham, Frank 50–1
Binham, Norfolk xxi, 195
Birchover, Derbyshire xv, 108
Bird in Hand, Ironbridge xx, 207
Birdlip, Gloucs xvii, 19–20
Bishop Auckland, Co Durham xx, 145
Bishop's Castle, Salop xii, 28–30, 207
Bishops Waltham, Hants 239
Black Cock, Eaglesfield xv, 132–3
Black Down, West Sussex 242
Black Fox, Thurston xiii, 201
Black Horse, Byworth xvii, 242
Black Horse, Checkendon xvii, 226–7
Black Lion, Cardigan xviii, 43
Black Lion, Consall Forge xix, 102
Black Swan, Parkgate xx, 145
Black Swan, Seahouses xvi, 150–1

THE QUEST FOR THE PERFECT PUB

Blakeney, Norfolk xxi, 193–4
Blanchland, Northumbria xiii, 152–3
Bledlow, Bucks xvii, 223–4
Blezard, Carl, of Barrow 136
Blicking, Norfolk xvi, 193
Blue Anchor ales 65
Blue Anchor, Helston xii, 64–5
Blue Ball, Malton xvi, 166
Blue Boar, Hay-on-Wye xviii, 55
Blue Lion, East Witton xvi, 163
Blue Ship, Billingshurst xiii, 242–3
Bluebell, Belmesthorpe xix, 110
Bluebell, Langham xxi, 194
Boat, Cheddleton xiv, 97–8, 101
Boddingtons ales 79, 128
Brain's brewery 22
Brakspear's ales 5, 221, 222, 223, 224, 226, 227, 245
Brampton Bryan, Hereford 26–7
Brancaster, Norfolk xxi, 194
Brassington, Derbyshire xiii, 101
Bratton Clovelly, Devon xiv, 73
Breconshire xviii, 48–50
Bredwardine, Hereford xviii, 20
Brent Walker Leisure 188, 191
Bretforton, Worcs xii, 56
Brewer, Timothy xii, 83–4
Brewery Inn, Langley xvi, 212
Bridge, Middleton-in-Teesdale xv, 146
Bridge, Topsham xii, 79–80
Bridgnorth, Salop xvi, 209
Brierley Hill, West Midlands 212
Brisley, Norfolk xiii, 190–1
Britannia, Leek xix, 96
Britannia Inn, Elterwater xix, 130
British Lion, Kings Caple xviii, 51
Broadley, Philip 132
Brocklebank, Agnes 133
Broom, Beds xx, 217
Broughton, Clwyd xv, 120
Bruce Arms, Easton Royal xiii, 229–30
Brunant Arms, Caio xviii, 47
Bryan, John 102–3
Buckinghamshire xxi, 221–4
Buckinghamshire Arms, Blicking xvi, 193
Buckland Dinham, Somerset 88
Buckleys ales 47–8
Bull, Long Sutton xiii, 180–1
Bull, Presteigne xviii, 26
Bull, Walsingham xvi, 191
Bull and Butcher, Turville xvii, 222
Bull I' Th' Thorn, Hurdlow Town xix, 103

Bull's Head, Craswall xiv, 23, 24
Bunch of Grapes, Bishops Waltham 239
Bunting, 'Lord' Ted 30
Burlinson, Paul and Evie xiii, 101
Burnham Market, Norfolk 186
Burnham Thorpe, Norfolk xiii, 186–8
Burnham-on-Crouch, Essex xvii, 202
Burton ales 96, 154, 203, 217
Burton Bridge ales 105, 245
Burton Bridge Brewery Tap xv, 105
Burton Hotel, Kington 169
Burton-on-Trent, Staffs xiii, xv, 84, 105, 106
Burtonwood ales 115, 118
Bury St Edmunds, Suffolk xvii, 201
Bush Inn, Morwenstow xiv, 67–8
Bushey, Herts xxi, 217
Butcher's Arms, Reapsmoor xv, 100
Butcombe's ales 85, 89, 237
Butley, Suffolk xxi, 199–200
Butt and Oyster, Pin Mill xiii, 200
Buxton, Derbyshire xix, xv, 103–4
Byworth, West Sussex xvii, 242

Cadeby Inn, Cadeby, Yorks xx, 172
Cadmore End, Bucks xvii, 223
Caio, Carmarthenshire xviii, 47
Cambridge xx, 182
Cambridge Blue, Cambridge xx, 182
Cambridgeshire xx, 181–3
Camelford, Cornwall 67
Cameron's ales 145, 165, 167
CAMRA 5, 60, 90, 161, 215, 244
Canllwyd, Gwynedd xv, 118
Cannon, Sid and Pat xii, 64–5
Cap and Stocking, Kegworth xv, 109
Capel Garmon, Gwynedd xv, 119
Captain Sir William Hoste, Burnham Market 186
Cardigan, Dyfed xviii, 43, 55
Cardiganshire xii, xviii, 43–4, 55
Carew Inn, Carew xiv, 53
Carey, Herefordshire xiv, 51
Carmarthenshire xviii, 47–8
Carpenters Arms, Walterstone xiv, 23–4
Carswell, Ken and Mal 24, 25
Carter, Les and Anne 15–17
Cartmel Fell, Cumbria xiii, 131
Case is Altered, Haseley Knob xvi, 214
Castle, Cardigan xviii, 55
Castle Drogo 76
Castle Eden Bitter 148
Castle Inn, Lydford xiv, 82

256

INDEX

Castleacre, Norfolk xxi, 194
Catherine Wheel, Marshfield xiv, 83
Cauldon, Staffs xii, 98
Cavalier, Grindon xix, 98
Cavan, Dan 169
Cenarth, Pembs xviii, 45
Central, Whitehaven xix, 135
Chacombe, Northants xx, 216
Chaddleworth, Berks xvii, 228
Chatteris, Cambs xx, 183
Chatwin, Bruce 23, 55–6
Checkendon, Oxon xvii, 226–7
Cheddleton, Staffs xiv, 97–8, 101
Chefers, N. and P. xii, 79–80
Chelmondiston, Suffolk xiii, 200
Chequers, Binham xxi, 195
Chequers, Gresham xvi, 189–90
Cheriton, Hampshire xiii, 240
Cherry Tree, Harleston xvii, 195
Cheshire xiii, xv, 115–18, 120–1
Chetwode Arms, Lower Whitley xv, 120
children 19, 50, 81, 194, 241
Christmas Common, Oxon xxi, 227
Chudleigh, Devon 4, 77–8
Churchill, Avon xiv, 85–6
cider 23, 26, 51–2, 55, 56, 85
Cilgerran, Dyfed xii, 43–4, 55
Clarendon, Folkestone 245
Clayton Arms, Marlow xvii, 221–2
Cleveland xiii, 160–1, 252
Clifford Arms, Chudleigh 77–8
Clodlock, Hereford xii, 22–4
Clovelly Inn, Bratton Clovelly xiv, 73
club/pubs 233–4
Clun Forest 30
Clwyd xv, 118, 119–20
Clyro, Powys 21, 26
Coach and Horses, Chudleigh 78
Coach and Horses, Rotherwick 238–9
Coate, Wilts xvii, 230
Coberley, Glos xvii, 19–20
Cock, Broom, Beds xx, 217
Cockpole Green, Berks xvii, 227
Cole, Maurice and Janet xii, 41–3
Colville, John xii, 73–5
Conan Doyle, Sir Arthur 26
Consall Forge, Staffs xix, 102
Consett, Co Durham 134
Constantine, Cornwall xiv, 69
Cooper's Tavern, Burton-on-Trent xiii, 84, 106
Corfe Castle, Dorset xiii, 236
Cornewall Arms, Clodlock xii, 22–4

Cornish Brewery 70
Cornsay Colliery, Co Durham xx, 145
Cornwall xii, xiv, xviii, 59–70
Corris, Gwynedd xv, 118
Corscombe, Dorset xvii, 237
Cotleigh ales 85
Cottage of Content, Carey xiv, 51
Coultiss, Tony 230
Courage ales 17, 63, 190, 209, 224
Cowap, Albert xiii, 116–17
Cowden Cross, Kent xiii, 247
Cows Hill Hotel, Weardale xv, 143–5
Cradley Heath, W Midlands xx, 212
Craster, Northumberland xvi, 152
Craswall, Hereford xiv, 23, 24
Cray, North Yorks xx, 164
Cresselly Arms, Cresswell Quay, Pembs xii, 41–3, 253
Critchlow, Eric 115
Crooked Billet, Leigh-on-Sea xvii, 203
Crooked Billet, Stoke Row xvii, 226
Crooked House, Himley xx, 213
Cross Keys, Epperstone xv, 110
Cross Keys, Gainford xx, 146
Croston, James 108
Crown, Churchill xiv, 85–6
Crown, Kelston xii, 84–5, 87
Crown, Lanlivery xiv, 60
Crown (Suddaby's), Malton 166
Crown, Newcastle-on-Clun xviii, 30
Crown, Nuffield xxi, 226
Crown, Old Dalby xv, 109–10
Crown, Southwold xxi, 196–7
Crown, Walton xviii, 32
Crown and Thorns, East Ilsley xvii, 228
Cumbria xiii, xv, xix, xx, 128–37
Cupids Hill, Pontrilas xiv, 21–2
Cwmcych, Pembs xiv, 54–5

Dalton, John 132
Daneway Inn, Sapperton xviii, 19
Darlington, Co Durham xx, 145
Davenport's brewery 207, 214, 215
Daventry, Warwicks xx, 215
Davie, J. R. xiii, 242–3
Davies, Alice 42
Davies, Dan and Nora xii, 56
Delph, Greater Manchester xv, 126
Denshaw, Manchester xix, 127
Derbyshire xiii, xv, xix, 99–100, 101–4, 106–8, 252
Derek (Bridgnorth barman) 209, 210
Devenish ales 69, 131
Devils Stone, Shebbear xviii, 73

Devon xii, xiv, xix 4, 70–82, 252
Devonshire, Ulverston xix, 133
Devonshire Arms, Sticklepath xix, 75
Dog and Muffler, Joyford xvii, 20
Dolphin Inn, Chudleigh 78
Donnington's ales 15, 216
Dorset xiii, xvii, 235–8
Dorset Arms, Withyham xvii, 244
Double Dragon ales 85
Double Locks, Alphington xii, 80–1, 253
Douel, Jean xii, 88–9
Douglas, Joyce xiii, 225
Downing, 'Dasher', 209–10
Draycott-in-the-Clay, Staffs xv, 104–5
Drewe Arms, Drewsteignton xii, 76
Drewsteignton, Devon xii, 76
Driffield, Humberside 167
Dryburgh's ales 151
Duck, Pett Bottom xxi, 247
Dudley, West Midlands xx, 212–13
Duke of Cumberland, Henley xiii, 241–2
Duke of York, Buxton xix, 103
Duke of York, Iddesleigh xii, 73–5, 78
Duke's Arms, Presteigne 25, 26
Duke, Fred 226
Dun Cow, Billy Row xiii, 142–3
Dun Cow, Daventry xx, 215
Dun Cow, Northmoor xiii, 225
Duntisbourne Abbots, Glos xii, 17–19
Durham Ox, Shrewley xx, 215
Durham, County xiii, xv, xx, 141–6
Duton Hill, Essex xxi, 203
Dyfryn Arms, Gwaun Valley xii, 52–3

Eagle, Skerne xiii, 167–8
Eaglesfield, Cumbria xv, 132–3
Earl Soham, Suffolk xiii, 199
Earl Sterndale, Staffs 100–1
Earle Arms, Heydon xvi, 84, 90, 192–3
Easingwold, North Yorks 143
East Ilsley, Berks xvii, 228
East Sussex xvii, 243–4
East Witton, North Yorks xvi, 163
East, Alan xii, 98
Easton Royal, Wilts xiii, 229–30
Eastwood, Notts xix, 110
Ebbesbourne Wake, Wilts xvii, 231
Edmond, Roy and Sylvia xiii, 167–8
Eldridge Pope ales 85, 237
Elliott, Nigel 193
Elsted, West Sussex xvii, 241
Elterwater, Cumbria xix, 130

Emlyn Arms, Newcastle Emlyn xviii, 47
Engine, Rugby xx, 215
Epperstone, Notts xv, 110
Erpingham, Norfolk 193
Essex xvii, xxi, 201–4
Everard's ales 126
Exeter area, Devon 79–81
Exminster, Devon xiv, 81

Falmouth, Cornwall xii, 63–4
Farmer's Arms, Presteigne xiv, 25
Farquhar, Careena 35
Faulkland, Somerset xii, 89–91, 252
Ferry Boat, Felixstowe, Suffolk 203–4
Fiddleford Inn, Fiddleford, Dorset xvii, 237–8
Firtree, Cornsay Colliery xx, 145
Fishers Hotel, Whitland xviii, 34
Fishguard Arms, Fishguard xiv, 53
Fishguard, Pembs xiv, 53–4
Five Mile House, Duntisbourne Abbots xii, 17–19
Fleece, Bretforton xii, 56, 132
Fleetwood Arms, Fleetwood, Lancs xv, 128
Fletcher, Bessie 163
Fletcher, John 3
Flower Pots, Cheriton xiii, 240
Flower's ales 214, 239, 240
Flying Horse, Leek xix, 95–6
Folkestone, Kent 245
Fonthill Gifford, Wilts xvii, 230–1
Ford, Glos xii, 14–17, 20
Ford, Mrs, of Kirk Ireton 108
Foster, Marjorie 164
Four Horseshoes, Throckenholt 181
Fox, Corfe Castle xiii, 236
Fox, Corscombe xvii, 237
Fox, Ysceifiog xv, 119
Fox and Hounds, Cwmcych xiv, 54–5
Fox and Hounds, Christmas Common xxi, 227
Fox and Hounds, Starbotton xvi, 164
Fox and Hounds, Stottesdon xvi, 209–10
Frederick, John xiii, 164
Free Press, Cambridge xvi, 182
Fremlin's ales 245, 248
French Horn, Rodsley xv, 107
Frilsham, Berks xvii, 228
Frisar, Ingram 3
Fritham, Hants 239
Fry, David 130

INDEX

Fuller's ales 85–6
Furness, Fred and Gwynn 101

Gainford, Co Durham xx, 146
Garnett, Carl 100
Gascoigne-Mullett, Peter xiii, 162
Gawsworth, Cheshire xiii, 120–1
George, Doris xiii, 245–6
George, Alstonefield xv, 99
George, Hubberholme xiii, 164
George, Norton St Philip xv, 90–1
George and Dragon, Ashbourne xix, 99
George and Dragon, Chacombe xx, 216
George IV Inn, Workington xix, 134
Gingell, Peter and Pat xiii, 152–3
Glen, Alan xiii, 147–8
Gloucestershire xii, xvii, xviii, 13–20
Goacher's ales 246
Godding, Mr and Mrs Joe 21
Golden Heart, Coberley xvii, 19–20
Golden Lion, Houghton-le-Spring xvi, 215–6
Goodwin, Linda and Frank 50
Goose Eye ales 164, 167
Goose Eye, West Yorks xvi, 167
Green Man, Little Braxted xxi, 202
Green Man Hotel, Malton 166
Green Man, Scamblesby 175
Greenall Whitley ales 116, 119, 120, 214
Greene King ales 179, 182, 183, 187, 188, 192, 194, 201, 216, 252
Gresham, Norfolk xvi, 189–90
Grey, David and Susan 82
Greyhound, Llangunllo xiv, 31
Greyhound, Tibenham xvii, 195
Griffiths, Mercedes 214
Griggs, Ada xiii, 190–1
Grindon, Staffs xix, 98
Grinning Rat, Keighley xvi, 167
Gwaun Valley, Pembs xii, 52–3
Gwent xviii, 22
Gwynedd xv, xix, 118–19

Hackett, Mrs, of Penrith 136, 137
Hall's ales 154
Hambleden, Bucks xxi, 222
Hampshire xiii, xvii, 14, 238–40
Hancock's ales 42, 53, 55, 60
Hand, William 83
Hanson, Neil 161
Hanson's ales 110, 213
Harbour Inn, Southwold xiii, 197

Hare and Hounds, Baconsthorpe xvi, 193
Hare and Hounds, Talkin xv, 134
Harleston, Norfolk xvii, 195
Harome, North Yorks xiii, 162
Harrington Arms, Gawsworth xiii, 120–1
Harris, Nobby 226
Hartford, Rob 74
Hartley's ales 155
Harvey's ales 241, 244
Haseley Knob, Warwicks xvi, 214
Hastings, Sussex xvii, 243–4
Hat and Feather, Bath 85
Hatherleigh, Devon xii, 72–3, 75, 78, 252
Haverfordwest, Pembs 34–5, 37–8
Hawksley, Peter xiv, 81
Hay-on-Wye, Powys xviii, 55–6
Heatons Bridge, Scarisbrick xv, 128
Helsby, Cheshire 117–18
Helston, Cornwall xii, 64–5
Henley, Sussex xiii, 224, 226, 227, 241–2
Henry, James xii, 75
Hereford and Worcester xii, xiv, xviii, 20–1, 22–4, 26, 27–8, 50–2, 56, 169
Hertfordshire xx–xxi, 217
Heydon, Norfolk xvi, 84, 192–3
High Force Hotel, Teesdale xx, 146
High House, Easingwold 143
Higson's ales 128
Hill, Albert xiii, 179–80
Himley, Staffordshire xx, 213
Holborn Rose and Crown, South Shields xx, 155
Holden's ales 209
Holly Bush, Tarset xvii, 152
Holly Bush, Little Leigh xiii, 116–17
Holt, Plant and Deakin's ales 212
Home Ales 99, 110, 111
Hook Norton ales 19, 216, 224
Hope, Pembroke 54
Horns, Ashbourne xix, 99
Horse and Jockey, Helsby 117
Horse and Jockey, Stanedge xv, 126
Horsehouse, North Yorks xvi, 163
Horseshoe, Llanyblodwel xv, 118
Horseshoe Inn, Ebbesbourne Wake xvii, 231
Horseshoes, Warham xiii, 194–5
Hoskin's ales 211
Hotel on the Strand, Trebarwith xviii, 67

259

THE QUEST FOR THE PERFECT PUB

Hough, Roger and Helen xii, 68
Houghton-le-Spring, Tyne and Wear xvi, 215–6
Hubberholme, North Yorks xiii, 164
Hughes, George and Elsa 73
Huish Episcopi, Somerset xii, 86–7
Hulme End, Staffs xix, 98–9
Humberside xiii, xvi, 167–8, 252
Huntingdon, Cambs xx, 183
Huntsman's ales 72, 222
Hurdlow Town, Derbyshire xix, 103
Hurt Arms, Ambergate xix, 102
Hurt, S. Le Fowne Alderswasley 102
Huthwaite, Notts xix, 111

Ibex, Chaddleworth xvii, 228
Iddesleigh, Devon xii, 73–5, 78
Ind Coope breweries 104–5
Ironbridge, Shropshire xx, 207–8
Itteringham, Norfolk xxi, 193
Ixworth, Suffolk xvii, 198

Jenning's ales 135
Jepps, Richard 216
John, Augustus 34–5, 236
Johnson, Dr Samuel 9
Jolly Fisherman, Craster xvi, 152
Jolly Sailor, Orford xxi, 200
Jolly Sailors, Brancaster xxi, 194
Jones, David xii, 45–6
Joyford, Glos xvii, 20
Jug and Glass, Newhaven xv, 102–3

Kegworth, Leics xv, 109
Keighley, West Yorks xvi, 164, 167
Keld, North Yorks xx, 161
Kelston, Avon xii, 84–5, 87
Keverne, Cornwall xiv, 69
Kent xiii, xvii, 244–8
Kershaw, Mr, of Stanedge 126
Kilnhurst, South Yorks xx, 172
Kimbolton, Hereford xviii, 51–2
King and Barnes ales 242, 243
King's Arms, Blakeney xxi, 193–4
King's Arms, Luxulyan xiv, 60
Kings Caple, Hereford xviii, 51
King's Head, Broughton xv, 120
King's Head, Ulverston xix, 133
King's Head (The Low House), Laxfield xiii, 198–9, 253
King's Walden, Herts 217
Kingsley, Staffs xix, 102
Kington, Hereford xiv, 52, 169
Kirk Ireton, Derbyshire xiii, 108, 252

Knight, Helen and Terry xiii, 106
Knowstone, Devon xii, 78–9, 87

Lamb, Audrey xii, 77
Lamb, Rotherfield Greys xvii, 226
Lamb, Sneed 88
Lambley, Notts xix, 111
Lampeter 47
Lancashire xv, 128
Lancaster, Harold xii, 39–40
Lane, Mrs C. xii, 27–8
Langdale, Cumbria xix, 129–30
Langdale End, North Yorks xiii, 165
Langdon Beck Hotel, Teesdale xv, 145
Langham, Norfolk xxi, 194
Langley, West Midlands 212
Lanlivery, Cornwall xiv, 60
Lawes, Winnie 190
Lawrence, D. H. 110
Laxfield, Suffolk xiii, 198–9, 252
Leeds Arms, Scarborough xx, 165
Leek, Staffordshire xiv, xix, 95–6
Leicestershire xv, xix, 97, 109–10
Leigh-on-Sea, Essex xvii, 203
Leintwardine, Hereford xii, 27–8
Lemon Arms, Mylor Bridge xviii, 69–70
Lewis, Keith xii, 208–9
Lewis, Margaret xii, 35–7
Ley Green, Herts xx, 217
Lifeboat, Thornham xxi, 194
Lincolnshire xiii, 175–81
Lions of Bledlow, Bledlow xvii, 223–4
Little Braxted, Essex xxi, 202
Little Chef restaurants 116
Little Dry Dock, Netherton xvi, 211
Little Leigh, Cheshire xiii, 116–17
Little Lumphammer ale 211
Litton, Derbyshire xv, 104
Llandovery, Carmarthenshire 47–8
Llangunllo, Powys xiv, 31
Llanthony Priory, Gwent xviii, 21–2
Llanyblodwel, Clwyd xv, 118
Llewellyn, Sam 52
Lloyd, Chris and Debbie 182
Lock-In 61, 66
Loftus, Simon 197
London Inn, Padstow xviii, 66
Long Sutton, Lincs xiii, 180–1
Longshoot, Leicester 97
Longworth, John 103
Lord Crewe Arms, Blanchland xiii, 152–3

INDEX

Lord Nelson, Burnham Thorpe xiii, 186–8
Lord Nelson, Southwold xxi, 197
Loughborough, Leics xix, 109
Louth, Lincs 175–9
Low Newton-by-Sea, Northumberland xv, 147
Lower Whitley, Cheshire xv, 120
Luddenham, Kent xvii, 248
Luxulyan, Cornwall xiv, 60
Lydbury North, Salop xviii, 28
Lydford, Devon xiv, 82

M & B ales 109, 215
Madeley, Salop xii, 208–9
Maid of the Mill, Atherstone xx, 214
Mainwaring, Dick xiii, 200
Malt Shovel, Oswaldkirk 162
Malt Shovel, Spondon xv, xx, 106
Malton, North Yorks xvi, 165, 166
Manaccan, Cornwall xiv, 69
Manchester, Greater xv, xix, 125–8
Manifold Valley, Hulme End xix, 98–9
Margate, Kent 244–5
Marlow, Bucks xvii, 221–2
Marlowe, Christopher 3
Marquis of Granby, Sleaford 179
Marshfield, Avon xiv, 83
Marston Inn, Marston St Lawrence, Northants xvi, 216
Marston's ales 51, 53, 85, 95, 96, 99, 100, 101, 105, 108, 109, 110, 119, 126, 136, 154
Martindale, Maud xiii, 165
Masham, North Yorks xvi, xx, 162–3
Mason's Arms, Cartmel Fell xiii, 131
Mason's Arms, Cilgerran xii, 43–4
Mason's Arms, Knowstone xii, 78–9, 87
Mason's Arms, Norham-on-Tweed xvi, 151
Mason's Arms, Strawberry Bank xiii, 131
Maxwell, Robert 48
May, Miss, of Kington 52
Maynard, Elsie xiii, 247
McEwan's ales 115, 155
McMullen's ales 203
Merrie Monk, Leek xix, 96
Merseyside xix, 128
Middleton, Lancs xix, 127
Middleton-in-Teesdale, Co Durham xv, 146
Mill Green, Essex xxi, 203

Mill House Inn, Trebarwith xviii, 67
Milner, Peter 29
Miners Arms, Huthwaite xix, 111
Minster, Kent 245
Mitchell, Mrs, of Long Sutton 180–1
Mole Trap, Stapleford Tawney xxi, 203
Monksilver, Somerset xiv, 87
Moog, Dr Robert 20
Moorcock, Langdale End xiii, 165
Moorends, South Yorks xx, 172
Morland's ales 225
Morston, Norfolk xvi, 189
Morwenstow, Cornwall xiv, 67–8
Moss, Joan xiii, 179–80
Mounted Rifleman, Luddenham, xvii, 248
Mudge, 'Auntie' Mabel xii, 76, 229
Museum Inn, Penrith xx, 137
Musgrave Arms, Shillington xx, 216
music 16–17, 24, 104, 121, 155, 169–71, 195, 247
Mylor Bridge, Cornwall xviii, 69–70

Nag's Head, Abercych xii, 45–6, 244
Nancenoy, Cornwall xiv, 69
National Trust 56, 132, 193
Navy, Pembroke St., Pembroke Dock xiv, 39
Near Sawrey, Cumbria xv, 132
Nelson, Horatio, Lord 186, 187
Netherton, Northumbria xvi, 148–9
Netherton, W Midlands xvi, 210–11
New Inn, Coate xvii, 230
New Inn, Ironbridge xx, 207
New Inn, Manaccan xiv, 69
New Inn, Newthorpe Common xix, 110
New Inn, Sampford Courtenay xviii, 73
New Inn, Stratfield Saye xvii, 240
New Inn, Tywardreath xiv, 59–62
New White Bull, Eastwood xix, 110
Newcastle-on-Clun, Salop xviii, 30
Newcastle Emlyn, Dyfed xviii, 47
Newhaven, Derbyshire xv, 102–3
Newman, Ray Charles xiii, 235–6
Newthorpe Common, Notts xix, 110
Newton, Cambridgeshire xvi, 183
Newton Bromswold, Northants xx, 216
Newton Cap, Bishop Auckland xx, 145
Newton St Cyres, Devon xiv, 81
Norfolk xiii, xvi, xvii, xxi, 14, 184–95
Norham-on-Tweed, Northumberland xvi, 151
North Shields, Tyne and Wear xiii, xvi, 84, 154–5

261

North Yorkshire xiii, xvi, xx, 161–6
Northamptonshire xvi, 216
Northmoor, Oxon xiii, 225
Northumberland xiii, xv-xvi, xvii, xx, 146–53
Norton Canon, Hereford xiv, 50
Norton St Philip, Somerset xv, 90–1
Notley Arms, Monksilver xiv, 87
Nottinghamshire xv, xix, 110–11
Nuffield, Oxon xxi, 226
Nutshell, Bury St Edmunds xvii, 201

O'Rourke's Pie Factory, Tipton xvi, 211
Oare, Kent xvii, 248
Oddfellows Arms, Alnwick xvi, 149–50
Old Brewery House, Reepham xxi, 191–2
Old Coaching Inn House, Chudleigh 4, 77–8
Old Crown, Skirmett xxi, 222
Old Dalby, Leics xv, 109–10
Old Dungeon Ghyll Hotel, Langdale xix, 129–30
Old Hatch Gate, Cockpole Green xvii, 227
Old Ship, Cadmore End xvii, 223
Old Ship Hotel, Padstow xviii, 66
Old Swan, Netherton xvi, 210–11
Olde Gate Inn, Brassington xiii, 101
Olde Ship, Seahouses xiii, 147–8, 253
Ong, Joyce xiii, 201
Orb, Margate 244
Orford, Suffolk xxi, 200
Orwell, George 9–10
Osborne, Ivy 203
Ostrich, Castleacre xxi, 194
Oswaldkirk, North Yorks xx, 162
Otley, West Yorks xvi, 167
Oxenham Arms, South Zeal xii, 75
Oxfordshire xiii, xvii, xxi, 224–7
Oxlade, N. xiii, 224–5
Oyster, Butley xxi, 199–200

Pack Horse, South Stoke xii, 83–4
Padstow, Cornwall xviii, 66
Page, Mr, of Marlow 221–2
Palace Bars, Hastings xvii, 243–4
Palmer's ales 85–6
Pandora Inn, Restronguet xii, 68
Pardoe, Doris 210
Parkgate, Co Durham xx, 145
Parkin, Steve xiii, 142–3
Parson Drove, Cambs xx, 181

Parsons, Janet xiii, 198–9
Parwich, Derbyshire xv, 99–100
Pembroke 54
Pembroke Dock, Pembs xii, xiv, 39–40
Pembrokeshire xii, xiv, xviii, 33–43, 45–6, 52–5, 252
Pen-y-Mynydd, Clwyd xv, 119–20
Penrith, Cumbria xv, 117, 128, 136–7
Penryn, Cornwall xviii, 62–3, 70
Penzance, Cornwall xviii, 70
Perfect Pub, Suffolk 196, 252–4
Perranporth, Cornwall 65–6
Perrett, Allen xii, 82–3
Petersfield, Hants xvii, 239–40
Pett Bottom, Kent xxi, 247
Peyton Arms, Stoke Lyne xiii, 224–5
Pheasant Inn, Madeley 208
Philleigh, Cornwall xiv, 69
Pickerel, Ixworth xvii, 198
Pickering, Ian 162
Pin Mill, Suffolk xiii, 200
Pittard, Eileen xii, 86–7
Plough, Ford xii, 14–17, 20
Plough, King's Walden 217
Plough Inn, Kingsley xix, 102
Plough, Ley Green xx, 217
Plough, Shenstone xiv, 56
Pocock, Tom 188
Point House, Angle Bay xiv, 38–9
Pompey Royal 235
Pontrilas, Hereford xiv, 21
Popples of Birchover 108
Port Gain, Pembs xviii, 54
Porth Madog, Gwynedd xix, 119
Portley, John 77–8
Pot Kiln, Frilsham xvii, 228
Powell, Lucy 55
Powers, Anthony 23–4
Powis Arms, Lydbury North xxi
Powys xiv, xviii, 24–5, 26, 31, 32–3, 48–50, 55
Pratt, David and Paddy 54
Presselli Arms Hotel, Rosebush xii, 35–7
Presteigne, Powys xiv, xviii, 24–5, 26
Price, Hugh xiii, 154–5
Priestley, J. B. 164
Prince, Olive xii, 100
Pub with No Name, Petersfield xvii, 239–40

Queen Adelaide, Snelston xv, 107–8
Queen's Head, Cowden Cross xiii, 247
Queen's Head, Newton xvi, 183

INDEX

Quiet Woman, Earl Sterndale 100–1

Racehorse, Arran Foot xv, 133–4
Racehorse, Ulverston xv, 133–4
Radnor Arms, Talgarth xviii, 48–50
Radnorshire Arms, Presteigne xviii, 26
Raglan Arms, Rugby xx, 215
Railwayman's Arms, Bridgnorth xvi, 209
railways 4, 36, 81, 125, 145, 209
    4.30 pm Liverpool Street to King's Lynn Special xvi, 185–6
Ram's Head, Denshaw xix, 127
Ramp, Cilgerran xii, 43–4, 55
Rampisham, Dorset xvii, 237
Rancho Del Rio, Co Durham 143
Rapier ales 192
Ray, Richie xii, 43–5
Rayment's ales 194
Reapsmoor, Staffs xv, 100
Red Lion, Birchover xv, 108
Red Lion Hotel, Bredwardine xviii, 20
Red Lion, Litton xv, 104
Red Lion, Llandovery 47–8
Red Lion, Snargate xiii, 245–6
Red Lion, Twyford 223
Reepham, Norfolk xxi, 191–2
Rees, John 47–8
Restronguet Creek, Cornwall xii, 68
Riding Stables, Crickhowell 34
Ridley's ales 202
Rising Sun, Duton Hill xxi, 203
Robinson's ales 103, 121
Rodsley, Derbyshire xv, 107
Rogers, Tim 85–6
Romney Marshes 245–6
Rose and Crown (Eli's), Huish Episcopi xii, 86–7
Rosebush, Pembs xii, 35–7
Roseland Inn, Philleigh xiv, 69
Rothbury, Northumberland xx, 151–2
Rotherfield Greys, Oxon xvii, 226
Rotherwick, Hants 238–9
Rougham, Suffolk xvii, 200–1
Royal Cottage (Olive's), Leek-Buxton Road xii, 100
Royal Oak, Fishguard 53–4
Royal Oak, Fritham 239
Royal Oak, Malton xx, 165
Royal Oak, Saundersfoot xviii, 41
Royal Oak, Wetton xix, 98
Royal Standard (Dolly's) xvi, 168
Ruck, Miss M. 17–19
Ruddle's ales 87, 110, 203

Rugby, Warwicks xx, 215
Rugglestone Inn, Widecombe-in-the-Moor xii, 77

St Austell ales 63, 66, 68, 75
St Elvis Island, Pembs 35–6
St Kew Inn, Cornwall xiv, 69
St Neots, Cambs xx, 183
Salmon, Iain xiii, 194–5
Salter, Ben 226
Sampford Courtenay, Devon xviii, 73
Sapperton, Glos xviii, 19
Saracen's Head, Lincs xiii, 84, 179–80
Saunders, Mrs, of Checkendon 226–7
Saundersfoot, Pembs xviii, 40–1
Scamblesby, Lincs 175
Scarborough, North Yorks xx, 165
Scarisbrick, Lancs xv, 128
Scottish and Newcastle 111, 149
Scoz, G. and A.-M. xii, 72–3
Seafood Restaurant, Padstow 66
Seahouses, Northumberland xiii, xvi, 147–8, 150–1, 252
Sealion, Leek xiv, 95
Seaman, R. xiii, 241–2
Sellafield 135
Seven Stars, Falmouth xii, 63–4
Seven Stars, Penryn xviii, 70
Severn Valley Railway xvi, 209
Seymour Arms, Witham Friary xii, 88–9
Shebbear, Devon xviii, 73
Shenstone, William 9
Shenstone, Hereford xiv, 56
Shepherd Neame ales 244, 246, 248
Shillington, Beds xx, 216
Ship, Chatteris xx, 183
Ship, Low Newton-by-Sea xv, 147
Ship, Porth Madog xix, 119
Ship Inn, Southport xix, 128
Shipwright's Arms, Oare xvii, 248
Short, Mary xiii, 108
Shoulder of Mutton, Stretton-on-Dunsmore xx, 215
Shrewley, Warwicks 215
Shropshire xii, xvi, xviii, xx, 28–30, 207–10
Siddle, Walton xv, 143–5
Simcock, Hedley 25
Skerne, Humberside xiii, 167–8
Skirmett, Bucks xxi, 222
Slaters Arms, Corris xv, 118
Sleaford, Lincs 179
Sloop Inn, Port Gain xviii, 54

263

Smarden, Kent xvii, 246–7
Smiles' ales 85
Smith's Tavern, Ashbourne xix, 99
Smith, Samuel 5, 20, 162, 168, 172
Snargate, Kent xiii, 245–6
Sneed, Somerset 88
Snelston, Derbyshire xv, 107–8
Sneyds Arms, Whiston 102
Society for the Preservation of Beers from the Wood 230
Somerset xii, xiv, xv, xix, 86–7, 88–91, 252
South Shields, Tyne and Wear xx, 155
South Stoke, Avon xii, 83–4
South Yorkshire xvi, xx, 171–2
South Zeal, Devon xii, 75
Southport, Merseyside xix, 128
Southwold, Suffolk xiii, xxi, 196–7
Sow and Pigs, Toddington xx, 216
Spondon, Derbyshire xv, 106
Spotted Cow, Malton xvi, 166
Spread Eagle brewery, Erpingham 193
Spreadeagle, Margate 244–5
Spudding, Mr, Mayor of Abercych 46
Square and Compass, Worth Maltravers xiii, 235–6
Squirrel, Rugby xx, 215
Staffordshire xii, xiii, xv, xix, 95–9, 100–1, 102, 104–6, 213
Stag and Huntsman, Hambleden xxi, 222
Stagge Inn, Titley xiv, 50–1
Staithe, Norfolk 194
Stalybridge Station Buffet xv, 125–6
Stanedge, Manchester xv, 126
Stapleford Tawney, Essex xxi, 203
Star, Bath xii, 82–3
Star, Harome xiii, 162
Star, Netherton xvi, 148–9
Star, West Leake xix, 110
Starbotton, North Yorks xvi, 164
Station Buffet, Stalybridge xv, 125–6
Steele, Michael xii, 84–5
Stein, Chris 66
Stephenson, H. and N. xiii, 131
Stephenson, Raymond 135
Sticklepath, Devon xix, 75
Stockton Cross, Kimbolton xviii, 51–2
Stockton-on-Tees, Cleveland xiii, 160–1, 252
Stoke Lyne, Oxon xiii, 224–5
Stoke Row, Oxon xvii, 226
Stone's ales 166, 172
Stonewall Hill, Powys 26–7

Stottesdon, Salop xvi, 209–10
Stratfield Saye, Hants xvii, 240
Strawberry Bank, Cumbria xiii, 131
Stretton-on-Dunsmore, Warwicks xx, 215
Strong's ales 239, 240, 229–30
Struggling Man, Dudley xx, 212–13
Stuart, Jamie xii, 80–1
Stuart, Kenneth 81
Suffolk xiii, xvii, xxi, 14, 196–201, 203–4, 252; The Perfect Pub 252–4
Sun Inn, Leintwardine xii, 27–8
Sun Inn, Stockton-on-Tees xiii, 160–1, 253
Surrey 251–2
Sussex 241–4
Swales, Joffrey and Peter 37, 38, 45
Swan, Addington xvi, 166
Swan, Bushey xxi, 217
Swan, Draycott-in-the-Clay xv, 104–5
Swan, Newton Bromswold xx, 216
Swan Inn, Parson Drove xx, 181
Swan in the Rushes, Loughborough xix, 109
Swift, Ivan and Glenda xii, 89–91
Sycamore, Parwich xv, 99–100

Talgarth, Powys xviii, 48–50
Talkin, Cumbria xv, 134
Tally Ho, Hatherleigh xii, 72–3, 75, 78, 253
Talybont-on-Usk, Powys xiv, 32–3
Tan Hill Inn, Keld xx, 161
Tandle Hill Tavern, Middleton xix, 127
Taplin, Lola 56
Tarset, Northumberland xvii, 152
Tavern, Kington xiv, 52
Taverner, Rev Richard 190
Tawney, Essex 203
Taylor, Jeremy 29
Taylor, Timothy; ales 103, 104, 126
Teesdale, Co Durham xv, xx, 145, 146
Teign Brewery, Teignmouth xix, 77
Telford, Salop 207, 208
Temple, Doris 189
Tennyson, Alfred, Lord 242
Terrace, Kilnhurst xx, 172
Tetley's ales 109, 115, 152, 154, 172, 203
Tewkesbury, Glos 20
Textor, Mrs, of Checkendon 226–7
Theakston's ales 108, 127, 143, 161, 162–3
Theson, Bill 31

INDEX

Thorne's ales 168, 172
Thornham, Norfolk xxi, 194
Three Chimneys, Biddenden xvii, 246
Three Horseshoes, Elsted xvii, 241
Three Horseshoes, Norton Canon xiv, 50
Three Pots, Leics 97
Three Stags' Heads, Wardlow Mires xix, 101
Three Tuns, Bishop's Castle xii, 28–30, 207
Three Tuns, Hay-on-Wye xviii, 55–6
Throckenholt, Lincs 181
Thurston, Suffolk xiii, 201
Thwaite Arms, Horsehouse xvi, 163
Tibenham, Norfolk xvii, 195
Tickell Arms, Whittlesford xvi, 183
Tiger's Head, Rampisham xvii, 237
Tinner's ales 60, 66, 75
Tintagel, Cornwall 67
Tipton, West Midlands xvi, 211
Titley, Hereford xiv, 50–1
Toby Carvery, Leics 97
Todd, Alex 152
Todd, D. and E. xii, 78–9
Toddington, Beds xx, 216
Tolly Cobbold ales 200, 202
top ten pubs 252
Topsham, Devon xii, 79–80
Tower Bank Arms, Near Sawrey xv, 132
Travellers Rest, Alpraham xv, 115
Trawsfynydd, Gwynedd xv, 118
Trebarwith, Cornwall xviii, 66–7
Trengilly Wartha, Constantine, Nancenoy xiv, 69
Truman's ales 203
Truscott, Celine 60, 61–2
Truscott, George 59, 60–2
Trust House Forte 26, 168
Tucker's Grave, Faulkland xii, 89–91, 253
Turf, Exminster xiv, 81
Turk's Head, Rothbury xx, 151–2
Turkey, Goose Eye xvi, 167
Turville, Bucks xvii, 222
Twyford, Bucks 223
Tyn-y-Groes, Gwynedd xv, 118
Tyne and Wear xiii, xvi, xx, 153–6
Tywardreath, Cornwall xiv, 59–62

Ulverston, Cumbria xv, xix, 133–4
Union Inn, Penzance xviii, 70
Usher's ales 87

Vaux ales 149, 150
Victoria, Earl Soham xiii, 199
Victoria, Huntingdon xx, 183
Vine, Brierley Hill 212
Viper, Mill Green xxi, 203

Wadworth's ales 19, 24, 72, 79, 85, 224, 231, 237
Waggon and Horses, Cradley Heath xx, 212
Walberswick, Suffolk xvii, 197–8
Wales 32–56, 118–20
Walker, Megan xiii, 160–1
Walpole Arms, Itteringham xxi, 193
Walsingham, Norfolk xvi, 191
Walterstone, Hereford xiv, 23–4
Walton, Powys xviii, 32
Ward's ales 172
Wardlow Mires, Derbyshire xix, 101
Warham, Norfolk xiii, 194–5
Warwickshire xvi, xx, 214–15
Wasdale Head Inn, Cumbria xix, 129
Watchet, Somerset xix, 87
Weekend Man 13–14, 185, 223
Wem; Davenport's brewery 207
West Leake, Notts xix, 110
West Midlands xvi, xx, 210–13
West Sussex xiii, xvii, 241–3
West Yorkshire xvi, 166–7
Westwood, Ron xiii, 197
Wethered brewery 221
Wetton, Staffs xix, 98
Wheatsheaf, Barrow-in-Furness xix, 135–6
Wheatsheaf, St Neots xx, 183
Whiston, Staffs 102
Whitbread breweries 76, 230, 247
White Bear, Masham xvi, 162–3
White Hart, Cenarth xviii, 45
White Hart, Pembroke Dock xii, 39–40
White Hart, Talybont-on-Usk xiv, 32–3
White Harte, Burnham-on-Crouch xvii, 202
White Horse (Nellie's), Beverley xiii, 168–9, 253
White Horse, Capel Garmon xv, 119
White Horse, Petersfield xvii, 239–40
White Lion, Barthomley xv, 115
White Lion, Cray xx, 164
White Lion Inn, Pen-y-Mynydd xv, 119–20
White Lion, Trawsfynydd xv, 118
White, G. xiii, 236

Whitehaven, Cumbria xix, 135
Whitland, Gwent xviii, 34
Whittlesford, Cambs xvi, 183
Widecombe-in-the-Moor, Devon xii, 77
Wiltshire xiii, xvii, 229–31
Winning Post, Moorends xx, 172
Winter, Les xiii, 186–8, 189
Wistanstow brewery, Salop 207
Witham Friary, Somerset xii, 88–9
Withyham, East Sussex xvii, 244
Wolsington House, North Shields xiii, 84, 154–5
Wood, J. & D. xii, 28–30
Wood's ales 207
Wooden Doll, North Shields xvi, 154
Woodford's ales 193, 195
Woodie's ales 210
Woodlands Hotel, Woodlands xvi, 171–2
Woodlark, Lambley xix, 111
Woodward, Glen 210
Woolliscroft, Trevor 97
Worcestershire *see* Hereford and W.
Workington, Cumbria xix, 134
Worth Maltravers, Dorset xiii, 235–6
Worth, Mrs, of Gawsworth 121
Worthington's brewery 36, 53
Wright, Peter 222

Yew Tree, Cauldon xii, 98
Yorkshire xiii, xvi, xx, 143, 159–60, 161–7, 171–2
Young's ales 203
Younger's ales 155, 248
Ysceifiog, Clwyd xv, 119